To Leslie

Nov 26/16

A Time to be Born

Memoir of a Canadian Mennonite

Peter Penner

Justina Penner

Peter Penner MA, PhD

FriesenPress

Suite 300 – 990 Fort St
Victoria, BC, V8V 3K2
Canada

www.friesenpress.com

The cover photos represent Peter's three generations:
1) The Vineland Church and parking lot with period cars, about 1939
2) Peter in McMaster gown, hood, and tie, about 1985
3) Peter and Justina relaxing in Minter Gardens, near Chilliwack, 2006

ISBN
978-1-4602-7933-5 (Hardcover)
978-1-4602-7934-2 (Paperback)
978-1-4602-7935-9 (eBook)

1. BIOGRAPHY & AUTOBIOGRAPHY, PERSONAL MEMOIRS

Distributed to the trade by The Ingram Book Company

TABLE OF CONTENTS

v   Foreword

xi   Preface

Part I, Mennonite Years

3   Chapter One, Early Years

32   Chapter Two, Education for Service 1947 to 1953

52   Chapter Three, Our BC Experience 1957–1960

59   Chapter Four, Five Years in Ontario 1960–1965

Part II, University Years 1965-1992

80   Chapter Five, Early Years 1965–1972

104   Chapter Six, Incredible First Sabbatical 1972–73

126   Chapter Seven, Two Decades of the Greatest
        Job in the World 1973 to 1992

147   Chapter Eight, Revisiting Mennonites
        during University Years

161   Chapter Nine, Family Story from Sackville to Calgary

184   Chapter Ten, Paths our Children Took

Part III, Retirement Years

200 Chapter Eleven, Our Years in Calgary

222 Chapter Twelve, Involvements and Travels

233 Chapter Thirteen, Voluntary Service
with Rotary in Siberia

243 Chapter Fourteen, Research and Writings in Retirement

259 Testimonials

261 Publications
Articles, Books and Reviews, 1951–2015

278 Select Bibliography

Foreword

The wonderfully complex, inspiring and splendid life–and–career of Peter Penner, with such remarkable features, cannot be explained without understanding its dual character. It represents a convergence of commitments to two life–long tasks. Faith and learning, religious and secular worlds are blended, both in the academy and in the ministry. The long trajectory of this nexus began in the vast steppe lands of Siberia to which his family had migrated voluntarily once the last Tsar opened up his vast Domains. It was there that Peter was born and then taken as a child by his *Russlaender* Mennonite family to lands nearly as vast in Canada.

In time Peter became an ordained minister of the Gospel among the Mennonite Brethren churches of Canada. Yet, with an ever enquiring mind and an interest in history, he also embarked upon an intellectual and scholarly journey into the secular academy. At McMaster University he completed a doctoral dissertation in British Imperial History with special reference to the growth of Evangelicalism within the Indian Empire of the East India Company. The excellence of his historical work led to a professorship at Mount Allison University in Sackville, New Brunswick. It was there, in the Maritimes, that Peter Penner found himself outside the confines of his MB community, but where the nexus of faith and learning continually challenged him to expanding and exploring new frontiers of historical understanding.

It was in London, at Orbit House, located at the corner of Blackfriars Road and the The Cut (not far from Waterloo Station), that we met while scrutinizing endless volumes of manuscript records of the East India Company, known as the India Office & Records. The name Penner immediately awakened my curiosity. Having grown up in the Telugu region of the Nizam's Dominions of Hyderabad, generic Mennonite names such as Penner, Hiebert, Wiebe, Unruh, Dick, and Voth were known from early childhood and had occupied a continual place in our family's vocabulary. My parents, American Baptist missionaries, were stationed at Nalgonda (east of Hyderabad City) in 1937 in succession to Cornelius Unruh (and before him Abraham Friesen), who had long been tenured in that grand compound. The John A. Wiebe family were MB missionaries stationed at Mahbubnagar; the John N.C. Hiebert family at Shamshabad; and the John Penner family at Suriapet, not far south of Nalgonda. What was especially fascinating about all MB stations, which we frequently visited, was how highly developed they were as centers of agricultural and educational activity, innovative technology in irrigation and vocational training.

My own deep immersion into this culture resulted from growing up with MB boys who were classmates and roommates in boarding schools of Breeks, in Ootacamund, and Highclerc, in Kodaikanal, both lovely "hill stations" located high in the Niligiri and Palni Hills (actually mountains of the Western Ghats)[1]. Accustomed to identifying each community in India by its caste name, I found it convenient and easy to think of these chums and their parents as belonging to the same *jāti* (birth-group or caste).

After instantly identifying Peter Penner at the India Office Records by his Mennonite name, I quickly gained a deep sense of mutual kinship, and soon thereafter developed a deeper intellectual and spiritual bond. Here was a person much like those with whom I had grown up in India. More than that, as I delved into results of his research, as found in his scholarly publications, my respect rapidly increased. Indeed, the bonds of rapport that grew up between us were such that, for a time, we toyed with the possibilities of teaming up on trying to jointly produce a more comprehensive and definitive History

---

1   Highclerc, now known as Kodai International School, has grown into an elite private school, brought to its highest distinction during the decade when Dr. Paul D. Wiebe was Principal – over half of its graduates having earned medical or academic doctorates, and not a few becoming internationally renowned diplomats and scholars.

of Evangelicalism an India. This dream was never realized due to many other commitments and priorities that surrounded each of us.

Two of Peter Penner's major contributions to historical understanding – *The Patronage Bureaucracy in North India: the Robert M. Bird and James Thomason School, 1820 – 1870* (1986) and *Robert Needham Cust: A Personal Biography* (1987) — brought him into close contact with leading authorities in Modern Indian History, especially within the "Oxbridge–London" triangle of institutions where some fifty such scholars were concentrated. One was C. H. Philips, author of *The East India Company: 1784-1834* (1940), who developed London's famous School of Oriental and African Studies (SOAS) into one of Britain's finest history departments. Another was Eric Stokes, author of *English Utilitarians in India* (1959, founder of what was later loosely termed the "Cambridge School" of Indian (South Asian) historians). He was Smuts Professor of British Commonwealth History at the University of Cambridge. A third was Ainslie T. Embree from Nova Scotia who, after teaching at a Christian College in Indore, became a renowned professor of history at Columbia University. Embree's seminal *Charles Grant and the British Rule in India* (1962) laid foundations for the study of Evangelicalism in nineteenth century India.

Peter Penner's work never became known for flights into theoretical abstraction (or ideological polemic) that would later afflict the historiography of modern India. His strengths lay in the depths of empirical exploration that he plunged and troves of fresh materials that he brought to light. Such work not only enabled him to make lasting contributions to historical understanding, but also has enabled later generations of historians to build upon foundations he laid.

In the meanwhile, faith commitments led to a remarkable outpouring of publications arising out of research into historical understandings of how the Gospel was spread – not only in Canada but in India and Russia. The most noteworthy was his history of Mennonite Brethren missionaries in India. This work, entitled *Russians, North Americans and Telugus: The Mennonite Brethren Mission in India 1885 – 1975* (1997), is a detailed description of both individual missionaries and of intricate connections and contentions between missionary institutions located in North America and India, between individual leaders, whose outlooks and personalities kept shifting as winds of theological and political change swept over the worlds they inhabited. These are reflected in the correspondence between them all that Peter Penner has examined. What began with the impulse and inspiration of Abraham and Maria Friesen, and their commissioning by the MB Church in Russia, eventually shifted with the coming of the Great War in 1914 to American MBs becoming more prominent from 1915 to 1945, and to Canadian MBs from 1945 to the end. In graphic details, Peter Penner describes both the triumphs and the tragedies, of which there were not a few.

The critical issue of missionary intentionality was faced squarely. The simple truth was that most Telugu MBs were Madigas or Malas (in a word, Dalits). This untouchable or outcaste community, in every Telugu village, has struggled to survive within an oppressive caste system that has, since antiquity, served as landless laborers, in conditions of dire oppression, poverty, and thralldom. MB missionaries, by comparison, came from an upwardly mobile, culturally and materially advanced, community that could deploy financial surpluses to support their mission in Telangana. The result was a situation of dependency: a patrimonial relationship between MB missionaries and Telugu MB leaders, who had been educated in mission schools and whose Telugu MB pastors and teachers depended upon monthly salaries that came from coffers in Russia and North America. Yet today, that Telugu community took over leadership of what is now, in numerical terms, the largest MB community in the world.

In conclusion, a personal reminiscence: It has been my privilege to occupy a "ring-side" seat on the career of Peter Penner, not only with reference to the academic historiography and prominent research historians with whom he interacted as a scholar in the secular world. Little could he know, when we first met at Orbit House, that he would be investigating the MB missionary venture that began in Nalgonda during the late nineteenth century. This study of the MB mission in Telangana brought together the accumulated and finely honed scholarly skills, both historical and theological, that Peter Penner possessed. This, indeed, was one of his finest works and, with his works on the British Raj in North India, constitutes the pinnacle of Peter's scholarly career.

Robert Eric Frykenberg
Professor Emeritus of History & South Asian Studies
University of Wisconsin, Madison

Preface

"For everything there is a season,
and a time for every matter under heaven:
a time to be born, and a time to die;
a time to plant, and a time to pluck up what is planted."
Ecclesiastes 3:1-2

This story has its foundation in a much longer Memoir I wrote some years ago. In that Memoir I took the trouble of documenting every-thing based on my correspondence and a daybook, both of which I had kept since age twenty-two. That Memoir also includes the stories of our families on both sides as far back as was possible. In this much shorter Memoir the story is mine, and Justina's, with few references.

Both Justina and I began life from within the *Russlaender* Mennonites of the 1920s. I know them about as well as anyone and I will explain what that designation means in Chapter One. The Mennonite years include the years of my youth in Vineland, Ontario, my marriage to Justina Janzen, and my preparation to serve in the Mennonite Brethren Church.

While this Memoir covers three generations, each of which has brought its unique experiences, excitements, and decision-making, one constant has been the Mennonite faith and culture with which I was imbued in those first thirty years.

I cannot expect every reader to find each generation's stories equally interesting. I could wish to have fleshed out more events, but I wanted to keep this memoir of manageable length and still readable.

Justina and I have touched many lives, have seen many things and have unique stories to tell.

In the mid-'sixties, by moving to New Brunswick, we joined that large group of Mennonites who live outside the organized Mennonite churches to which they once belonged, perhaps only as children or young people. In my case, as these pages will show, I never got away from them completely. While working far from the Mennonite epi-centers like Winnipeg, Manitoba, Abbotsford, British Columbia, and Fresno, California, as well as worshiping in mainline churches such as the United Church of Canada, I was invited to do two books, one on Mennonite Brethren (MB) church planting in Canada and the other on the MB Conference Mission in southern India. While I am grateful for the warm reception we received while researching these projects in the 1980s and 1990s, and for the continuing friendship with people of our background, I have particularly to thank Mount Allison University where I taught from 1965 to 1992 for the strong support I received for these and other projects throughout those years, and especially for a third sabbatical in Fresno, California, for the school year 1988–89.

This memoir is **dedicated to Justina** because without her I would hardly have succeeded in what became my passion, writing about the Mennonite communities and ultimately finding my niche in univer-sity teaching as a career with British imperial history as a research focus. It is this area that Robert Eric Frykenberg, contributor of the Foreword, knows so well and for which he has given me high marks. This pursuit, however, did not happen without creating a strain for Justina as I shifted from Church Ministry to the University. As these pages will show she always found a way to serve as an exceptional volunteer, while at the same time working part-time and bringing up our two children. She has always been my first proof-reader and valued critic.

I wish to thank those who have encouraged me to write this memoir, particularly Justina, also my friend of long standing, Harry Loewen, a most significant scholar, who much to our sorrow died in Kelowna, BC, in September 2015 after a severe struggle with cancer, Mel Gray of our Rotary Club of Calgary South who helped to prepare my photos for publication, many friends in Grace Presbyterian Church, and Vern Heinrichs of Toronto, prominent in some chapters.

I must particularly thank my friend Robert Eric Frykenberg for his generous Foreword, and those who have written testimonials to my integrity, among them Marlene Epp, University of Waterloo, with whom I sat on the board of the *Mennonite Reporter*. Her statement actually echoes what Frykenberg has written: ``Peter Penner's rich and varied life exemplifies bridge-building between the worlds of church and academy. Situated as he was on the physical 'edge' of Mennonite communities for much of his career, his perspective on their history and identity is full of insight. As pastor, teacher, scholar, and volunteer, he has brought a critical yet gentle and loving eye to a lifetime of service.``

Justina and I are grateful for all the friends we have made among people not of our background and with whom we feel as Canadian as they and with whom we want to share our story.

Peter Penner, Calgary, 1925 –

PART I

MENNONITE YEARS

Chapter One

Early Years

In order to make the Mennonite years and my background more understandable, I offer this brief introduction into Mennonite history.

Mennonites stem from the time of the Protestant Reformation triggered by Martin Luther in 1517. Menno Simons, a Dutch priest in Witmarsum, Friesland, Netherlands, was converted to evangelical faith in 1535, and soon identified with the Anabaptists, at first called Swiss Brethren in Zurich, Switzerland. They had split from Ulrich Zwingli, the Swiss reformer, ten years earlier, in 1525. Like the Anabaptists (those who baptized again), Menno wanted a church of adult believers prepared to live out their faith. All Anabaptists, including the early Hutterites, were persecuted to the death for their radical stand in that decade. Lutherans, Catholics and Reformed could agree that these folk who wanted freedom to worship in a communion free of the state and who would not participate in public life, including military duty, could not be tolerated.

The first martyr for his stand was Felix Mantz who was executed by drowning in the river at Zurich on January 5, 1527. Zwingli is said to have called this his 'third baptism' since he had been baptized as a child, rebaptized as an adult, and was drowned in a 'baptism of death.' A decade later Jakob Hutter, founder of the Hutterian Brethren, was burned at the stake in the public square in Innsbruck, Austria.

Menno Simons (1496-1561) also had to flee in order to escape death at the hands of his persecutors. Those who followed him as a wandering pastor were nicknamed Menists or Mennonites. In time Dutch Mennonites tended to migrate to safe havens eastward across Europe

until they found a new home in what is today Poland and Lithuania, but was then under the Electors and later eighteenth century Kings of Prussia, including Frederick the Great. Unlike them, the Swiss and South German Anabaptists were either able to stay where they were or migrate to the Thirteen Colonies which formed the United States of America in 1783.

As is well known, Catherine the Great, Tsarina of Russia, and her successors invited Germans to settle in the vast realms of Russia in 1765 under a very generous set of Privileges. The very first were the *Volgadeutsch.* Two Mennonite groups, domiciled and Germanized in Prussia, took the opportunity under successive Tsars Paul and Alexander I to migrate into today's Ukraine in 1789 and 1804. They thus formed the first major colonies of Khortitz and Molotschna, respectively.

Astonishing as it may seem, these German-speaking peoples multiplied and spread over Russia to number more than two million before the Great War. Mennonites formed a relatively small group in this total number. All of them were overwhelmed by the Communist Revolution led by Vladimir Lenin, beginning in 1917–1918, and many, by 1923, were prepared to leave Russia forever.

Youth, 1926 to 1943

We came to Canada from Orlovo, the Altai, south-western Siberia. My grandfather Peter Franz Penner had taken his family there from Neu-Samara in 1909. Orlovo was the leading village in a new settlement on the Kalundasteppe, 400 kilometres south-west of Novosibirsk.

How we got there is a long story by itself. In short, however, the two original colonies outgrew their boundaries and launched new colonies such as Sagradowka to the west of Khortitz and Neu=Samara to the north in the upper Volga region. Then Tsar Nicolas opened his Siberia Domains to settlement, beginning in 1906, and Mennonites from these outliers, seeking new opportunities, moved onto the promising Siberian grasslands, eventually to build up more than forty

villages. Major settlements were also developed along the new Trans-Siberian Railway west of Omsk.

My mother's father Peter Jacob Wiebe also moved from the south, from Sagradowka, in 1909. He had some education, was trained as teacher and served the new colony as minister, teacher, and book-keeper and brought with him some talent in music leadership. Even then, life was a struggle for all of them. In those circumstances, both my mother and father probably received no more than grade six schooling and had worked from age fourteen.

Peter Peter Penner and Katherina Wiebe married in 1919 and, with me and elder sister Erna in tow, decided in 1926 to join the ongoing Mennonite migration to Canada. We came via Riga, Latvia, the United Kingdom, and disembarked at Quebec City on the *Montclare*, landing November 21, 1926. Grandfather Penner, who was travelling with us, was delayed in England at the Atlantic Park Hostel because of eye problems. We arrived at an immigration centre in Winnipeg, and were soon settled on Canadian Pacific Railway (CPR) land near Rosenfeld, Manitoba, in the West Reserve.

We had no money, so how could we emigrate? We were sponsored by Abe and John Braun, Bergthaler Mennonite families farming near Altona. We came courtesy of the CPR whose chief officials believed that we and the more than 20,000 others who were allowed into Canada by Order in Council of the Mackenzie King Government between 1923 and 1927 would actually pay our *Reiseschuld* (travel debt). The Mennonite Colonization Board led by David Toews, Rosthern, Saskatchewan, worked until well into the 1930s and in some cases beyond to have that debt repaid by this large wave of immigrants from Russia.[2] I remember how when I was about ten years old (1935) David Toews accompanied by C.F. Klassen came to visit and collect from us while living on Green Lane.

---

2   The full story of this migration may be found in Frank H. Epp, *Mennonite Exodus: The Rescue and Resettlement of the Russian Mennonites since the Communist Revolution*, Altona: D.W. Friesen and Sons, 1962; a very recent account of Colonel Dennis' role was given in an address by Archivist Conrad Stoesz, *Mennonite Historian*, December 2015, 2, 4

What made *Reiseschuld* collection difficult in most cases was not human perversity, but economic adversity – the unexpected depression of the 1930s.

Manitoba:

The Rosenfeld farm, near Altona, where we lived from 1927 to 1931, was located on Highway 14. I remember our farmhouse, rather small, and the much bigger barn, the machine shed and a horse-drawn binder. There were at least two horses, probably more than one cow. But the Manitoba experience was not rewarding financially. Life for Erna and me in Manitoba meant a somewhat settled sadness. Death was not far away. We knew two infants borne by my mother had died; my grandfather Penner died in 1928 (my grandmother Anna Nikkel Penner had died in Siberia in 1921). We were poor, indebted, probably resigned to inequalities; *life was a struggle*.

Since I was the second child to survive, I had only Erna three years older to pester. Alongside such activity I seemed to indulge one passion. I could draw well enough from an early age to think that I might have developed that talent in later life. Life became more exciting when Marianne was born. She survived because Mother could go to Winnipeg for this delivery on Christmas Eve, 1929, whereas Jacob who was born about sixteen months earlier only survived a week.

Some gladness came with the arrival from the Soviet Union in March 1930 of my grandparents Peter and Katharina Wiebe, with two unmarried children, Uncle Jacob and Aunt Mary. By this time Stalin had ordered Collectivization as part of his First Five Year Plan. This meant that a number of villages like Orlovo would be collapsed into one large administrative unit, thereby losing all their former rights and privileges. Thereupon thousands fled to Moscow hoping for exit visas. My grandparents with their children were among the lucky ones in late 1929 to get to Weimar Germany temporarily and then to Canada through our sponsorship.[3]

The interlude of their visit remains a pleasant memory for me personally because I got a precious crafted gift – a box sleigh with four horses in tandem, harness and all, about six inches high – made by my grandfather, a meticulous craftsman.

When they left for Ontario later in 1930, we decided in those depressing times to follow them. At least we were free in Canada to make that decision. Though life was not easy in Vineland of the Niagara Peninsula at Chris Fretz's huge fruit farming operation, our adults all found work and we became berry pickers at an early age.

Ontario, 1931 to 1944

During the spring or early summer of 1931 we left the rented place in Manitoba behind and headed by car for the Niagara Peninsula. Taking our trusty Chevrolet we set out and had uneventful travelling once we had replaced all the tires! Erna and I sat on a trunk, I believe, filled with food, probably *Geroestetes* (roasted *Zwiebach*, two-decker buns), and cookies. As it turned out, at age six, this was my first of many long trips across the Canadian and American landscape by car. Erna, three years my senior will have learned enough English to introduce me to the Burma Shave ads planted along American highways. One of these read:

If you don't know whose signs these are,
you can't have driven very far.
Burma-Shave

We joined our grandparents at Vineland Station in the Niagara Peninsula, living in a house just south of the big farm owned by Christopher Fretz. From this first dwelling in Ontario we soon graduated to a much larger, square-constructed, two-story house. This

---

3   Peter Penner, *Let My People Go! A Catastrophic Episode in Russian/German Emigration, 1929,"* Journal of AHSGR, Fall 1995, p. 38-45

was one of three situated in the lane behind the Red and White Store, run by Mr. Richardson, and across the lane from the Knight family who tended the acres and acres of Fretz greenhouses (for tomatoes, cucumbers, and other vegetables destined for the market.)

Christian Fretz

Peter and Katharina Wiebe with Jacob and Maria, my parents Peter and Katharina Penner on the right with Erna, Peter, and Marianne, 1931

During the 1980s I did some research in what is now the Municipality of Lincoln. Christian Fretz (1869-1944) was the first fruit farmer many of our Mennonite families met. He was a respected member of First (Old) Mennonite Church in Vineland, a descendant of the 'Loyalist' Mennonites who came up from New York and Pennsylvania between 1786 and the 1790s. He was sympathetic, I think, to our kind of immigrants because we were part of the larger Anabaptist Mennonite family. Their minister was S. F. Coffman who was my first Daily Vacation Bible School teacher. Among these Mennonites were the Kolb (Culp) and Hoch (High) families, each of whom started at the time with fifty acres of sandy loam topsoil, much of it in woodlands. No one should think their beginning was easy then, but the potential in that sandy loam for fruit orchards was enormous.

Christian Fretz was an aggressively successful farmer and entrepreneur. He owned three farms of fifty acres each. His home place featured an enormous complex of greenhouses for vegetable growth for the market, fruit and vegetable packing sheds, and his own residence. Because of this diversification he could employ people all year round. His place could be seen for miles because of the towering chimney lettered with F-R-E-T-Z emitting smoke from his large heating plant. One of the heating 'engineers', whether licensed or not, was John Wichert, later *Aeltester* (Bishop, Elder) in the United Mennonite Church, with whom my dad worked in the winter months as a fireman.

Dad began with Fretz in 1931, as did others, at ten cents an hour, and worked hard sixty hours a week, bringing home $6. While I came away with the jaundiced view of Christian Fretz as a hard driver, he provided seasonal if not year-round employment for many, and we survived on something less appetising than butter, *Griebenschmalz* (cracklings, fat) on our bread. In time I came to the conclusion that Chris Fretz was not much different from many *Russlaender* entrepreneurs (or *Gutsbesitzer)* in the so-called Mennonite Commonwealth in Russia.

Four Mennonite Migrations into Canada

In order to understand who we are, the reader must be able to distinguish the various Mennonites. They differ remarkably according to their migrations into Canada. The Post-American Revolution era saw the so-called 'loyalist' Anabaptist/Mennonites (who never were in Russia but came from Switzerland and South Germany) deciding to move to Upper Canada, beginning in 1786. We have already seen one such Mennonite, a successful fruit grower, Christian Fretz. They settled in Jordan Valley, Waterloo and Markham counties. Among them were some Amish who are also Anabaptist.

These Mennonites moved into what was Upper Canada at approximately the same time as Mennonites first migrated from Prussia to what is today's Ukraine.

The next strong migration of Mennonites into Canada came almost a century later. Between 1874 and 1878 about **7,000 Mennonites came to Manitoba** from Russia. At the same time about 10,000 settled in the USA, principally in Kansas. Those in Canada were of the more conservative groups that had been formed in the Russian Mennonite colonies mentioned above. While there were some very progressive entrepreneurial families among them making famous such places as Steinbach, Altona, and Winkler, the majority decided by 1922, and another group in 1948, that they could not adjust to Manitoba's education laws and left for Mexico, spreading to British Honduras (Belize) and Bolivia.

A considerable number of the conservative groups – Sommerfelder, Old Colony – stayed in Canada, tending to migrate within the country, for example, to Osler in Saskatchewan or La Crete in Alberta, rather than leave.

During the **Inter-War Years** there was a large migration of Mennonites, the largest of all. These came to be known as the *Russlaender* in contrast to those of the 1870s who were known in common parlance as *Kanadier*. The *Russlaender* came 20,000 strong over the years from 1923 to 1927, and then another 3,000 in early 1930, including my grandparents as illustrated.

This was my (our) group. In Russia they were basically one large, growing, conference until the secession of one group in 1812, the so-called *Kleinegemeinde* (Little Church), and another in 1860. The latter became known and recognized officially as the Mennonite Brethren, as opposed to the general church, in Russia called *die Kirchliche*. Once in Canada, those of the latter identified with or joined the General Conference (GC) formed in the USA in 1860, and the other group, Mennonite Brethren, joined their American counterparts in a general conference.

How these two interacted with one another in Vineland, Ontario, will be discussed in the next section.

It may be safely asserted that the descendants of this Mennonite immigration and also of the 1870s have made a significant contribution to Canadian life, at all levels, perhaps out of proportion to their numbers. That may sound a bit boastful, but here and there in the telling of our combined story, there are evidences of Mennonites in all walks of public life and business, the universities, entrepreneurship of all kinds, and service. Think education, politics, literature, music, and health services.

Among the Low German Mennonite names they brought with them, occurring frequently, are the following, in alphabetical order: Dyck, Epp, Friesen, Harder, Janzen, Klassen, Neufeld(t), Pauls, Penner, Reimer, Thiessen, Toews, Wiebe, Wiens. (The Internet shows the variations of some of these and many more names.)

The Road Between GC and MB

Both General Conference and Mennonite Brethren families were church-going people and church attendance and Sunday afternoon visiting made up most of our social life. We brought that with us from 'the old country.' There were many social and cultural reasons to think twice before separating for doctrinal or ecclesial reasons. Yet this is what happened. The secessionists pointed to general 'decadence' and indifference to standards of Christian living for church membership. They wanted to start over, as it were. Ultimately this forced many church adherents to choose up sides, a division which they brought with them to Canada.

Gerhard Lohrenz gave an example of the difference from Sagradowka, Province Kherson, in his *Sagradowka* (Echo Verlag, 1947). In Russia in those years before the 1920s emigration some preachers were convinced that to start a new church you needed to 'come out and be ye separate' and be baptized by immersion. Others like one Elder Wilhelm Voth held to the principle that his church needed to serve all the youth, not separate them because they had not had Damascus Road-like experiences of conversion. The reference is to the conversion of Paul who became the noted Apostle to the Gentiles (Acts of the Apostles 9:1-31).

What took place in the attractive village and area of Vineland, Ontario? When many of our people left the dry prairies, those who moved east came to Vineland first, as our family had done, before perhaps moving on to Virgil in the Niagara region. In1931 we found a small GC congregation called, in English, the Vineland United Mennonite. And this is where I learned to know Elder Wichert and his group. It was almost as though I was there at an early age to welcome the new arrivals as they came east throughout the Dirty 'Thirties from Manitoba, Saskatchewan and Alberta locations.

At first the United Mennonite (*Kirchlich*) fixed up an old abandoned sawmill and welcomed new arrivals in Vineland to worship with them. Many did, as did we. When Johann Wichert, elected *Aeltester* (Elder or Bishop) in 1927, found his membership growing by this influx from the West, his members built a new meetinghouse on the west side of Victoria Avenue, mostly by voluntary labour, completed by December 1935.

At much the same time some Mennonite Brethren leaders began to gather up those who leaned toward the MB and by 1932 they had twenty-seven members and their own church council. They started a Sunday school, a monthly youth service, a church choir, and even a Saturday school of German language teaching. For a short time, the MB gathered in the neighbouring Town of Beamsville. The Brethren however purchased that old Vineland sawmill in 1937, renovated it and used it until 1959.

So, by 1937 new arrivals could be told that in Vineland there were, for their convenience, ready-made congregations to welcome them. Some joined on the west side of Victoria Avenue, the others on the east side, culturally speaking the same language, for them the colloquial Low German (*Plautdietsch*). They sang many of the same songs and some members were related by marriage. Both the Mennonite Brethren and the General Conference of the 1920s tried to keep German as their language of worship until about 1960.

Meanwhile, our family continued to worship with John Wichert. This was natural since we were not MB then. My father had been baptized on his avowal of faith by sprinkling in Orlovo in 1915 and my mother in 1919 (both at about age nineteen or twenty). About 1936, however, this all changed. Influenced by a preacher from Kitchener who was a family friend, Henry H. Janzen, my grandparents and my parents were re-baptized by immersion in Lake Ontario. And thus we became Mennonite Brethren.

By and large there were no ill feelings, but what did those ignorant of our history think, the passerby who stopped to ask questions? As said, on the one side of the road the United Mennonite had built a church sanctuary with room for all. Across the street the MB created their own church with different assumptions about membership, and tried to make sure, so it seemed to me, that all who knocked on the entrance door understood the reasons for the road between. There were unfortunately many Mennonite Brethren who did not recognize the General Conference path into membership as a valid and effective conversion.

In Vineland there were now preachers like Dietrich Klassen who called us out, while Bishop Wichert, our friend since 1931, held to convictions similar to Elder Wilhelm Voth in Sagradowka. Thus the lines were drawn creating **'the road between!'**

This became a problem for me from a very early age. Why carry into a new country the differences created in the old? Even then, as life turned, I grew up among the Mennonite Brethren in Vineland and found my wife and life-long partner there in the post-War years.

My Youthful Conversion

Whatever confusion all of this created in my mind, I have to confess I was not any different from a lot of kids. During one summer five or six of us, largely unsupervised while Dad and Mom worked, ran about the yards and warehouses. We tried smoking a whole variety of things, including cigarette butts. After all, we did not have money. We were therefore tempted to steal cigarettes and chocolates from Mr. Richardson's store.

That summer I had a fit of conscience over this activity. After waking my parents one night, I confessed all my wrong doings and felt as though I had been cleansed by confession and repentance. I went to Mr. Richardson to confess, ask for forgiveness and offered restitution. He did not take money, as I recall, but he accepted the apology and our friendship remained unbroken. Often, since then, I have told people who asked whether I would like a cigarette that I once smoked at age ten and have not touched tobacco since!

I did not consider that experience to have been my conversion. I had another experience of contrition at age fourteen and two years later, in 1939, I applied for membership, for which there were guidelines, in the Vineland MB Church. This meant being baptized by immersion rather than by sprinkling as was done on the other side of Victoria Avenue. We had to give a testimony to the whole congregation before being asked to step outside the worship hall while the congregation voted on our eligibility.

Green Lane

When I was about ten, in the fall, we bought two acres of land on Green Lane, a street which branched off Victoria to the west. We thus became neighbours to the brothers John and Jacob Wall, with their families of children our age. John was MB and his eldest son Frank became a close friend. Jacob who was GC had two lovely daughters to whom I could talk over the back fence. Across Green Lane lived the family of **James Platts**. He was a war veteran. His son Jim became my friend. Some other English boys were sons of people working for Martin Farms, where Dad became employed, or for the Vineland Horticultural Experiment Station. My first introduction to Europe came as a result of hearing the ranting, raving, voice of Adolf Hitler over the radio in the Platts home.

From that location in the Rittenhouse school district at age ten I began to work for Alvin Culp and his son Isaac each summer. All of these farmers, some still speaking the Pennsylvania Dutch dialect, seemed to balance their open space and their orchards on this good soil so that there was something to do all summer, from asparagus cutting in May, to strawberries in June, cherries and raspberries in July, peaches in August and September, grapes and pears in September, and apples in October. I learned about all of the varieties of fruits of that day, how to thin peaches and pick them, and eventually also how to trim fruit trees back in the later winter and spring. Many of these families were active members of Bishop Coffman's church, and Alvin Culp used his truck to pick up as many kids as he could for Daily Vacation Bible School with the Bishop.

I can't recall what age I was, perhaps sixteen, when I was asked to paint Alvin Culp's barn. I can hardly believe that I did it! Its end gable measured more than thirty feet up, and I was expected to go up there with a can of paint and a scraper and brush on a long extension ladder, made of hard wood and round rungs. I also painted his round silo, made of wood, and just as high up. Only some nail pegs kept the ladder in place at the top. There was no provision for protection in case of a fall. At this stage of life I shudder at the thought of what I did or was expected to do. It was reckless of all parties....

Pleasant Memories of Rittenhouse School

Rittenhouse was a special school, founded by United Empire Loyalists and Pennsylvania Dutch people long before. It was located next to the Vineland Horticultural Station that encouraged lovely gardens and shrubbery and attracted professional people. The school boasted a large library, an auditorium, a fully equipped carpenter shop with all the tools and a lathe, as well as a skating rink.

While at Rittenhouse School I was an avid hockey fan, especially of the Toronto Maple Leafs. I listened to Foster Hewitt regularly and began to collect hockey cards of, say, the *Kid Line*: Charlie Conacher, Joe Primeau, and Boucher Jackson, later of Sylvannus Apps. For every card I needed a Bee Hive Golden Corn Syrup label. My sister Marianne helped me hunt for these in garbage dumps and we collected from friends and neighbours. In this way I got quite a good collection of hockey pictures from the eight teams then in the National Hockey League. I eventually gave them to Corney my only brother who added to them. I was no more than fourteen years when I drew members of Toronto's team on large sheets of art paper and sent them to Maple Leaf Gardens. I got a letter saying that they liked them and had posted them in a gallery. Should I believe that? I lost the letter and never got there to check things out until years later.

At Rittenhouse School I developed a strong interest in athletic games of all kinds: baseball, soccer, hockey, as well as gymnastics.

By frequently playing with us, our teacher Elwood Cook helped us develop our talents outside the classroom as well as inside. He also taught us to appreciate birds. We became avid birdwatchers, having learned to identify about eighty birds. Most of my schoolmates were English or Scottish, though there was a sprinkling of Mennonite children.For this reason, much to the chagrin of my Mennonite schoolmates I joined *Trail Rangers* at the United Church, led by Agronomist Upshaw. In this way I showed my independence at a fairly early age. These choices may have created a distancing from some parts of my Mennonite community as I never seemed to be willing to be poured into a mould, rather wanting to retain my individuality.

Meanwhile, I completed my elementary schooling at Rittenhouse School with good grades in 1939. It was because I felt well liked at Rittenhouse by these friends whose families hailed from the British Isles that I took an early and intense interest in all things British and I learned to appreciate the strong Canadian identity within the British Empire.

Leo Rittenhouse Martin (1887-1956)

Meanwhile, while living on Green Lane, Dad became employed at Leo Martin Farms. Many Mennonites also got their first employment here in those years. Martin Farms specialised in vegetables for the Toronto market, especially celery, peppers, and tomatoes. They too had vast green houses, and Dad had employment there year round. At the same time, while we ran off to Rittenhouse School, my mother worked seasonally at the Culverhouse Canning Company situated at the end of Victoria Street, at the edge of Lake Ontario. She walked that distance, over a mile, past Rittenhouse School. In this way our parents struggled through. I've forgotten how much my mother was paid (some of it piecework), but Dad worked for 12 1/2 cents, rising to 15, and then 17 1/2, and so on as the 1930s progressed.

Cherry Avenue

We made another move to a larger place about 1938. This was on Cherry Avenue, one mile further west, next to the family of Abram H. Harder who was a lay minister in the Vineland United Mennonite Church. Here we had ten acres of fruit, not the best soil, like Alvin Culp's, but the Harders and others on Cherry Avenue to the Lake shore were doing well enough. So we hoped for better things. The Harder couple had seven sons, one of whom, Abram, became my father's good friend who also did some custom work for us.

Our residence at Cherry Avenue coincided with the construction of the Queen Elizabeth Way, opened in 1939, joining Niagara Falls and Toronto. While living there, unfortunately, I dropped out of Beamsville High School in the fall of 1941, having only completed Grade Nine. I enjoyed high school and did well, but I became discouraged by our continuing poverty and was convinced I should find employment to help the family income. Whatever the combination of factors, the decision was made that I would go to work for the rest of the fall term at Alvin Culp's fruit farm and take other jobs subsequently.

My early years – the first two decades – should have seen me through high school. But entering high school at age fourteen and doing five years of it was still not a given for young people attending our church – recent immigrants that we were.

The Vineland Young People

Those years, if wasted in terms of education, were happy years nevertheless. We had great young people and had good clean fun. Vineland was the best. Our choir leader, George Reimer, and his wife opened their home at Jordan for almost any Sunday where we could, and did, gather and enjoyed ourselves and were given Mennonite high tea, *Zwiebach und Kafe* (doubledecker buns and weak coffee) and whatever else went with that! This was *Zwiebach* hospitality as Katie Funk Wiebe called it! I was happy with these young people from Mennonite Brethren families.

Many, my closest friends among them, also came to visit at Cherry Avenue on Sundays. Like Mrs. Reimer, our mother was always prepared and served all of us gladly. We also circulated round to the Penner home at Jordan Station (with five daughters) or Peter Dirksen's in Vineland proper. A few years later I found my life's partner, Justina Janzen, among them. She had come with her family from Steinbach, Manitoba.

Peter and Katharina Penner, with Erna (husband Abe Friesen), Peter, Marianne, Thelma, Cathy, and Corney, 1942.

In the midst of these years most of them were baptized upon confession of faith at about age sixteen/seventeen. There were no baptismal classes in preparation as was the case in the congregation across the street. We simply made our way to the home of the moderator, Peter Dirksen, to declare ourselves ready for baptism and prepared to give our testimony in front of the congregation.

One of the fine memories of these years was the frequent visit to the J.K. Janzen family at Grimsby, about eighteen miles from Vineland. There were six sons and one daughter, though the eldest were married and away from home. I would be invited to drive home after morning church in their Packard car, and return for the evening service, thus enjoying two of Mrs. Janzen's meals, and the good fellowship there, except at the table. No one talked while eating until spoken to by the patriarch J.K., formerly Laird, Saskatchewan. I shall introduce J.K. in another way later.

I had a particularly good group of fellows as friends. The one we depended on for transportation was Otto Bergman from St. Catharines. A little older, he was earning well and had his own car and preferred our Vineland companionship to that of others near his home. Together with John Wall and a few others we did Sunday afternoon trips to Niagara Falls, Queenston Heights, or even Toronto.

During one winter I divided my time between attendance at the Vineland MB church school and a job at Weston's Bakery in St. Catharines. However, because the language used in this school was German, and it was wartime, we were investigated by the RCMP. Our teachers, supported by the church council, decided to close the school. Unfortunately, there were a few admirers in Canada among Mennonites of Hitler's National Socialism.

From this mistake of dropping out of school it followed that I lost valuable years when I could have completed high school, even Grade XIII before being called into War service.

Alternative Service

What I could not avoid was the Conscription of 1943. Like thousands of others I was called up to serve my country in wartime service at the age of eighteen and a half. That was the year I had chosen to seek employment at Isaak High's place rather than continuing at Alvin and Isaak Culp's.

That was also the year that I contracted typhoid fever. We were residing in the house on Cherry Avenue. Our family doctor in Vineland, who visited patients in their homes, had the water tested, and found no trace of typhoid germs. Interestingly, there was only one other case in the Niagara Peninsula at the time that I knew about. Both of us survived after going through the three-week crisis period of fever, which reached a climax when it either broke or killed one. My dear mother nursed me through all, the fever, crisis, and recovery which took six weeks. I returned to Isaac High's in mid-summer, thin as a rail.

In the midst of those maturing years I chose to take Canada's provision for Alternative Service as a conscientious objector. Why did I do that?

Such a choice stood out clearly. While my Rittenhouse school friend, Jim Platts, for instance, volunteered because that is the way he was brought up, I chose this other path because that was my understanding at the time as to what I should do. We were in Canada only thirteen years when war broke out, German speaking though not German sympathizers. Some of us believed we as Anabaptist Mennonites had a commitment to conscientious objection to war just as our fathers had declared themselves in Tsarist Russia and served in Forestry Camps or as Red Cross Medics on military trains. My father, living in Siberia since 1909, at age 20 in 1915, also worked in these camps.

Clearly, it was an issue of conscience for me, as it was for many Mennonites. There was however no agreement among Mennonite leaders across the country on how the issue of the conscientious objector should be handled. On the Prairies there was some interest in joining the defence forces in a medical corps attached to the military. Actually, roughly sixty percent of eligible Mennonite men declared for CO status, forty percent joined the various forces. The number of active conscientious objectors was never more than 7,500. [4]

In Ontario the Historic Peace Churches, made up principally of Mennonites, Quakers, Amish, and Brethren in Christ, had made advance provision for those who would choose Alternative Service. This was facilitated by the long-term residence in Ontario of the (Old) Mennonites in Waterloo County. They had claimed the traditional military exemption given to Mennonites on entirely biblical grounds since their days in Upper Canada.

Once conscription became a reality, I was able to get a note from our church moderator that identified me as a conscientious objector to official participation in war. When the call came I presented myself at the Selective Service Office for military service. I had in hand the slip of paper (and a mere slip it was) that indicated that I was a member of the Vineland Mennonite Brethren Church, and that I was applying for alternative service to participation in the military. Since there

---

4   Nathan R. Dirks, *War Without, Struggle Within: Canadian Mennonite Enlistment During the Second World War*. Master of Arts Thesis, McMaster Divinity School, 2010 [Available on the Internet].

were many precedents in Ontario which I cannot explore here, I was treated with equanimity.

The first Alternative Service Work camps were set up in May 1941. The government's designation in 1942 of reforestation as a work of national importance focussed on replanting the Sayward Forest in BC, destroyed by fire in 1938. By 1944 more than 4,000 alternative service workers were serving in the B.C. Forest Service (BCFS). During the War years, these conscientious objectors planted about 17 million trees in various parts of the country, mostly in BC. Selective harvesting of second growth forests began in 1991.

Both Justina and I Have Stories

Several years before we met, while Justina was still living in Steinbach, Manitoba, she contributed importantly to the War effort. At age 17, following Grade Eleven, she helped to alleviate the shortage of teachers. It was 1943 and with a teaching permit in hand she was sent to Moosehorn in the Lake District to take over a one-room all classes school!

Following that exhilarating experience she found employment as *opere* in an upscale home on Wellington Crescent in Winnipeg. She told her mistress that she wanted to learn how the wealthy ran their households. She even had the experience of serving at Tea when Lady Eaton from Toronto came as a guest. There was once a different guest who asked Justina whether she had any brothers and had they volunteered to join the defence forces! When Justina told this woman that her brother Henry had asked to be recognized as a conscientious objector, Justina was subjected to quite a lecture, presumptuous on many points about advantages that COs were enjoying by being exempt from service overseas and having well-paid jobs. To this Justina calmly replied that her brother had been sent to serve as an interpreter to a camp for German Prisoners-of-War, was being paid $25 a month and room and board. The remainder of his earnings were being sent to the Red Cross.

This more or less silenced the critic.

My story is this: In 1943 four of us from my Vineland congregation were called up. Each was a good friend. One joined the RCAF, two did not declare themselves as conscientious objectors because they assumed they would get deferment and would therefore obviate the stigma society attached to those who chose alternative service. I however did make this choice and thought the decision of the two was a cop-out.

Late in life I learned that I belong to the *silent generation*, those born between 1925 and 1942. (At no time have I been very conscious that I was living through generations so variously described in recent years as Generation X and Y.) That *silent* generation includes thousands upon thousands who tried to stay out of fighting by seeking deferment. Michael Stevenson in his exhaustive study of mobilization efforts in Canada during the War has shown that the Mobilization Board heard 750,000 requests for postponement of military service.[5] About fifty percent of those who were medically examined were called up for service.

Official attitude of dislike for me was indicated by being sent a ticket to proceed to Green Timbers, BC, leaving home two days before Christmas, 1943. Meal vouchers were enclosed. On Christmas Day, the train nearly empty, while having a special meal, we rolled into Winnipeg, where I knew no one at that time, even if I could have gotten off for a day.

Arrived in Green Timbers, New Westminster after Boxing Day, I was taken in a pickup truck across to Vancouver Island, to plant trees. I was soon settled in C-2 Camp, Lake Cowichan, where we had very good cabins, good meals, were supplied with rain proof clothes and spiked logging boots (some charge for these), and were paid fifty cents a day.

I met good fellows everywhere, some from Mennonite Brethren and other families in Ontario, but most of them were from the Prairies. Admittedly, it was a great learning and growing-up experience. We

---

5 Michael D. Stevenson, *Canada's Greatest Wartime Muddle: National Selective Service and the Mobilization of Human Resources During World War II*. McGill-Queen's Press 2001

were all sent home at the end of March 1944. All of us had to continue in other forms of alternative service until the end of the War in May 1945. During the summer months I was allowed to go back to work on the fruit farm I was fully acquainted with – that of Alvin Culp. During the winter months of 1944-45 I was consigned with two others to the Canada Packers Meat Plant in Toronto. There we were sent to work with mainly Maltese men in the hide cellar. As was the case with Justina's brother I received $25 a month while the rest of my wages went to the Red Cross.

What Should I Do?

In 1982 I had a totally unexpected invitation to tell my story and that of Alternative Service in a town-wide **Remembrance Day Service** in Sackville, New Brunswick. That year, the Chaplain of the local Legion, the Rev. George Lemmon, a former Baptist who had become an Anglican minister (and later elevated to Bishop of Fredericton) came to me and said: 'Peter, we need to hear something different. You come from a different background, and we want you to speak to the town!'

This was most unusual. Normally we listened to a veteran, a military historian or the university president. In those days, schools, banks, and many businesses were closed in Sackville for Remembrance Day. Veterans and Legionnaires always marched from the Cenotaph – rain, shine, or snow – accompanied by the town band, the volunteer firemen, the police officers, the IODE (then a service club for women of which Justina was a member),[6] the service clubs (Rotary, Kinsmen, and Lions), the school band, and church representatives.

George Lemmon knew that I had worked in the Mennonite Brethren Conference before I came to Mount Allison University. He also knew me as an Associate Professor of History who had joined Sackville United Church, and yet of Anabaptist/Mennonite background

---

6 When the IODE was formed in 1901 upon the death of Queen Victoria, it was declaratively the very patriotic Imperial Order of the Daughters of Empire

theologically. There was an informal ministerial in town in which I represented that wing of the church.

What should I do? By that time we had lived in Sackville for seventeen years and everyone knew me, Justina, and our two children, Robert and Ruth. With some hesitation I decided to tell my story in the third person! I intended to be self-explanatory, to answer some of the frequently asked questions about conscientious objection to war, and to satisfy the need to remember. It was an unusual-sounding speech for that audience.

This is a page out of that speech:

> You may say, given the protected and privileged position of the Mennonites that they never have come to grips with the issue of war. How wrong you are. Mennonites throughout their history have had to come to grips with war, anarchy, destruction of their property, and personal assault in a way that Canadians who remained at home have not. ...

> The Mennonite anti-war stance was made in the 16th century, in the very midst of war. In Frederick the Great's Prussia in the 18th century they dwelt in a warfare state and were asked to leave for reasons of state, but were then welcomed in Russia. There the Mennonite villages lay in the path of the Red Army fighting the Whites in the Civil War (following Lenin's takeover), and were laid waste by the Anarchist Nestor Machno and his roving bands (1917-1919). There was the knock on the door, the pistol at the head, and the demand, first for food for the men and fodder for the horses. Next, they wanted the villagers' horses, and wagons, and eventually their women. Non-compliance meant the trigger, or the tearing away of the father, leaving the women defenseless.

> In this way Mennonites quite literally faced the question often asked of them: What would you do, if you were attacked? They faced it in two ways: One group

said we must organize our own self-defense against these marauding bands. They did, under the aegis of the White armies, and the results were shattering. This was a complete denial of their principles. They were already too much identified with the wealthy classes, and the retaliation was all the more fierce in a war that the Whites lost.

The other group said: No, we must not resist the aggressor: we must "heap coals of fire on his head," we must "turn the other cheek." [The murderous assault in 1919 on some of the villages of Sagradowka provides a case in point. I will give an example later.]

There was one protest in the press, from a student who was enrolled in the Reserve Officer's Training Course at the University. He argued that such Remembrance Day services should be reserved as a memorial to those who had died. They should not be given over to a pacifist. But no one else objected. Afterwards I was seated at the head table at the Legionnaire's lunch and asked to say the blessing. Some veterans even thanked me for my talk, while others kept their distance but were respectful. Many of my fellow Rotarians were present at the service as well as at the lunch.

Tufford Road

While I was still in Alternative Service, my parents in April 1944 relocated to Tufford Road, about half way between Vineland and Beamsville. The nineteen acres they bought had a peach orchard, a very large pear orchard, and quite a good vineyard, and some open land for tomatoes. We were within a quarter mile of Lake Ontario, near the school, and across the street from a brother and sister after whose family the Road was named. Though the Lake was more polluted than we knew then, we resorted there for a swim or just to cool off during the hot summer days.

Our home on Tufford Road, with its stone veranda round the front and large lawn and trees, lent itself to family and larger gatherings. This included Uncle Jacob and Alice (Enns) Wiebe, and David and Aunt Mary (Wiebe) Unrau, with all their children. These were happy times as I recall. We had this larger family over frequently, headed by the patriarch Peter J. Wiebe and his wife Katharina (Kroeker), whose Golden Wedding we celebrated on April 27, 1947.

When Grandfather Wiebe sat down on a Sunday to *Vesper (Faspa)* at the head of the table at such gatherings, we may as well have been back in Siberia. He usually read a portion from the Bible, gave a brief homily which included gratitude for 'freedom in this country of Canada' and an exhortation to all to live so as not to disgrace the family or church or country in any way.

This and his prayer lengthened out the waiting period for the younger set. If there was room for all, we were asked to join the first sitting. If not, we had to wait, or eat in the kitchen. This delay-of-the-meal pattern was possible only because there were *Zwiebach*, sugar-coated rolls, and *Kruemmelplatz* (a coffee cake) or cookies (*Plaetzchen*) during this *Russlaender* substitute for "high tea." In those days we did not need hot dishes for invited guests. What a blessing for the hostess!

The Singing Years

Our parents could not afford voice lessons for me, though money was fortunately found for Marianne's piano lessons. She learned to play well, and as long as we were together – Marianne, Thelma, Cathy, and I – we did an inordinate amount of singing at Tufford Road in the post-War years. The house frequently rang with music, a great part of our lives. We also grew up singing four-part harmony in church during the congregational hymns. This was not reserved for the choirs. Though we learned the rudiments of singing parts from self-taught choir leaders, four-part singing was a beautiful tradition brought from Russia and done without conscious effort.

My solo attempts were less successful, I think, though there were several memorable occasions, such as one at Prairie Bible Institute, Three Hills, when I sang "Asleep in the Deep," a song ending in E-Flat. This was under the bright platform lights of the huge tabernacle with Principal L.E. Maxwell standing behind me. At the conclusion I remember his saying loud enough to be heard: 'Don't let that go to your head!'

Back to School

In later years I asked who was to blame for the loss of those educational years. Why the lack of vision, courage, common sense, about the need for education? While it seemed difficult for my parents to see that need in 1940, yet they supported my three sisters, Marianne, Thelma, and Cathy, five, seven, and nine years younger. They all went through Beamsville High School uninterrupted and even took cadet training! In Manitoba by comparison many Mennonites went to university without attending Bible school first. Those of us who came from the West in the 1930s were still being urged to have a Bible school experience first. That is what you need, we were told!

For *Russlaender* immigrants coming to Canada without any knowledge of English, it seemed most natural to think of giving young people an education in Bible knowledge, in German of course, using the Martin Luther translation, but also to tie them to the church, to train them for Sunday School teaching, to provide some training in music and choral work as support for choirs in home churches, and last, but not least, it was thought there was no better place to find a life's partner, even when open dating was usually not permitted.

The Winkler Bible School, Winkler, Manitoba, was launched in 1925, with experienced, well-known and qualified teachers and preachers who had just migrated from the Crimea, and another in Hepburn, Saskatchewan, two years later. Hepburn is one of a cluster of Mennonite villages north of Saskatoon.

The rationale for Vineland youth going to Winkler Bible School seemed quite self-evident, so why did I go to Prairie Bible Institute, Three Hills, Alberta, instead? Why would I risk being different? What did I become as a result? While there was no complete rationale for going to PBI when discharged in 1945, instead of returning immediately to complete secondary education, I spent two winters at PBI. Only after that, skipping Grade Ten altogether, did I take Grade Eleven at Eden Christian College, Niagara-on-the Lake, Grade Twelve back at Beamsville High School, and after marriage in 1949, Grade Thirteen at St. Catharines Collegiate Institute.

For all that, having chosen Alternative Service followed by two years at PBI, I had gained experience, had seen the country, learned my Bible, become wiser, but I was in fact twenty-five years old, married, when I went to Mennonite Brethren Bible College, Winnipeg, in 1950.

The Prairie Bible Institute Interlude, 1945-47

In the West it was not an unusual thing for Mennonites to choose Prairie Bible Institute, in Three Hills, Alberta, 130 kilometres north-east of Calgary or Briercrest Bible Institute in Caronport, Saskatchewan, west of Moose Jaw. Indeed, many, perhaps most Mennonite young people interested in some form of mission service, wanted to be at Prairie at least one year. In Vineland, however, it was a different thing. There I was seen either as the 'black sheep' who would not go to Winkler, or as one who thought he knew better, or wanted something different. I guess that was *the quester* in me. My future girlfriend, Justina, heard various statements about me when she became secretary of the Vineland young people's 'Christian Endeavour'. She however understood.

PBI's Beneficial and Detrimental Influences

At PBI where the main textbook was the King James Bible, I had bought the Scofield Reference edition which had dispensationalism worked into its Notes. This was a novel approach to the Bible developed by the English John Nelson Darby, an Anglican priest, in the 1830s. In 1909 Cyrus Ingerson Scofield, an American theologian, produced an annotated Bible incorporating Darby-like views. Wikipedia sums it up neatly: dispensationalism is a Christian evangelical, futurist, Biblical interpretation that believes that God has related to human beings in different ways under different Biblical covenants in a series of "dispensations," or periods in history.

Though this must sound as though we thought only within a closed shop, it was the wider world of mission, PBI's major interest, which was fostered and which I appreciated, even though it suggested a non-denominational approach. Missions was inculcated by a constant stream of graduates coming back to speak as missionaries-on-furlough, from all over the world, and Principle Leslie E. Maxwell's emphasis prepared many of the nearly 1,000 attendees to go if not called to stay home. This was how I received my interest in mission studies with reference to India and China. This helped me later to choose British Empire studies because this enveloped many of the areas about which I had learned at Prairie Bible Institute.

As well, though I did not realize it fully, I had a good course in church history for which Mr. James Murray used a two volume text by Albert Henry Newman (1852-1933), considered a premier historian of the Baptists, but also of the Anabaptists with which I came to identify. Though I was not fully aware of how important this course might have been to me, not having been introduced to Anabaptist history within the Mennonite Brethren church, this two-volume work, which I kept for many years, made a significant impact on me.

My two winters at PBI were rewarding, in that I developed good study habits, though (in retrospect) somewhat restricting in terms of social contacts. I received some good musical training, led a disciplined weekday life, including gratis work to keep down the costs. One

Sunday a month was a fast day, that is, we went without lunch. The substantial meal of meat and potatoes was served at the supper hour.

I made many friends at Prairie, among them the Janz brothers (Aron, Hildor, and Leo) from Main Centre, Saskatchewan, and Corny Enns, Steinbach, Manitoba, who started to sing together while at Prairie and who became well-known for their evangelistic campaigns in Europe. Roger Kellogg came in his own plane. I remember being permitted to go to the Cornelius C. Toews home at nearby Linden for each of two Christmases. They were Mennonite Brethren. Many years later, already living in Calgary, I was able to meet members of that family and thank them for their kindness to me fifty years earlier.

My Own Immersion into the Fundamentalist Camp

I guess I had gradually been drawn into this stance through our own approach to the Bible, a biblicist, literalist interpretation that seemed so believable when our local Brethren discussed portions of the Bible in our traditional *Bibelbesprechungen* (planned Bible discussions) held annually. What was damaging intellectually was our families' exposure and participation in the activities of the Associated Gospel Church (AGC) in Beamsville during what I earlier called 'the singing years' while living on Tufford Road. My sisters found friends at school from this congregation and were invited to sing there. Their pastor and his family were guests at our place between Christmas and New Year's in 1947.

Through them our family was introduced to The Faith Mission of Canada and their superintendent J. Allan Wallace. (This Mission directed a number of travelling evangelists on the 'faith mission' principle [expecting love offerings] and used tents for their own missions where possible.) My mother liked to entertain them as they brought a tent meeting to the nearby Montmorency family farm along the shore of Lake Ontario.

On a group picture there was the familiar figure of Rev. H. H. Janzen and his wife seated beside the Wallace couple. The Janzen couple, friends of our family, were visiting from Kitchener where he was the leading minister and had become a prominent MB Conference leader. As I remember it, there was no question raised over the Gospel emphasis of the tent meeting. Janzen with his linkage to Toronto People's Church and its Russian Bible Institute and Wallace of The Faith Mission of Canada seemed very compatible with each other.

Chapter Two

Education for Service 1947 to 1953

Reorientation

Yet for all this, I returned to the Mennonite Brethren (MB). In my second year at Three Hills I communicated with Jacob K. Janzen, Grimsby, parent of my Janzen family friends. While I don't remember exactly what I asked him, he came back with some pertinent questions: Where would Prairie, without high school and college, lead me? As a leading preacher of the Vineland MB church, he asked me why I was attending PBI. He feared that I would turn away from the MB church as a result. He did not like the 'faith mission' emphasis at PBI, the inter-denominationalism which destroyed loyalty to one's own people and church. He thought he could understand some of my feelings because he had indulged similar ones when he was young in Russia and studied in Germany. He recommended that I return to high school, meaning Eden Christian College, Niagara on the Lake, where he was teaching then, and then follow this by taking a degree course at Mennonite Brethren Bible College, a fairly new school launched in 1944 in Winnipeg, Manitoba.

The years that followed saw me encumbered in high school studies, in somewhat traditional courtship and wedding plans, and in changing residences as I went to three different high schools between 1947 and 1950.

Completing High School

In short, I went to Eden Christian College, located in Niagara-on-the-Lake where I could begin at Grade XI, thus skipping Grade X altogether. Anne Wiebe, Kitchener, and Arthur Harder, a son of our neighbour on Cherry Avenue, were my favourite teachers in English and Mathematics, and they helped me complete that grade without difficulty.

In the fall of 1948 I decided to do Grade XII at Beamsville High School, when I could live with my parents at Tufford Road and attend the same school as my sisters. Mr. Welch the Principal thought that having four of us from the Penner family at Beamsville was quite unique in his experience. While there, encouraged by very good marks, I began to think of completing Grade XIII in Ontario.

For this I chose St. Catharines Collegiate. As I was already married, Justina and I drove from Jordan Station to St. Catharines and we often ate lunch together, since Dodd's Machine Shop where she was employed as secretary was not far from the Collegiate. I was in a Grade XIII class with fellows who were repeating Math just to upgrade their marks to get scholarships at Queens University! It was a hard grind, yet at the end of my high school career in June 1950 I wrote seven papers, and got firsts in all but two, even in Trigonometry and Geometry. This gave me a convincing university entrance, and acceptance at Mennonite Brethren Bible College, Winnipeg.

Marriage and MBBC

Once I had met Justina Janzen she encouraged me to consider Bible College and ministry in the MB Church. This would mean a residence in Winnipeg for three years after which I would be twenty-eight years of age. For all of this we would need finances and that goal also determined, in many ways, a modest approach to courtship and wedding preparations. This attitude was of course in tune with our actual circumstances as relatively new immigrants in Canada. Neither of our families came from a background of substance and wealth, and most of our friends were in much the same boat.

Courtship began with Justina's enquiries about me in 1946-47 when I was away at Prairie Bible Institute. She was the eldest daughter of Abram P. and Justina (Steingart) Janzen and had moved with her family from Steinbach, Manitoba. In Vineland she soon became secretary of Christian Endeavour and was mailing reports to Vineland young people who were away from home. When she discovered that I was a member, but was not on the mailing list (apparently because I was at PBI and not Winkler!), she wrote me a note with the news report. I was naturally grateful that here was a western girl who was above discrimination. As a result, when I got back home in April 1947, I thanked her for this kindness.

During the 1947-1948 year while I was at Eden Christian College, Justina and I met on several occasions, usually with family present. In September we had our first serious talk about our relationship to each other. We were parked at Jordan Harbour in my Ford with the rumble seat until late. I think the moon was shining on Lake Ontario, or was it Jordan Pond? Did it matter which? It soon became clear that we were in love and meant for each other. We exchanged gifts at Christmas and Justina, as a teacher of young children spent much time in preparation for the Christmas Eve Sunday School program. As the winter progressed, dormitory life and classes at Eden seemed never ending as we looked forward to weekends together or special events in our church and social groups.

Interesting perhaps to this generation, our courtship followed a pattern established in Sagradowka, Kherson, Ukraine. After one year of courtship we went to her parents to discuss "*Verlobung* (the formal engagement)" and set the date for it, September 26, 1948. Our engagement was announced in church that day and all the relations came to the Janzen home for the occasion. After this we could feel at ease about being seen together in public. We were now treated as *Brautleute* (an engaged, betrothed, couple, literally).

Our Wedding Day, Saturday, 9 July 1949

Preparations for our wedding had of course begun in 1948. Justina bought her wedding veil in Hamilton in December 1948 during a Christmas shopping trip. We shopped for rings in April 1949, and I bought a wedding suit. Early in May I bought a 1932 Chevrolet from a Jordan farmer for $275. As the wedding date approached we purchased various other things for our residence at the Janzen's. They had an apartment with a separate kitchen at the west end of their house and kindly lent us that for one year. In May a friend had a shower for Justina while Mrs. Dodd helped generously with the cost of the wedding bridal flowers. In addition to a crescent of gardenia, as shown, Mrs. Dodd gave Justina a set of silver in the 'Remembrance' pattern. We received various gifts from our families.

Our wedding portrait,
Peter and Justina, July 9, 1949

The wedding day was warm and pleasant. We walked into church together, without attendants, as prescribed at the time and Rev. Peter Goertzen, a kindly gentleman of the old school, officiated. The entire congregation was invited, and came, and the ladies of the church served up the reception food prepared by Mother Janzen: *Zwiebach*, *Zuckerkuchen*, *Platz*, and sandwiches.

You have to agree, this was a truly Canadian Mennonite wedding, everything done 'decently and in order!'

Yes, we had a brief honeymoon, done on a shoe-string, so to speak, in Ontario when, of all things, one day we needed a policeman to open our car door because I had left the keys in the car. What next? We returned to work, Justina at Dodd's and I at the fruit farmer named Phil Wismer, Jordan Station.

The Year 1950-51 at MBBC

In order to raise funds for the first year of MBBC, we did what I knew how to do. In 1949 we put in 3,000 strawberry plants on the productive soil at Jordan donated by Dad Janzen. That promised some income a year later, though it meant the plants had to be fertilised, cultivated, and blossom-plucked. All this I had learned while working in fruit culture during my years at Culp's, and Justina and I could do together. As it turned out, the strawberry harvest in June 1950 was good, but coincided with my Grade XIII final exams. Much of the picking fell to Justina and anyone who could help.

Justina and Peter, in our Ebenezer Hall apartment, 1950-1951

Once in Winnipeg, we got settled in Ebenezer Hall very quickly. This was a residence for married couples built by the C.A. DeFehr family, widely known in Canada for their business enterprise. We bought a davenport (for sitting and sleeping) and, like many others, built desk and shelf space from bricks and boards cut to length. We were soon quite caught up with activities at the North End MB Church on College Street. To begin, Justina found work at Eaton's on Portage Avenue and I began classes on the first Monday of October. I was now a student enrolled in a Bachelor of Religious Education course to last three years.

MBBC was, since 1944, the senior college of the Canadian Mennonite Brethren, fielding the best teachers this Conference could find at the time, among them the noted Bible expositor Abram H. Unruh and historian/theologian John A. Toews. The president was the Conference leader Henry H. Janzen whom I have introduced as from Ontario. The school was located on the east side of the Red River just off Talbot Avenue in Elmwood.

We were of course made aware that the Conference of Mennonites in Canada had launched a Bible college on the other side of the City south of the Assiniboine River in an area named Tuxedo. This was named the Canadian Mennonite Bible College and opened in 1947. We exchanged visits once a year and the music departments in each cooperated in festive works.

Though the years at MBBC, 1950–1953, were not entirely liberating in terms of fundamentalism, we became closely attached to the MB position on many points and came to admire the strong contribution that the denomination was making to missions, both at home and aboard. Once classes began I was chosen to sing in the *a cappella* choir of about twenty voices led by Ben Horch, head of the Music Department.This choir did two tours in 1951, one to Minnesota congregations, extended to Ontario, and the other to Saskatchewan and Alberta. This latter tour, by trying to reach as many MB congregations as possible in early spring, occasionally found our bus sliding off wet shale roads and having to be pulled back on the road by local farmers with their tractors. By Christmas I had become integrated into what might be called the MBBC quartet of that year, featuring Clarence Hiebert as the leader, Wendolin Mann as tenor, George Dyck (at the piano) as baritone, and I as bass. We sang in many Manitoba churches, often taking the entire service.

An Active Social Life while at MBBC

When Justina was offered the job of College secretary in 1951, she held that position for the next two-and-a-half years, providing a faithful and efficient service to the administration, and an anchor in the office for many students. As Justina worked for Conference leaders, mostly in German, she found herself in July 1951 called on to serve during the General Conference meetings of the MB churches of North America at Winkler. The American Mennonite Brethren had already switched to English and wanted the major Canadian reports translated and transcribed into English. Does anyone remember those Gestetner mimeographing days?

We became active socially, especially once we became close friends with Clarence and Ferne Hiebert from Hillsboro, who had come for one year. Clarence was the youngest son of C.N. Hiebert, whose family Justina knew so well from his days in Winnipeg as city missionary. They had a 1932 car and we did many enjoyable and sometimes crazy things together. For example, on May 19 Clarence stopped at a local restaurant and ordered one brick of 'Neapolitan' ice cream, one knife, four saucers and spoons and four glasses of water. He simply sliced the brick in four quarters, laid each on a plate and said: Take, eat, drink, and be merry! After we had eaten that we went out to the court to play volleyball in moonlight.

For me a highlight of 1951 was a July visit from my parents. Together, we visited the Heinrich Penners at Petersfield, north of Winnipeg. They were related to us because Tina Penner, wife of Heinrich, was a Kroeker, mother's cousin. My folks also visited the Abram Braun family at Altona, a family that sponsored us in 1926. On the way home to Ontario my parents took Justina with them for a well-deserved vacation to see her family. She returned by bus mid-August 1951.

The Year 1951-52

Without belabouring the matter, each three-month term was packed full of course work, complete with exams. I did nine terms in all and maintained an A average. Though we missed the Hieberts, we soon found a warm welcome at the family of Ben, Esther, and Viola Horch. This came about because two of my sisters arrived in the fall of 1951, Marianne as a student for the year and Catherine to work. The latter found a welcome place with Esther Horch and Viola who were alone while Ben Horch was away on study leave in Germany.

Justina enjoyed a visit from her mother in November. Taking my sister Cathy with them, they visited old friends and relations in the Steinbach area. Justina's mother left at the end of November for Sioux Lookout, Northern Ontario, to visit Henry and Vera for the occasion of their firstborn, Arthur Henry. Henry was teaching in the local school. Only two months later on February 6, 1952 we had an unexpected holiday on the death of King George VI and the accession of his young daughter Princess Elizabeth to the throne. We took the occasion to visit Henry and Vera at Sioux Lookout. We had an enjoyable visit, all told, and among other things, heard Charles Forsyth, the United Church of Canada minister, speak on Sunday February 17. We would later meet him in New Brunswick.

Camp Arnes, 1952 and 1953

In the midst of a busy year we were invited by Abram A. Kroeker to consider working at Camp Arnes during the summer of 1952. Arnes was organized by Mennonite business men as the Lake Winnipeg Mission Camp Society. We had learned to know the families of the Kroeker brothers: Peter and A.A. Kroeker, the latter formerly of the Winkler Bible School who then became a prominent agribusiness entrepreneur. They were 'Kanadier' of the 1870s migration. When Kroeker exceeded the speed limit on the gravel roads north to Arnes, he boasted that he had more money than time!

We accepted the challenge and Camp Arnes (north of Gimli on Lake Winnipeg) provided an entirely different experience during the summers of 1952 and 1953. This was our first child–related work on such a scale in such a setting. I was camp manager the first summer, with Alfred Kroeker as director. After one year I replaced him and had Abe Quiring as camp manager. During our stints at Arnes Justina served ably as secretary.

My responsibility during that first summer involved getting everything cleaned and ready for the first batch of boys and then girls. The work was enjoyable and volunteers were willing to work hard. A bad dose of poison ivy, however, plagued me much of that summer. Strangely, on July 23, in the act of digging and staring down my four-foot hole for an outside latrine, the thought came to me that my personality and ability might be better suited to the profession of teaching history and theology!

Taking on this responsibility of Camp direction meant that, alongside my classes, studies, papers, and other activities at MBBC, I had to write all the lessons for Camp Arnes. Why not? Wasn't I earning a Bachelor of Religious Education Degree? Actually, I was amazed at how easily our teachers could use the lessons I prepared.

All told, during these two summers we made many good friends, among them A.A. DeFehr whose son Arthur [later of Palliser Furniture] was there as a camper. We also consolidated our friendship with the sons of C.A. DeFehr: Cornelius, Abram, and William, because their children were either in Sunday school at North End Church, Winnipeg, or at Arnes during this time. For us the most endearing person was our cook, Helen Willms, the mother of Herman, Betty (Bergman), and Helen (Litz, of Winnipeg Children's Choir fame).

The Year 1952-53

This last year proved to be a very busy year. All told it meant a seventy to eighty hour week, everything included. As editor of the 1953 *Rainbow* I was also a member of Student Council. The year proved challenging in another way. We were asked to serve as house parents to a batch of male MBBC students. This large house at 72 Carman Avenue, Elmwood, meant walking from there to MBBC each day. This proved healthy for both of us. Among these fellows were David Harder and Bill Reimer from Yarrow; Jake Friesen and Bill Redekopp from Abbotsford; Lawrence Fast, Jake Klippenstein, and Henry Braun from Saskatchewan; Jake Doerksen, the loner from Gem, Alberta;

and Karl Bartsch and Ben Toews from Ontario. The young men who became doctor, music professor, social worker, teachers, and farmers, loved Saturdays because Justina would send a nice aroma through the entire house when she baked *Zwiebach*. Many found an excuse to pass through the kitchen on the way to the laundry or the outdoors on those days. She did other things for them that reminded them of home.

Justina and Graduation

Justina was not without her misgivings about our employment prospects. For the most part, however, she thrived on her association with people through her position as College secretary. During the last year she practised with the oratorio choir with Ben Horch, and sang in his *a cappella* choir. He produced a performance of Handel's *Messiah* in March 1953 and the smaller choir travelled during the end of March and early April as far as Coaldale and into the Fraser Valley.

Having guests in and feeding them was of course Justina's department, and often her delight. Our daybook is filled with references to guests who came to Carman Avenue, probably as many as ninety during the course of that year, besides having the boys 'in and out' for *Zwiebach* every weekend. John B. Epp and Hugo Jantz were among my closest friends during this year. They came frequently. Justina had Terry Tsuda and Junko Matsuna from Japan as friends. After Justina got back from her choir tour, we had a multi-birthday party for our boys.

Convocation ceremonies took place over two weekends. There was a recreation day, a Baccalaureate service. The last weekend offered a banquet, *a cappella* choir concert, and Commencement, as it was called. George Konrad was valedictorian of our graduating class, while Frank C. Peters, then at Tabor College, gave the commencement address.

"What Shall I Do with My Life?"

My experiences in trying to find a gratifying field of service within the Mennonite Brethren Conference were a bit disappointing, somewhat confusing. First, of course, I went to Waterloo College to complete the requirements for a BA degree. This College then was in reality a Waterloo campus of the University of Western Ontario in London. In Waterloo we were looking for that first opportunity to serve somewhere in the Conference.

There were many 'unpaid counsellors.' Some were very good, especially Isaac Redekopp. He strongly suggested Tabor College and a USA assignment. Not far off the mark, he viewed me as an introvert who had enough talents to go in a number of directions. Ministry was not my only option, perhaps medicine or administration. In the midst of less than helpful negative critics I asked "What shall I do with my life?" While not yet too daring, I concluded from one self-analysis that I was probably best suited for teaching! This turned out to be a portent of the future.

Though I was quite happy while at MBBC, I was shaken when in 1952 some Saskatchewan MB congregations lobbied our faculty to take a stand against the new *Revised Standard Version* (RSV) of the Bible. Only the reading of the balanced assessment of the RSV two years later by H.S. Bender and Millard Lind of Goshen College helped me to see the scholarly integrity in the translators. The Christian anti-Communists of the day wrote the translators off as 'pinkies' (near Communists). As a result of this intellectual upheaval, in the midst of my full year in Waterloo College, I journalized that I was "no longer a fundamentalist, but an evangelical. There is a difference as between sanity and fanaticism, between scholarship and obscurantism, especially as revealed by the attack on the RSV of the Bible."

The Call to Sawyer MB, North Dakota

Whatever discouragement I was feeling at this time was lifted when we were steered to the prospect of a pastoral position in the Sawyer,

North Dakota, church, albeit a 'small country church.' Had not I.W. Redekopp suggested an assignment in the USA and completing the BA requirements at Tabor College, Hillsboro, Kansas?

Well, our acceptance of this position began the year-long-and eventually failed-process of trying to get a visa for work in the USA. In July 1954 I made the long trip via Chicago, on the Soo Line. I wondered about my host Mr. Beck who told me he had driven twenty-seven miles in nineteen minutes [!] to pick me up. I seemed to please most of the people with German-sounding names, Bechtels, Fauls, Heintzlmans, Liebelts, as opposed to Mennonite names. They paid me $76 expense money, and offered about $200 a month plus some allowances. I played lawn croquet with Evelyn Beck, a MBBC student, and her four sisters. On the return trip I had nearly six hours waiting in Chicago, my first experience of the famous Loop.

Ordination of *Mitarbeiter* (Ministers-Elect)

The decision to make this venture in faith meant facing the prospect of ordination, something that Sawyer wanted to know was done in a congregation that knew us. It did not take long for the Kitchener MB Church (where we had our membership in 1953-1954) to vote in favour of that and we got our Canadian passports in short order, but we never did succeed in getting a USA visa. This time the excuse was that we had not been in 'ordered ministry' for a period of at least two years.

Justina's family: Abram and Justina Janzen, holding Arthur, Doug and Mary Coombs, Henry and Vera Janzen, Peter and Justina, Susie, 1953

Ordination for a pastoral position in Ontario required a doctrinal and ethical questionnaire. Not only that, I had to do an *Eintrittspredigt* (induction sermon) in the home congregation, and then also 'do the circuit,' preaching in all six Ontario Conference congregations, east to west: Virgil, St. Catharines, Vineland, Kitchener, Port Rowan, and Leamington.

Lindal, Manitoba, 1955-57

Very soon the vigilant I.W. Redekopp wrote asking whether we would consider an appointment in Manitoba's *Randmission* (home mission), either at Lindal or Winnipegosis. We could hardly say 'no', and when the official call came from the committee, we were concerned only to finish our degree work first. This meant postponing the departure until the fall of 1955. As Harry and Gertrude Loewen had consented to take Winnipegosis, we accepted the call to Lindal, a work to be taken

up following summer school. Lindal had its beginnings in the 1930s among German and Czech people who had settled on the edges of the Pembina Valley about fourteen miles south-west of Morden. Our postal address was Thornhill, west of Morden, with its traditional railway station.

Thornhill, Manitoba, Railway Station, 1956

Having opted for completion of the degree work at Waterloo College, I was allowed, as an exception, to take a necessary course in New Testament Greek by correspondence (in which I did well), as well as two summer courses at McMaster University, located in the west end of Hamilton. This circumstance forced us to take my parent's offer to live at Tufford Road, near Beamsville, where I could be picked up by a car pool. I took first year Biology and Ancient History, and commuted with other summer school students from the St. Catharines and Vineland area. This was the hot, humid summer of 1955 (without air conditioning) when we spent as much time in Lake Ontario as possible. It was also the last summer with my Dad who died of cancer the following spring.

Following a successful summer school and the joy of access to the Lake for swimming in that hot summer, we left for Lindal, arriving about the middle of August. We were to succeed Wilmer and Evangeline (Willms) Kornelson who had followed Abe and Helen (Penner) Goerz.

When we took our first worship in this Pembina Valley location on August 28th, we landed feet first into a troublesome family affair of which our predecessors had told me. Since it was said to be a serious problem even as we arrived, I thought it best, encouraged by Rev. Jake Quiring, then serving the Winkler Church, to treat the so-called errant as a brother rather than continue the disciplinary procedures of my predecessors. Whatever his misdemeanours, we had to leave judgement up to God in a matter that had been festering for nearly a decade. I won a friend and relative peace was restored.

Unfortunately, this couple had a son who was ill from sleeping sickness.[7] They wanted to take him to a faith healer named Valdez who had been mesmerizing the countryside. In this matter I was as firm as Abe Goerz before me. I discouraged this. In fact, during the winter of 1956–57 I wrote an article entitled "Faith Healing or Fake Healing" and sent it to Orlando Harms at the *Christian Leader*, Hillsboro, Kansas. He welcomed it warmly and published it in 1957. I had studied the matter carefully because I knew of others who were being misled by Oral Roberts, Tulsa, Oklahoma, whose literature was widely read.

While I found the two-year Lindal experience less than rewarding, it was clear that even a small Christian community tucked in the Pembina Hills fourteen miles from Morden could dish up problems to test one's patience and also one's wisdom. There were also some wonderful people in that group, a joy to get to know, especially Harry and Edna Guderian with their family of four, also the Balouns, the

---

7   Though sleeping sickness has a name, narcoplexy, it remains a puzzle to the medical profession

Browns and Rachuls, whether German, Czech or Mennonite. Harry and Edna, a half mile away, provided the most help, social time, and intelligent discussion. We played *Scrabble* with them many times, having introduced the game. It was always amazing to me how frequently Harry won at *Scrabble*, sometimes with what was a 'poor hand' (set of letters). He was a successful grain farmer who had built his own seed-cleaning plant. He would go out to check his operation during the course of a game!

Norman Guderian, a nephew, completed a barn-raising one summer with only me as his helper, while his wife Bertha had her first child in the midst of the worst snow-filled roads imaginable. What a story! Mine, as it happened, was the only car that could get out. Norman brought Bertha to our place by tractor. Harry Guderian had to use his tractor to pull me through otherwise impassable roads. By a very circuitous road we reached the number 3 highway and got to Manitou's hospital just as she 'broke water.' This was three days before Christmas, 1955, and Karen Joy turned out to be a fine baby.

Reynold and Alice Rothenberger with son Norman became fast friends. They were United Church people, our nearest neighbours. They had a team of horses, a box sleigh and heavy blankets. Because I once helped Reynold rescue one of the cows of a Czech family, the latter prepared a thirteen-course Czech meal, reserved only for special occasions. We were considered good people, trustworthy, not constantly haranguing. They even sent their children to our Daily Vacation Bible School.

Lindal Experiences

Experiences in the Pembina region were so varied. We once witnessed a complete hail-out at Snowflake, a second outpost of ours, on August 19, 1956. Hail took out the whole section of grain in full head belonging to a Goerz family. We drove there the next day to commiserate with them. Expectations of thousands in harvest earnings were wiped out in less than five minutes.

The new radio 'good music' station CFAM came to Altona in 1957. This was about the same time as the appearance of a Fargo, ND, Christian radio station. This really set us apart from our indigenous community. Members kept asking: do you like what is being offered. Having been introduced to classical music by our good friend Ben Horch, we found it difficult to be fed one half-hour program after the other featuring fundamentalist preaching and promising a book or tape for a donation.

When we were deluged with ninety inches of snow during the severe winter conditions of 1955-56, and were in consequence unable to use the church building, we began to think of alternatives to living in the little house near the church. Could I be usefully employed at Winkler Bible School during the winter, and still serve Lindal? The big question "why are we here" kept cropping up. Are we really cut out for rural work? Circumstantial signs again pointed to study and teaching, as the following account will indicate.

Shortly after our arrival in Lindal we joined the Morden MB church as it was the closest one while Lindal was still an 'at-arm's-length' mission. We were accepted first as members, and then I as a minister, on November 6, 1955. Frank Friesen, a delightful man, a business associate of John Wiens [father of Rotarian Bob], was then the moderator. We enjoyed our association with this church, especially through the medium of Abe and Frieda (Penner) Riediger. They proved to be one of the strong compensating elements for the difficult situations that we had to cope with at Lindal. The Riediger family had a feed and grain business in Morden. Frieda, who hailed from Vineland, used to invite us for dinner and allowed us to use their proper bathroom facilities. We had only four rooms and a PATH!

Lindal (and Peter Penner) at the Cross-Roads

Much of our thinking about the MB Church and Conference seemed to crystallise at Lindal while Harry Guderian sensed that the next year, 1956-7, would be crucial for Lindal. Certain young people needed to be baptized, others needed to commit themselves to meet their pledges for a church basement, while the eyes of the Manitoba conference were on Lindal. Harry recognized that self-support was difficult to attain and the geographical location remained a problem. Jake Quiring in Winkler thought the group should be responsible for about $1,000 annually in order to continue to have a conference worker. Some of these questions oppressed me and led to considerable introspection. On June 6, 1956 I had "fleeting pains in the chest."

Baptismal Service, Lindal church, at Pembina river, 1957

The best possible climax to our work at Lindal was the baptism of seven candidates: Dorothy and Russell Brown, Doris, Bertha, and Ronald Guderian, and Joyce and Ronnie Rachul. This was the first baptism, I believe, since before the MBBC graduates began to come. Jake Quiring came as speaker to the Pembina river site.

The question of our staying reached an acute form in November 1956. We did not really fit in too well; we were not really missionaries; and the congregation, though they wanted college graduates, never went out of their way to push penetration into the community. How to form a believer's church out of the disparate locations and situations of Lindal and Darlingford and Snowflake to the west was the frequent subject of discussion. *Never was so much driving done in so many different directions with so little accomplished.*

Similar to two years earlier, I had many unpaid counsellors about what to do. When Anne Schmidt, Justina's successor as secretary at MBBC, came to visit in 1957, she told us Professor J.A. Toews was sending her to Lindal "to solve all our problems." While exploring the opportunity and advisability of going to East Chilliwack Bible School where my friends John Wall, Hugo Jantz, and Hans Kasdorf had taught before me, three other suggestions popped up. At least we were not without choices.

With all of this on my mind I had a chance to talk to John A. Harder, Yarrow, who happened to be in Winnipeg at MBBC in March 1957. He had the wisest idea of all: begin in BC with the Bible School, "get to know the BC folk" and then there will be other opportunities if what I started with did not work out. This rationalisation of our aptitudes and situation at Lindal led inextricably, it seems, into accepting an offer to take a position at the East Chilliwack Bible School. That the choice for BC at that time was not quite right could not be foreseen.

The First of Our 'Chosen' Family

Though we were wont to think that it was Justina that was infertile, it turned out that it was I who proved to be sterile. A St. Catharines doctor discovered that I had a negligible sperm count. The only conclusion we could draw from this as to cause was my severe bout with typhoid fever at age eighteen. On the basis of this discovery we decided that we would adopt children rather than remain without them.

We adopted our first child in Manitoba in 1956 while at Lindal. We made application to Children's Aid in Manitoba and were directed to the office in Portage la Prairie. Albert Hoeppner, a local friend, offered to drive us on that first winter trip to Portage la Prairie, on a roundabout way because of wintry conditions.

We were pleasantly surprised that Children's Aid would even consider us eligible, given our meagre income and somewhat uncertain future. We were even more surprised, having just arrived back from a quick trip to Ontario, and having waited only ten months, that Margaret Boux had a baby boy for us in Winnipeg. We met with her in Morden on October 17, 1956 and were very pleased with this child's history. Following a shopping trip to Winnipeg, where we stayed with Bill and Erna DeFehr, we picked up the one we named Robert Gregory Penner, born August 22, and took him home. We notified the *Mennonite Observer* that "our chosen son" had come to live with us.

At the next social occasion, a Lindal wedding, Robert was the centre of attention. This seemed to be everyone's first experience with an adoption, and he was blond and blue-eyed and liked to run on gravel on all fours.

During this period of searching out the employment options, and waiting for finalization of the adoption process, I put Justina and Robert on the CPR's *Canadian* for a trip to Ontario to show off Robert to the grandparents.

With Margaret's generous help we were able to complete the process before we left Manitoba for BC, and just before the woman we loved to call "our Miss Boux" herself left the Portage la Prairie office. We applied for Robert's birth certificate and for the "absolute decree" on May 24th and received this court document in due course.

My First History Thesis, an Earnest of the Future?

It was in February 1956 at Lindal that I took steps to earn another degree by researching the home mission work of the Canadian MB conference. Upon completion I would earn the Bachelor of Theology degree and would at the same time be kept from idleness on the field during inclement weather. As told, we had 90 inches of snow which reduced the use of the church to two occasions that winter!

This was a good exercise in thesis writing and made me more fully versed in the history of the MB Conference. I was fortunate to find that Abram H. Voth, a Morden member, had a complete collection of the Northern (Canadian) District Conference yearbooks, from 1910, and allowed me to take them to Lindal. It was Doctor David Ewert at MB Bible College who had cleared this path for me and helped in this my first extensive research and writing project to set me on the path of historical research as a vocation.

Once the roads were cleared of snow and ice, we took a trip to Winnipeg where I was able to research the Mennonite papers for which I had already written some articles. Frank Epp of the *Canadian Mennonite* (1953), Leslie Stobbe at the *Mennonite Observer* (1956), and

Orlando Harms at the *Christian Leader* (1934) had become receptive to my style of writing and my choice of subjects.

Leaving Lindal

Having completed our work for this small congregation, we were given pleasant farewells at both Lindal and Morden. We packed up everything for shipping by train to Chilliwack. One of our members took our truckload to Winnipeg free of charge and he and his wife kept us for the night until we departed on September 7. The shipping costs were $220.89 for which we were **not** reimbursed by the school board that hired us.

Susie, Justina's sister, a nurse, came to join us and, after making some visits in Winnipeg, we got under way in our 1956 Dodge. We travelled via Herbert, Saskatchewan, where we visited Rudy and Erica Janzen and then, at Medicine Hat we took Highway 3 to Coaldale, Alberta, east of Lethbridge, where we stopped with Aron and Aunt Mary (Steingart) Janzen. From there we drove through Washington State and arrived in Chilliwack on September 12, 1957.

Chapter Three

Our BC Experience 1957-1960

Though we enjoyed getting to British Columbia (BC) and looked forward to teaching at the East Chilliwack Bible School (ECBS), we felt some unease about this appointment. The years in the Fraser Valley, however, brought us unusual opportunities, one of which would lead to the production of a first book, be it ever so modest.

The East Chilliwack Bible School

Our first home in the Valley was in Rosedale just east of Chilliwack. A surprise grocery shower staged by board members was a huge gift. Perhaps its total value was more than, or the equivalent of, the sum we were out of pocket to get ourselves and our things moved from Manitoba to BC. While the grocery hampers were wonderful, we could not however make ends meet on the initial salary. After a frank discussion with board member Kroeker, we were paid $225 a month retroactive to the beginning of October and then only for the teaching year.

Were These two Years Necessary for My Education?

The discussion of this Bible school's viability, a question I had asked before I came, was never far below the surface. Some local members agreed that their congregation should have been willing to combine with other Fraser Valley MB congregations in support of such a school. But congregational selfishness prevailed: this was our school! It was not until early April 1959 that Henry Dick, Chilliwack businessman, told me that he had once (before we left Manitoba in September 1957) composed a twelve-page letter "advising me *not* to take on [this Bible school] job". In that statement he had recounted the history of failure by Greendale, Broadway Chilliwack, and East Chilliwack churches to work together on a Bible school project. He then changed his mind because he did not want to be responsible for choices I might make. Given the great uncertainty of that period in my life, I think I would have been grateful if he had sent the letter. I might [should] have stayed in Manitoba.

My one colleague told me at our first meeting that he had a personal problem which he designated in New Testament terms as his 'thorn in the flesh.' While I was not competent to diagnose his problem, I was more than a little concerned about his feeling of insecurity in handling his share of the school program and serving as principal. Early in 1958, at his request, the East Chilliwack church leadership decided to follow the prayer sequence suggested in the Epistle of James, 5:13-16. As we placed hands on his head, we prayed that he might have a rapid, or gradual, recovery, or receive "grace to bear his burden." It was a victory for him because he came to feel better after that, and felt buoyed that he knew others were praying for him. My colleague turned out to be quite an effective speaker and promoter of mission in BC, was ordained to the Gospel ministry at East Chilliwack and had a varied and successful career in social work.

He wrote an autobiography in 2001 and was good enough to let me read it. While he skirted some of these personal things, I did not think he was fair to his previous colleagues when he referred to them as persons who came in for 'various staff needs.' I wrote him: "I don't think Hans Kasdorf or Henry Warkentin would be too thrilled to read that. I think all of us were full-fledged, full-time teachers, though you had the responsibilities as principal, correctly enough."

The Closing Down of ECBS and Finding a New Position

During my second year I began to show the strain of teaching, writing articles for the press, and having the church choir. What was troubling, however, was the uncertainty about the future of this Bible School. So I called John J. Esau, chairman of the board, to unburden myself of these things, and to tell him about plans to return to school, and to leave BC after one more year. The process of the second adoption was the only thing that would detain us that long. This came to him as a *Hiobsbotschaft* (commiseration by 'Job's comforters!').

When my colleague left to study social work at University of BC, and I went to the Mennonite Educational Institute (MEI), Abbotsford, ECBS was left without a teacher. Our combined resignation effectively shut down this school. As I had suggested, quite a number of young people now decided to go to the MB Bible Institute, Abbotsford, as this was a much better situation for them in every way.

When one of my fellow graduates from MB Bible College wrote to ask about ECBS in April 1959, I told him that East Chilliwack represented a 'one-church affair,' *whose board expected two to do the work of three on the salary of one!* I also told him that "I am actually quite proud of my role in helping to close down ECBS in 1959 because it was better for the young people." I also wrote that if he were to accept a position at another school, he should ask for moving expenses!

As it turned out, there were vacancies both in Mennonite Educational Institute (MEI) and MB Bible Institute, Clearbrook (became part of Abbotsford), and I could have chosen the latter. To the puzzlement of my close College friends who took positions at the Bible Institute, I decided for MEI because I would earn $3,600 spread over twelve months, while working only one more month than at the Bible Institute.

How different our departure was from that of our arrival in the East Chilliwack community. In 1957 we were "glad-handed, dined, showered with groceries, praised, loaded with work – and many assured us: 'We want to have you down sometime'!" As it was, except for J.C. Willms (whose daughter attended school) and who moved us to Abbotsford (by sending his son and a three-ton truck), nearly everyone was *silent*. Of the church leaders, lay ministers and deacons, Gerhard Thielmann and P.S. Thiessen were considerate to the end and in later contacts.

"Getting to Know Some BC People"

That the East Chilliwack congregation could treat people roughly in those days may be illustrated from the vicissitudes of a namesake, Peter H. Penner, Rosedale, from whom our first house in Rosedale was rented. Details aside, the case of Penner's bankruptcy 'trial' in a church forum was not pretty and goes far to explain why people turned away from the church in those decades. Penner survived by moving to Mutual Life as an insurance salesman and did very well.

We were quite upset by all the hypocrisy, disunity, and slander we discovered in East Chilliwack in those years. Moreover, some of the very preachers who led the church to discipline P.H. Penner, and were negative about women, were not immune from criticism and most of them failed to some extent to retain their own children for the church. Fortunately, we also got to know many exceptional people while living in what was then called Clearbrook and teaching at the MEI, but that is part of the next section.

The West Coast Children's Mission (WCCM)

In 1958 I was elected to a two-year term on the board of the West Coast Children's Mission and thus got involved in BC conference activities. This was the home mission arm of the BC/MB conference. I was soon appointed secretary. It was my privilege to do a tour of the WCCM stations all the way up to Port Edward, near Prince Rupert. All told I was away ten days, travelling by bus, and spent five nights sitting up in my "brown casual suit." I was not out of pocket and became well informed in the matters of the Mission. Justina had her sister Susie as company in Chilliwack.

Once elected chairman of the WCCM board in 1959 I became the *Vertreter* (representative) to the Conference and was expected to give the semi-annual report. I was also asked to write the history of this work from its beginnings in 1939. To help me verify information and see the locations again, by car this time, I was able to take Justina and Robert with me. Visiting the MB mission work sites in the towns of Vanderhoof, Hazelton, Terrace, and Kitimat, was an enlightening experience. Besides some articles for the press, I got considerable satisfaction out of researching, writing, and publishing what was entitled *Reaching the Otherwise Unreached*. I believe 1,000 copies were printed and distributed to all the congregations in BC. I was able to include pictures of all the workers and I drew two maps for the book.

Even though it came thirty years later, I was pleased to receive a certificate from the BC conference in recognition of that historical contribution.

No one was prepared for the tragic news at the beginning of July 1961 that Peter Neufeldt, our associate in the WCCM, along with his son-in-law Walter Sawatsky (missionary), and Herb Martens, a former director, were killed at Bonners Ferry, Idaho, on their way from Yarrow, BC, to the Canadian Conference in Winnipeg. Though we wrote our condolences to Peter's widow, it was believed that the accident was the result of excessive speeding.

The Second Adoption

Completing our 'million-dollar family' was most important to us. In the late fall of 1957, following our move to British Columbia, we took steps to contact the department that looked after adoptions in the province. Our social worker made her first visit on November 27. Her main concern was that the Rosedale house rented for us was too draughty for a new baby. The question of the cost of heating that house came up again in December. The East Chilliwack Bible School board then helped us find a warm house (completely renovated) on Cleveland Avenue in Chilliwack. Living on Cleveland Avenue brought us just a few doors away from

Justina with Robert and
Ruth, Chilliwack, BC, 1960

Peter and Katie Harder, and their children David and Louise. As I shall explain, Justina and Katie had known each other since they were children.

We received a little baby, born May 3, 1959 into our home on July 29, 1959. We named her Ruth Catharine Jeannette Penner. [Later on we regretted not giving her the name Justina instead of Jeannette, for then she would have carried forward the favourite first daughter designation in the Steingart family!] She was beautiful and we were glad to show her off to the new friends we made during our year of residence in Abbotsford when I taught at the Mennonite Collegiate Institute.

Our Year at Mennonite Educational Institute, 1959-60

As told, I found employment at the Mennonite Educational Institute in 1959. That year of teaching, a trial run so to speak, turned out to be a wonderful experience. The atmosphere was so different from what I had sensed in East Chilliwack. For some reason, however, I did not write much in my daybook about this year. We were abnormally busy with class preparation and were having such a very satisfying and active social and church life. We were much happier and our interests widened by our involvements in the WCCM board.

The year proved "interesting, challenging ... and satisfying since I [was with] a good companionable staff," including Principal Bill Wiebe. Among the most interesting was Cornelius C. Peters, 63, the father of Frank C. Peters. Other colleagues whom I remember with affection were Jacob Toews, John Ratzlaff, Henry Klassen, and Cornelius D. Toews. I managed to establish good discipline and a learning atmosphere in my Grade Eleven home room. As I wrote, "We found kindred minds, interests and aspirations there." We joined the large membership of the MB church where I had many invitations to speak, and we shared in church activities, especially with couples our age.

Chapter Four

Five Years in Ontario 1960-1965

Daring to Make a Change

Except for a short period for educational purposes, 1953–55, we had been away from Ontario for a decade. I was coming back with a nagging question: did I want to be a minister or historian? Why was I daring to consider a change? Little did we know that this return to Ontario would lead to a sharp break with the past, nor could we conceive what the issue would be to help us make such a decision. Actually, the decision to go into teaching was easier than to leave the MB church and to perhaps even give up the ordination status.

As the MB church turned to professional ministry, 'vocation' and 'career' became one and the same for many. As I turned from ministry to teaching as a profession (beginning in 1965), I rationalized the change by thinking of profession as the way I earned my living, and my calling (vocation) to be a witness to those around us. Did I really have to do full-time ministry just because I was already ordained?

My foray into producing articles which were warmly welcomed by Mennonite editors, and my satisfaction at being able to put together a readable historically integral book in the Fraser Valley helped put me on a path of less and less reliance on the church for a living.

During this period I developed a rationale for studying history. My interest in history was real and English history could do for me, I conjectured, what theology did for others. Much of English history is religious as well as political and imperial. In the long run, this proved to be the right path for me. My knowledge of the Bible remained and history taught me all the practical theology I needed.

Ontario, 1960-61

Notwithstanding our good experiences in BC, I was determined to return to Ontario to pursue a Master's Degree and to do it at McMaster University, Hamilton. As soon as we completed the adoption process for our daughter Ruth we left June 13, 1960 and drove back to Ontario. Along the way we discovered that Ruth was not a good traveller. Given that we stopped to visit along the way, we subjected our dear Ruth to seven different beds in as many nights on the road.

The trip was not entirely enjoyable for Justina either. After all, she had married me twelve years earlier thinking that I was going to work in the church. Until 1957 I had given her the impression that "I was pursuing studies and situations leading toward a settled occupation in the ministry." Now I was heading back to school.

I cannot easily gloss over the first year back in Ontario. Altogether, it was not our best year in terms of accommodation and church fellowship. As was our custom, we joined the local church, Scott Street MB church, then under familiar pastoral leadership. Though some people welcomed us 'back home,' so to speak, this congregation and that at Vineland were different from the ones we had left a decade earlier. In Vineland, my former home church, I was made welcome by Henry H. Voth who had previously started the MB fellowship in Toronto while pursuing theological studies.

My reception at McMaster was, however, most satisfying. Doctor E. Togo Salmon, then head of the history department, remembered me, remarkably, from summer school ten years earlier. Doctor Arthur Bourns, dean of the graduate school (later president), assured me that I could enter the MA program in history after a make-up year. Having done well enough previously, I registered for six history courses, and Togo (as he was affectionately known) asked me to correct his student's Ancient History essays, and I was also awarded $1,750 as a teaching assistant for the Master's ahead.

My Master's Year at McMaster, 1961-62

There were decisions to be made. Robert was now of kindergarten age, Ruth nearly two years, and I nearly 36! When I seriously worked out a budget for another year at McMaster, implying residence in Hamilton, I realized that with summer employment I could make it without too much indebtedness. All that was necessary was to finish my 1960–61 course work on a strong note, move to Hamilton, and together work our way through another year of studies, this time at the Master's level.

We enjoyed a four-day visit to my sister's home in Smithville, Ohio, six hours away. On a previous occasion we had helped John and Cathy (Penner) Lerch with their *Lerch's Donuts* at the Wayne County Fair, an annual event. I did an article on John's enterprise entitled "Twelve Thousand Dozen Donuts [made and sold in 10 days!]."

A friend loaned his truck to move our earthly goods from St. Catharines to Hamilton in September. Others who helped with the move were my brother Corney, his wife Sondra, and my brother-in-law Abe Friesen. We moved into an upper duplex apartment on Main Street West, within walking distance to McMaster University. While Justina got a job in Mills Memorial Library, I registered for courses with Charles Murray Johnstone in British Imperial history, and with Herbert McCready in Nineteenth Century Britain. Between the two major reading and writing courses, I was allowed to do some topics of interest to me. In my MA seminar were three Anglicans, one Presbyterian, and one Mennonite, not that church affiliation was intended to be our major identity.

These fellows, especially W. Fox-Decent, Winnipeg, were the first to challenge me about our Mennonite Brethren approach to film, theatre, and the arts generally. Why the MB prohibitions (against movies, TV), why the protectionist, exclusionist, policies? Why the ban on this and that when enterprising Mennonites in Winnipeg were entering a variety of professions, business, and contracting without being challenged! At this time, as I was aware, there were about 600 Mennonite students in Canadian universities.

Though we as a family had some good times, all of us found the second year at McMaster more stressful. For Justina the gradual orientation toward teaching and the pressures related to my studies and her busyness as a mother and a part-time employee brought on fatigue, nervous exhaustion, and repressed anxieties over the immediate future. She was also getting the brunt of parental criticisms of the course we had taken. That she needed my love and encouragement as well as a good friend was obvious.

Justina made some new friends among the Library staff at Mills Memorial Library. Robert started Kindergarten, while Ruth was able to stay temporarily with our sister-in-law Vera Janzen in Kitchener. Meanwhile, I was getting to know professors Johnstone and McCready. They would prove to be most helpful for many years. Taking two major reading and writing courses, as well as doing seminars with the other MA students posed a new challenge. I was in a new world of scholastic demands in writing, articulation, and retention of material. My Master's year in History included a critical study of the remarakable career of David Livingstone, missionary-explorer in Africa.

Hamilton Christian Fellowship Chapel

During this year of 1961-62 our church life revolved around the relatively young Hamilton MB church, still run as a mission, and then served by David Nickel in succession to my friend from MBBC, John Unger. The group was still meeting in a basement chapel, a situation that remained until John D. Reimer came from BC.

It soon became clear that some fellow College graduates in Hamilton would have liked me to serve them as pastor. They knew we would be with them for one year and that they would need a replacement for Nickel who was leaving after one year. The trouble was that my name was also being mentioned as a potential candidate for Toronto when Herb Swartz decided to return to studies. It eventually came down to making a choice between Toronto and Hamilton, as both sent committees to interview us.

At the Ontario conference in Leamington (June 1962), we indicated our preference for Toronto, and were announced as the new Toronto workers. As a result I had four summer months to complete my MA work. The Hamilton congregation took the John Reimer family, somewhat on my recommendation, as I was the only person in Ontario who knew John intimately from our years in BC. Once they had committed themselves to Hamilton and had moved into the area, John soon led the congregation in relocating to a new church building at Stoney Creek.

Two Years in Toronto, 1962-64

What an unbelievable convoy on the Queen Elizabeth Way it was. For our 'midnight move' from Hamilton to Toronto siblings and friends helped out with a two-ton truck. This was loaded to capacity and the remainder of our things was taken in cars, our own little Simca, inside and roof-top, and one of Justina's friends at Mills Memorial Library. This convoy arrived at Yorkdale between Dufferin and Bathurst after midnight on September 1. Graduate students in various fields, Herb Swartz, Alex Redekop, and Elmer Stobbe, bless them, were waiting to help us unload and carry our things into a fairly spacious house at 272 Ranee Avenue, located on the edge of Lawrence Heights. We were indeed grateful to Margaret Swartz who had left the house spotless.

Herb Swartz had ministered in the Lawrence Heights area since the fall of 1959. The good news was that the adult membership made up of Mennonites had increased by fifty percent, while the Sunday school was expanding under the guidance of teachers drawn from a commuting congregation. The bad news he reported was that the people living in subsidized housing, while sending their children to Sunday school, were quite indifferent to our ministry.

Be that as it may, at our first service held in the home of Jake Wiens, with thirty persons present, we were pleased to receive Jack and Ruth Neufeld as supportive members of this congregation. They had recently moved from Edmonton where Jack worked with Hudson's Bay. As it turned out, we were fortunate later to form a lasting triangular relationship with them and Vern and Frieda Heinrichs who also joined our fellowship at that time.

During our time we won the adherence of a painter, Hannu Aalto, who lived in the community. He painted landscapes and seascapes designed for over the living room davenport. He was making a living by selling these by knocking on doors. He seemed more successful than those of us who knocked on doors to deliver invitations to our worship services and Sunday school.

During that fall of 1962, we had the fascinating experience of seeing a church edifice arise from the ground up. This construction brought us a great deal of attention. Getting it ready for occupancy in March 1963 was ably assisted by David Warkentin, a practicing physician. He often drove sixteen miles from Agincourt early in the morning to do certain jobs, and left in time to open his practice at nine o'clock. The general contractor was Jacob Reimer, St. Catharines. Aside from the mainly Italian workmen who came as crews of skilled tradesmen, his chief assistants were Low German speaking Paraguayer, we called them. They came on Monday morning; at night Mr. Reimer slept in an upstairs room in the house; and the Paraguayer made do in our basement.

Frieda Heinrichs, assisted by her parents Anna and Peter Dick, Kitchener, much to my surprise and delight, fixed up a cozy office for me in a small room at the bottom of the side entrance. It was carpeted, draped, furnished, housed my modest library of books, thus helping me in the preparation for preaching and my writing ministry.

Years later I was able to write the history of the beginnings of this congregation and of the construction of a commodious chapel in some detail in my book *No Longer at Arm's Length* (1987).

The 'Writer in Residence'

In March of 1963 I became aware of a new initiative called Student Services. I was asked to accompany John Wiebe, Vineland, to meet in Chicago with a committee of the MB General Conference. This resulted in a request that I write a series aimed primarily for the burgeoning crop of university-bound young people. As my List of Publications shows, these were printed in the *Mennonite Brethren Herald*, and often also in the Hillsboro *Christian Leader*. Spread over 1963 and into the fall of 1964 there were eight in all. This and other writing activity created news for and of our Toronto church.

Peter and Justina, Robert and Ruth, 1961, Ontario

While the Student Services committee liked my series, I was criticized by the Home Missions Committee for putting so much effort into student services and also "inter-Mennonite activities" which grew out of our relationship with other Mennonite churches in Toronto. Actually, most of my opportunities to be away and give talks that I translated into articles for the *MBH* were MB-related. At the end of June, 1963, I was invited to give the commencement address at Eden Christian College at Virgil, and in February, 1964, I was privileged to attend the annual course for ministers given by the professors at MBBC in Winnipeg. While there I chose for my talk in Chapel the theme "Reclaiming Marginal Men" and then published it as one of my series for students.

It was not what the HMC had bargained for, a person who sometimes seemed like a 'resident writer' for the MB papers. In fact, not to boast, during my two years in Toronto I wrote about twenty pieces for the *MB Herald*.

The Guest List

Under the Toronto agreement we had the free use of the house at 272 Ranee Avenue, utilities, but a very minimal salary which created at best a marginal existence. When we asked for an increase with the assistance of another home mission pastor and David Warkentin, the HMC agreed to pay the medical insurance. However, its members concluded from a comparison of salaries with other conferences that they were paying "a handsome average" as ministers' salaries went. As a result we just scraped by in consideration of our obligations to the children, ourselves, our guests, and a small insurance premium we had started in Morden, Manitoba, in 1957.

Even then, Justina was very guest-friendly (*Gastfreundlich*) so nearly everyone that came to see what we were doing in Toronto, or attended one of our services was invited to the house. How we managed to have so many guests as shown in our Guest Book is beyond me now! There are 320 entries in our Guest Book between September 1962 and August 1964, many of whom received a modest meal, and some stayed overnight and were given breakfast. Justina had a remarkable ability to stretch every dollar into wholesome food. Once Justina found a ten dollar bill under a plate as she cleared the table! One Christmas the church members surprised us by bringing together everything conceivable for our pantry.

The Difficult Synthesis

Though we had some experience in working under the guidance of a conference committee, we developed some misgivings with the structure in Ontario. We were supervised by a Home Missions Committee which answered to a small executive of the Ontario MB Conference. In time they appeared somewhat interlaced in matters of our supervision. Together they had determined that we should be located in a low income community and that our major thrust should be to families living in subsidized housing, to wit, in Lawrence Heights. The HMC would not support a group whose main aim was to build an independent Church, something that would have been possible had this growing congregation stayed in Willowdale, north of Yorkdale, where it had its beginnings in 1957.

Except for those living in Lawrence Heights on whose doors we were expected to knock, nearly everyone else drove in from a distance, some as far away as Oshawa and Brampton. Having commuters who were loyal to the MB church, wanting the congregation to succeed, was most encouraging. Many were supportive of an emphasis on mission outreach to the disadvantaged, the subsidized, in the community, but were not in a position to help personally.

To help me sort out the best methods for reaching into the community, I discovered that the pastors of the churches in Lawrence Heights got together once a month for fellowship and discussion. I was warmly welcomed and took my turn at hosting Anglican, Baptist, Presbyterian, and United Church ministers. I provided tea and coffee and each brought a 'brown-bag' lunch – a sandwich. I found that all of them at some point faced the same kind of questions and problems in trying to minister to low-income people living in subsidized housing as I did. Having such meetings provided good fellowship, mutual sharing, and an on-the-site quick course on how to do my job!

The Toronto MB Church

We liked to think of ourselves as a full-fledged church, keeping in mind that my salary was coming from the Ontario Conference via the HMC. My church council had the wisdom to run things responsibly towards a self-supporting congregation. Our guest list shows that there was a potential for a self-supporting church in the right location. Council members and others were mostly younger professionals, certainly under forty, who were in the beginnings of their careers, most of whom had good chances for advancement.[8]

---

8 Among those who served on the Council in my years, in alphabetical order: Bill DeFehr, Ben Doell, Rudy Dueckman, Vern Heinrichs, Henry Kliewer, Jack Neufeld, Alex Redekop, and Dave Warkentin

I remember doing a series on the Apostle Paul's letter to the believers in Corinth. These arose out of our experiences in Toronto with Don Watt who came to our Toronto church about May 1963. He became intensely interested in the revival of interest in the gifts of the Spirit (1 Corinthians, chapters 12 to 14) created by Dennis Bennett. He was the Episcopal priest who in 1960 launched what became the charismatic movement, whose influence moved into Mennonite Brethren congregations on the West Coast. He came to Toronto and when Don Watt wrote an article for the *MBH* about his visit to hear Bennett, Henry Warkentin, chair of the HMC, considered Watt's article to be a 'caricature' of Mr. Bennett. It was then in May 1964 that I wrote, preached, and published "The New Penetration: the Current Tongues Movement," and "Shall We Concentrate on Glossalalia or Proclamation?" My statements were really an exposition of the MB position on these Gifts of the Spirit. They however led to considerable correspondence in the *MBH* in May 1964.

In addition to preparing sermons that satisfied expectations, in the adult Sunday school class we studied the old (1902) MB Confession of Faith. While some deemed this as showing some lack of respect, according to an officer of the highest board in Fresno, our submission was one of the first to trigger consideration towards a revision of that Confession.

The other most attractive part of our services was the quality of our music – first the congregational singing – under the inspiring leadership of our two excellent pianists, Frieda Heinrichs and Ruth Neufeld. In the spring and early summer of 1963 Frieda put together an inter-Mennonite choir which prepared Haydn's *Creation* for a performance at Conrad Grebel College, University of Waterloo, to be conducted there in July by Victor Martens, then teaching music at MB Bible College. This event, heralded in the *Kitchener-Waterloo Record*, and which I wrote up for the *Canadian Mennonite,* also brought our congregation considerable attention.

Without Frieda, Victor Martens would not have had an opportunity to receive recognition from some of Toronto's most highly qualified music critics. A scheduled deputation visit to Ontario churches from MBBC at Easter, 1964, brought Professor Jacob Quiring with Martens and his *a cappella* choir. Frieda arranged to have Victor's choir perform a concert in Hart House on the University of Toronto campus. Fortunately Professor Quiring accepted our premise that this was an occasion to do a concert performance and not the traditional promotional meeting in church. Some notable individuals of the music world were in the audience at Hart House, and their reaction was in marked contrast to the reception in a number of MB churches, or among his current critics at MBBC, where Victor had performed Schuetz and Pachelbel music as well as Ben Horch's *Kernlieder* (hymns germane to Mennonite expressions of faith).

The Globe and Mail music critic reported,

> "Easter music has fared well in Toronto this season, but probably nowhere quite as well as it did last night at great hall, Hart House. The cause was the superb musicianship and interpretive sincerity of the *a cappella* choir of the MBBC, Winnipeg, conducted by Victor Martens, presented in a free concert. ... In feeling, clarity of musical line and enunciation, flexibility, lightness and balance it would be difficult to find their superiors." Martens obviously is one of the rare choral conductors who is able to inspire their singers to almost impossible achievements – and that within varied stylistic frameworks ... the lightness and warmth of sound served the choir to perfection in a group of religious folk songs sung in german and english ...."

Our Relations with Conference

It was also in Winnipeg that the issue of Rudy Wiebe's virtual dismissal from his position as the first editor of the MBH was aired. Some members of our Toronto congregation, very disturbed by Rudy's dismissal in 1963, had voiced their objections in a letter to the publications committee of the Canadian Conference. When I met J. H. Quiring at the triennial General Conference of MB churches in Winnipeg that summer, he considered it wise that I as pastor had not signed that letter of complaint to the publications committee. He as much as told me this group really had no business writing that letter. The matter was in the hands of the publication committee, and its members had done the right thing.

We were fortunate to get to know Rudy Wiebe and his wife Tena in the years 1963 and 1964. When Rudy first came to Lawrence Heights as a guest he was already teaching at Goshen College, Goshen, Indiana. He came to Toronto to research his second novel, *First and Vital Candle,* his first having been the controversial *Peace Shall Destroy Many.* Several times he brought Tena and their children as our Guest Book shows.

Vern and Elfrieda Heinrichs

Their names appear in these pages frequently. Without them, and a few other true friends, we could hardly have survived in Toronto. We had known Frieda [Dick] since our days in Kitchener (1953-54). We learned to know Vern as a result of their marriage. Both were graduates of the University of Toronto, she a high school teacher and he an engineer with Shell Canada.

Beginning in 1963 we frequently had them in for meals, fellowship, and discussion. When Frieda noticed that Robert had musical talent and should be taking piano lessons, she offered to come in after school once a week to teach him. At first Justina offered her loaves of fresh bread, and then, because she would not take money, Vern began to join her and us for dinner. In this way the friendship grew and became cemented long before they were even in a position to buy a first house.

Our Departure from Toronto

Though it might have been reasonable for me to continue taking Sunday services in Toronto during the time of our residence in Hamilton during 1964–1965, close friends suggested that I make a complete break and let the church carry on. I had followed through on my desire, the MA behind me, to pursue doctoral studies in history at McMaster University and now I recognized that the congregation could carry on under the able leadership of Rudy Dueckman, our senior council member.

The church did not let us go empty-handed as was demonstrated on September 27, 1964. The reception committee led by Vern and Betty Isaac had a farewell for us in June. Assisted by Frieda Heinrichs there was a tasteful presentation with flowers, an array of gifts, topped by the gift of a silver tea service. Other Mennonite pastors who were invited for this occasion spoke appreciatively of our inter-Mennonite fellowship, and Vern Isaac mentioned what Justina had contributed by way of hospitality, and that my most signal contribution had been my journalistic efforts in the larger conference.

One most rewarding experience was the confidence that my friend and supporter David Warkentin placed in me. He phoned me in Hamilton to request that I be the speaker at the funeral of his eldest son, Bruce, who was killed on the morning of December 5, 1964 while out delivering his papers. He was not quite thirteen, a good lad. I was somewhat overwhelmed, but David assured me that "if he did not have confidence in me as always, he would not have asked me to speak at so important an occasion as the funeral of his son." Quite apart from any other consideration, this event was proof that we were appreciated and my participation in this funeral helped to erase much of the feeling of rejection. This was actually a momentous event in the life of the Toronto congregation. Never had so many young people and strangers, and people from the congregation and the community packed the church. "It was a tremendous opportunity for me and for the Warkentin family to give testimony to a triumphant faith out of seeming tragedy."

Among other things I said:

> We normally expect young people and children to advance through years of schooling, working, and taking an increasing share of the responsibility of man's stewardship under God to that maturity and wisdom which speaks of having more fully completed the mandate of the Creator.

> But it has pleased God for reasons which are hidden in his inscrutable counsels to take Bruce before he had, as we think, much of a chance to make his mark. Hence it behoves us to give thought to that world 'where mortality is swallowed up in immortality', where this dying body is unwrapped, unshrouded from the undying soul.

Launching Into a PhD Program in History

Knowing that McMaster University was launching a PhD programme in history in the fall of 1964, I had contacted Professor McCready to see whether the department thought I could make it and whether there would be a job for me at age forty. In January 1964 I made formal application to be one of the first students admitted to the PhD programme and also wrote Margaret Meikleham, Librarian, about a possible full-time job for Justina. Both applications were successful. Before the end of May it was clear that I would have $2,000 from a Graduate Fellowship, as well as another $600 as an assistantship, while Justina would earn about the same in the serials department of Mills Memorial Library.

Having settled the matter of finances for the year 1964-65, we took an apartment in Hamilton on the road to Ancaster. While getting adjusted to full-time work proved difficult for Justina, settling into PhD studies was "alarmingly difficult." This meant planting my feet squarely on four areas of historiography and interpretation: Modern Britain with Herbert McCready (who was in Massachusetts for the year); British Empire with Charles M. Johnstone; Canadian with Goldwin S. French; and Renaissance and Reformation, including a section on Anabaptism, with Edward M. Beame.

The children, by the way, were in Grade Three and Kindergarten in nearby schools. Ruth was away only half days, so I stayed in the apartment for my reading when she was home, so that Justina need not worry about her. But really, the latter's perpetual fatigue, and need for a better location and greater income seemed overriding. McCready seemed to understand my predicament as "the dark night of the scholar's soul." He allowed there was "no unhappier lot than that of the man who is half way to the PhD."

Finding Full-time Employment

With these things in mind I asked my professors about the possibility of getting full-time employment as early as the fall of 1965. By April the History Department strongly supported that idea and the committee for graduate studies proved amazingly insightful. Friends at McMaster as well as Henry C. Klassen, Toronto, and especially the Heinrichs, were supportive also. All were very firm on this: you must steer clear of teaching at the secondary school level. All these discussions helped us to feel better and see our way clearer. However, I had to agree to spend the next three summers (four months each) either at McMaster or at a "suitable research centre."

When I canvassed about a dozen universities, the only clear offer came from Mount Allison University, Sackville, New Brunswick, on the Atlantic side of Canada. This University deserves to be placed in context, but I will reserve discussion for Chapter Seven when I am on site in Sackville.

Professor Philip Lockwood, head of the History Department, was leaving for "down under," thus creating a vacancy in precisely the fields for which I was preparing. It was all done before the end of April. I had an appointment for **one** year, hired sight-unseen. Lockwood did not have the time or money to have me come out for an interview. I would be starting as a Lecturer at $6,500 at a time when full professors started at $10,500 at this eastern University. I would do an introductory survey course, English history and European history at the third year level. President L.H. Cragg, whom I learned to know very well, confirmed the appointment on April 28, stating that he hoped it could be renewed by "mutual consent." In preparation for this relocation I was able to indicate what our moving expenses would be, and could also request some assistance in finding housing.

When family and friends heard that I had a teaching position, they were delighted for us, and things began to look up! The prospect of having a mover take care of our goods sounded absolutely wonderful in contrast to our personal relocation costs in 1957, 1959, and 1962. Though we were getting good advice by letter about accommodations, we thought it best to drive to Sackville to have a preview of the town, the University's History Department, and to choose a house. We took Robert and Ruth to Justina's parents in St. Catharines and left for Sackville on June 12.

Briefly, we liked what we saw, and chose a small three bedroom bungalow on Squire Street. Jim Cole, treasurer, and his wife Barbara were most helpful and we enjoyed staying one night in the famous Marshlands Inn presided over by Herb and Alice Read. We rented a mail box which we held for twenty-nine years. We opened a bank account and had our cheques deposited there from the beginning. Murray M. Tolmie, medievalist, gave me good advice how to get started and what to expect by way of standards, student workloads, and departmental routine.

Before we left Hamilton in the summer of 1965 Frieda Heinrichs had a farewell for us and the Neufelds who were moving to Montreal. On the way to New Brunswick we looked up Jack and Ruth Neufeld at their new location in Beaconsfield, west of Montreal and arrived in Sackville on August 26. As my notes indicate, it took a few days to get settled into our small house. We did some early sight-seeing, introducing Robert and Ruth to Sackville vistas, and to the ferry terminal at Cape Tormentine – the road to Prince Edward Island, and Avonlea.

This was a different world.

Writings of This Period

While these are listed in the Appendix, a few remarks about beginnings might be helpful. It is clear that my journalistic interest developed before I ever imagined publishing a first book in 1959 for the West Coast Children's Mission. As mentioned, while still in Manitoba I began to write for the Mennonite press, mainly for the *Mennonite Observer* edited by Leslie Stobbe. Long before the *Mennonite Brethren Herald (MBH)* was launched in 1962, I had also written for Orlando Harms of the *Christian Leader (CL)*, Hillsboro.

Once I had contributed some articles that Frank Epp really liked, he invited me to consider coming back to Manitoba to work with the *CM* as an editor on a full-time basis. While Ben and Esther Horch in Altona encouraged me, there were hindrances. We had just moved to BC and were committed to East Chilliwack at least until 1959 and we were in the adoption process for our daughter. The other was the serious hang-ups of a number of leading Mennonite Brethren who had been canvassed by Jake Quiring. It is hard to imagine this now. To be told that such a move would be "something objectionable to many brethren" was more than an eye-opener. Quiring asked: "Have you come to rest within you with reference to the true nature of your life's work?" Leslie Stobbe claimed to know that the Friesens in Altona and Frank Epp intended to use the *CM* as a vehicle to "return all the 'lost' sheep to the 'fold'!" Where his views were formed can be guessed. What absurdities!

As it was, I wrote Frank that I was being "strongly dissuaded from all sides" but assured him I would continue to contribute to his paper.

There was encouragement from a few key sources. Esther Horch, who had an eye for effective writing, wrote Justina in March 1962 that she always carefully read anything I contributed to the Mennonite press. "I do this," she wrote, "because it's Peter, and then also because he writes so very well, stimulates thought, and occasionally makes an appropriate 'dig'." Most of my articles came out of my involvements with what was called 'student services.'

One of these, "reclaiming marginal men," drew an interesting response from Adolf Ens, graduate of Canadian Mennonite Bible College, Tuxedo:

> Many students will join me in expressing sincere thanks to Peter Penner for his courageous defence of our freedom to doubt honestly. We hope that many will hear his plea and enter into serious discussion with 'marginal men' on those issues where they differ from the mainstream of church life ... We will show genuine acceptance of our marginal men (especially students and scholars) when we not only discuss differences of view but actually open ourselves up to the possibility that they may be more correct than the 'pillars' in their traditional [roles]. At that point we can begin genuine reclamation.

Once or twice in subsequent years I wondered whether this particular piece was prophetic. Even more significant for me was the opportunity in April 1966 to respond to Delbert Wiens' review of the MB church entitled *New Wineskins for Old Wine*. One of three reviewers, this turned out to be the first occasion I had to speak openly about my own metamorphosis since about 1952. I was critical of the conference's scuttling of the joint Sunday school materials which could have kept us away from the use of that "un-Mennonite" material from Scripture Press; for the 'absurd stance' against the use of television, the new media instrument; and for its preference of the "golden apple of North American evangelicalism" over what I vocalized for the first time, my new Anabaptist-Mennonite position.

Leaving Ontario with a New Perspective

Once I was accepted as a graduate student in 1964, I was eligible to attend the Mennonite Graduate Seminar at Elkhart, Indiana. What made that seminar eminently attractive was the promise of hearing papers from those who had devoted years to the study of Anabaptism, especially John Howard Yoder who came from a Smithville, Ohio, family. As many are aware he was then already considered the leading expositor for Anabaptism while teaching at the Mennonite seminaries at Goshen and Elkhart. At Elkhart I gained sufficient insight into the meaning of Anabaptism as the central core of Mennonite faith to consider making it my guide, my *Weltanschauung.* What had been undervalued in the Mennonite Brethren guidelines for faith and life was here adjusted for me.

More recently, Stuart Murray, an English Anabaptist, has sparked an interest around the world.[9] In his book he asks why North American Mennonites "have so little interest in Anabaptism when so many spiritual seekers outside of our tradition are 'coming home' to a 500-year-old belief system in this post-Christian era." He had found numerous examples of Anglicans, Presbyterians, Catholics and Quakers finding Anabaptism "surprisingly relevant" in contemporary culture.

Perhaps this coincided with the movement toward reconciliation initiated by the Reformed congregations of Switzerland, the Catholic Church of Austria, and the Lutheran World Federation between 2003 and 2010 for the purpose of bringing healing through repentance for wrongful persecution of the Anabaptists in the 16th Century.

Palmer Becker of Mennonite Church Canada in his *What is an Anabaptist Christian?* (2008) puts it simply: being a Christian from an Anabaptist perspective is a combination of 'believing in Jesus, belonging to community, and behaving in a reconciling way.' One does not need to be in a Mennonite church to carry that theological orientation.

---

9 *The Naked Anabaptist: The Bare Essentials of a Radical Faith.* Scottdale, PA, Herald Press, 2010

PART II

UNIVERSITY YEARS 1965-1992

Chapter Five

Early Years 1965-1972

Settling in Sackville and Mount Allison University

For many people life begins at forty. For me, this was the beginning of my second generation. Everything in Sackville was new and much to our liking. I had a full-time job, and Justina, not having to work, could concentrate on settling Robert into Grade Four and Ruth into Grade One in the primary school on Allison Avenue. They adjusted well and seemed content. We were conveniently located to almost everything, within easy walking distance to grocery shopping, church, schools, and university. Life seemed restful.

It helped that we had been introduced to the town in a newspaper article dated May 13, 1965. Where actually were we?

Though we soon learned about the Acadians who were deported from this area in 1755, we were now in an old mainly Anglo town dating from 1763, filled at first with Baptists from the south, then Wesleyan Methodists from Yorkshire, England, and Anglican Loyalists from the new United States. Sackville as we came to know it numbered about 3,000 people in 1970. It was served by the Canadian National trans-continental railway.

What I found in 1965 was a small liberal arts school enrolling about 1,200 students and offering courses in History, English, and in the sciences, Biology and Chemistry, to name just a few of the departments. Two other schools, one of Fine Arts, and the other of Music, attracted our attention. All of this was situated on a hill, what the

English would call a rise, above the town site, hence the mount in Mount Allison.

We soon learned that Sackville and the University had a most unique history, well told by William B. Hamilton in his *At the Crossroads, A History of Sackville New Brunswick.*[10] Yes, truly at the crossroads, at an important mid-point in the geography of the Maritime Provinces, where the Cumberland Basin of the Bay of Fundy was swelled by the highest tides in the world, flowing in and out twice a day, and where the road past Sackville went to Nova Scotia or veered off eastward to Prince Edward Island.

In 1839 Charles Frederick Allison, a wealthy merchant and devout Wesleyan Methodist, donated land and money for an educational institution intended for both elementary and advanced courses. In his inaugural address he uttered a line which bears repeating here:

> The Lord has put it into my heart to give this sum [initially 100 pounds sterling] towards the building of a Wesleyan Academy ... [Then, following a dramatic pause] I know this is of the Lord for I am naturally fond of money.

Much larger sums from Allison and enlarged aims made possible a Ladies' College as well as University division for the liberal arts and the sciences. Though there were voices calling for a federation of the many schools that had sprung up in the Maritimes, this fell through in the years after Church Union in 1925. Not only that, Mount Allison University stood independent supported by the Maritime Conference of the United Church of Canada.

All of this appeared like small change once Ralph Pickard Bell, hugely successful entrepreneur from Halifax, came on the scene as the University's first Chancellor. We saw the evidence of his vision and personal investment in Mount Allison. Between 1961 and 1969 twelve new buildings rose up on the campus. And the one that just took our breath away was the University Chapel dedicated in the very year we arrived in Sackville. It is beyond my ability to describe its

---

10 Gaspereau Press, 2004, pages 89, 128, 153, 191, 209–216

architectural perfection and the powerful message of the four stained glass windows, but it became for many a quiet place for reflection as well as the place for beautiful music from its special Casavant organ. Topping the tremendous spurt of growth was the construction, on the brow of the mount, of the Ralph Pickard Bell Library and Crabtree Building, thus replacing the venerable Beethoven Hall and also Allison Hall in which I had my first office for six years.

There, when I pulled up the lower window and looked out from my fourth-floor, I saw the rope dangling there. What, a fire escape? Yes, this rope was there to help one descend gradually rather than hurtling oneself out the window in case of fire! Allison Hall had to go!

But first, a brief interruption.

Leaving the Mennonite Brethren Church, 1967

Once settled in Sackville, NB, I wrote Isaac Tiessen, my successor in Toronto, in August 1967 that "we have decided to request release from our membership obligations to the MB church" in order to join the United Church of Canada (UCC). There were good reasons for making what seemed like a radical shift. By that time it was clear we wanted to stay in Sackville; we enjoyed living there; and we were "more or less oriented to our new field of witness, both as Christians and Anabaptist-Mennonites, a field which included a university community, a large congregation of the UCC, which was open to people of our convictions...." Brother Tiessen was not happy with us, and objected specifically to the liberal theology rampant in the UCC, but the Toronto church did send our baptismal certificates, thus releasing us from membership.

Then Tiessen followed with a reminder of my responsibility to the Ontario Conference as an ordained minister. I replied: 'Yes, but the MB leadership of Ontario also has a responsibility to me.' In September 1967 I requested that the Committee of Reference and Counsel send me a letter stating that when I left the Conference I was not only a member in good standing, but also a **"minister in good standing."**

Supported by Isaak Tiessen and Frank Peters, I received this letter in November 1967:

> "This letter is given to certify that our Brother, Peter Penner, was duly examined and ordained to the gospel ministry by the MBC of Kitchener on October 10, 1954. Until his transfer, he was a minister in good standing and his name is registered in the official records of this conference." Signed, Peter J. Dick, secretary.

I wrote to thank Tiessen for his generous assistance, while Peters, then president of Wilfrid Laurier University, Waterloo, wrote to say that it seemed most logical to transfer to Sackville, since church was not a membership roll, but a fellowship. He said he was writing out of a "feeling of debt I owe, and a desire to express it, clumsily perhaps.... [but] your deep Anabaptist convictions and your concern for open communication among the brethren have been appreciated...."

I thanked the Toronto church for helping to make the withdrawal "as painless as possible," though it was no easy step to take. All family members except our parents were happy with our decision. Some wondered about our affiliation with a liberal church, supposedly wishy-washy on the fundamentals. Strangely, *hardly anyone assumed that we would be able to survive simply because we were well enough grounded in the faith and in our history!*

Beginning our 'Mission'

We were encouraged to be involved in church and community in line with our Anabaptist persuasion by President Laurence Cragg. He told both Justina and me, as the only Mennonite family in Sackville, to take every opportunity to contribute to the entire community from "the left wing of the Reformation." By this he meant from an Anabaptist position. He was a well-read, active, United Church lay person. That suggestion was more appealing than the possibility of having my ordination recognized by the Maritime Conference of the UCC. I wanted to be at ease within the organized church.

In those first years I gave some lectures on Anabaptism. I took every opportunity to inform, dispel misinformation about Mennonites, and indicate 'contemporary postures.' Because Justina was being asked, when do you wear your head covering, where are the 'bonnets and buggies?' it seemed necessary to show the differences between the Old Order and *Russlaender* Mennonites. We did not have head coverings in our background as part of our religious identity. By using a set of slides on Ontario Swiss Mennonites, those living in Elmira and St. Jacobs, Ontario, Justina was able to tell her audience that we had had our own ways of being modest (or immodest) in an entirely different background in Russia.

Our family made an impact early even though Justina had some difficulty in adjusting to the Sackville/University reality. She did not have an academic degree, a matter of which she was occasionally reminded by the somewhat snobbish university women's club. Nevertheless, Justina gave presentations about who and what we were, beginning with the IODE which she was invited to join in the spring of 1967. She was a member of this service club for women until 1994. More of her role later.

Robert came to notice in school for his fine singing, sight reading, and good tonal quality in an excellent music program in the lower school. In 1965 he began his violin career (as it turned out) by joining a Susuki class conducted by Rodney McLeod of the University's Music Department. By spring Robert was helping Rodney tune violins for others in the class. At age ten Robert joined the New Brunswick Youth Orchestra conducted by Stanley Saunders of the Music Department. But the most memorable event of April was his reading from Luke's Gospel on Baden-Powell Sunday. Among many congratulations the person most impressed was **Alex Colville**, the Canadian artist who became famous beyond Canada. Colville was then still living and painting in his Sackville Studio and also attending the United Church. He phoned us to congratulate Robert on his splendid rendition.

We soon had many friends among faculty and some related to Church. There were a surprising number of Christians on faculty, in all fields. It became clear that Mennonite parents of the old school worried far too much about students losing their faith position, if they came with one. Of course some did. My Mother, for example, thought university students were a pretty wild bunch and some professors were surely to blame.

Looking back, there is no doubt that moving to the Maritimes where few Mennonites had settled, none as immigrants, meant that life would be different. We could expect many interesting experiences to come our way: research in Harvard's Widener Library, a renewal of my summer Canada Council doctoral fellowship, our first visits to England, promotion to Assistant Professor and, of much greater significance to me, a letter in March 1969 assuring me of "permanent tenure." In all of these years Cyril Poole, who came from Bishops University in the same year as I and who became Dean in succession to Clayton Baxter, was most supportive.

My First Colleagues

Having been hired without an interview, I had no clear idea who my colleagues would be in the small history department at Mount Allison University. Once arrived, I met the senior people soon enough. Professor David H. Crook, Acting Head, told me how the courses were divided into American, Canadian and Medieval Studies, and that I would do the British courses. Though I had some butterflies in my stomach at meeting my first ever university classes, I soon felt confident that I could handle myself and the material well enough. I even consented to take two students in a fourth-year seminar course in British History. By this time I had also engaged to give one course in the University's Extension program in Moncton.

Some of the euphoria evaporated when the Acting Head told me on November 25 that my position in British history would be thrown open to more senior applicants, if any applied. I was naturally crestfallen to be placed in such a precarious position so soon after beginning to teach. Soon, however, the Administration (President Cragg and Dean Baxter) came to me to explain that, while Crook as Acting Head was permitted to advertise as he said, they were looking for someone to replace him as Head of the Department! That is, he was never going to be put in that position. Obviously, I had made a good start and a good impression on the Administration.

David and Susan Crook were not inhospitable. He was just one of several wannabe intellectuals who dotted the campus in those days and who wanted to make of Mount Allison an Ivy-League type of school. During an invitation to dinner it became clear these historians felt themselves too good for the community and had nothing to do with the local people. David was a graduate of Dartmouth who had visions of being called to teach at Harvard! His senior colleagues were much like that. They were willing to give themselves to the brightest graduates in Honours History so they could get into good graduate schools, but they cared little for the average history duffer. In a word, elitism was at work.

In this milieu it was most gratifying to have a long discussion in early December with Clayton Baxter, the philosopher then serving as Dean. He had reservations about the current crew in History and was hoping for good to come out of new appointments. In January 1966 he contacted me at least three times, and by February 8 he was quite certain he could offer me a position if I was flexible as to courses. It was clear by the end of January that Crook and his two colleagues were leaving because they resented the fact that the Dean had gone over their heads to encourage me! They left disgusted because their agenda was undermined.

Even though a senior historian from Ireland had been engaged to take my position, I was assured by February 1966 that the adminis-tration wanted to keep me as long as I was willing to move into the Canadian field. Thus David Crook had no choice but to offer me a second year as Lecturer at $7,500 to teach the introductory course, my European history course, and a senior Canadian seminar for which I had a good preparation. He was however very upset by this development, since Baxter had pulled the rug from under him, both as to my appointment, and also with respect to the general direction of the Department. The Philip Lockwood system of concentrating on the honours people would be changed.

Two Surprising Invitations

Though the above seems like a linear development, it was by no means so. A degree of the former feeling of 'indecision' returned when out of the blue I was asked in November 1965 to consider taking Ottawa Mennonite Church; and in January 1966 I got a call from Fresno Pacific College, Fresno, CA, asking me to consider taking a position with them, a Mennonite Brethren-related school.

The invitation from Fresno was easily set aside as its administrators offered very little for moving expenses compared to Mount Allison's generosity, and their course suggestions did not really fit with my training more suitable to British Commonwealth schools. Taking the Ottawa Mennonite church, as successor to my friend Frank H. Epp, was more appealing. Looked at squarely, however, it pointed in the wrong career direction.

Some Local Anomalies, Anxieties, and Adjustments

Meanwhile, in spite of my precarious employment situation, we enjoyed our first year in Sackville. Justina and the children were happy, even though our first house, a rental, was sold. By this time, however, it seemed we were so well known and liked that Frank West (a former Vice President) and his wife Marjorie (Bates) invited us to consider taking the third floor in their house at 74 Bridge Street directly across the street from the famous Marshlands Inn. This flat to which we moved on April 26, 1966 was 60 by 40 feet and built on those proportions in 1910, reflecting some good years in Canada. Not having thought anything of carrying so many heavy objects to the third floor, I felt the physical strain of that move for some time. Much later, when asked to help the cardiologists determine when I might have had my 'silent heart attack,' I thought of this time, having forgotten that I had recorded chest pain at least twice before.

While we were firmly committed to returning to Sackville for a second year, there were some anomalies in my position. None of the new people David Crook had hired were any more sympathetic to me than his former colleagues. While John Boyle and his wife were hospitable, the others hired to do English Medievalism and Tudors and Stuarts kept their distance. Their general attitude toward students was almost identical to their predecessors. This was unacceptable.

The other person hired by Vice-President Bill Crawford to do Canadian and American diplomatic history, replacing Crook, was David Pearce Beatty, from Michigan. He turned out to be a strong supporter of the University and a good friend. We had an active correspondence until a few years ago. To the regret of many David died in 2015.

One of the leading proponents of the concept that we must serve all students, not only the elitist, was Doctor William Godfrey. He and his wife Clementine (Pickard) had a long association with Mount Allison. He was my near neighbour and we had a discussion about this. It was soon clear that the administration favoured my staying for a third year and was prepared to put me on a tenure track, in which case I could soon be an assistant professor. Cyril Poole, the new Dean, assured me that Boyle would not be considered for the headship of the department, even though he had associate ranking.

The Changing Scene at Mount Allison, 1968-72

There was great frustration in the Boyle camp when during the first week in April 1967 Graham Adams Jr. from Columbia University came for an interview. When he, an Americanist, born and raised in New York, was hired as Head with authority to shape the Department, John Boyle was most upset. Because he believed that Adams had been indoctrinated about the History Department, perhaps with my help, he turned to me one day at tea time and blurted out: "And by God, Penner, if you had anything to do with that, I'll have your life!" When Baxter heard of this he soon reviewed for me all the people who had been very bad for Mount Allison students and who had left one by one. "You had a hard time this year – just forget them – the world is large." Meanwhile, David Beatty and I were made to feel secure in our positions.

As long as John Boyle was there we felt 'an air of conspiracy' within the department and beyond. Every effort was made to discredit Graham Adams whether it was his headship, or to find fault with his one book. Boyle seemed jealous of the fact that in 1969 we began to have considerable increases in history enrolments and to give every student a chance to excel. We were no longer interested in pursuing the Excellence Report standards of one-third failure rates.

What aggravated tensions was the Catherine Daniel case. The Canadian Association of University Teachers had brought censure against the University's alleged mishandling of her dismissal from the Music Department. It seemed very clear to me that some hoped to blacklist the University sufficiently to induce faculty to resign in protest and seek employment elsewhere and deter potential faculty from seeking jobs at Mount Allison. When not much of this happened and Boyle as a senior published historian found employment at the University of Guelph in 1971, there was less tension in our Department of History.

After that David Beatty and I tended to reminisce about the years with these predecessors, and compare how solidly the Department was being built up with Graham Adams, William Godfrey, Eugene Goodrich, myself, John Reid, and the high profile George Stanley in Canadian Studies.

Pressure to Complete the Doctorate

Given these changes in staffing, it was imperative to complete the doctorate to assure the administration that I had the makings of a satisfactory candidate for teaching their students and seeking to bring out the best in everyone. During the summer, as promised, I was back at McMaster in Hamilton, getting ready for my final written and oral examinations in all fields. I had to read 200 pages a day in addition to fitting in eight hours of seminars during July. I was most relieved to be successful in those comprehensive examinations in September. Once it was all over I had warm and sincere 'congratulations' from my professors.

There was of course the small matter of the third language requirement. My German language was accepted as the second without question, but instead of letting me elevate my beginning Russian from a course taken at MBBC, Winnipeg, as I requested, McMaster men insisted I learn to read and translate French historical prose. I would have to do a "sight translation" of such prose in the spring of 1967.

On the Road to Cambridge, Massachusetts

Reading in the Widener Library at Harvard University was a mind-boggling experience, given that it had seven million volumes, among them nearly everything I needed except for the primary sources. With a letter from Mount Allison in hand, I received a stack pass from the Librarian at Harvard and could read during the day, reserve books overnight at my desk, and copy materials inside at very reasonable cost.

But first I must tell of my reception in Cambridge.

A long day's drive from Sackville in south-eastern New Brunswick to Cambridge next to Boston during the third week in June 1967 took me to my destination. Where would I find a place to live? Arthur DeFehr, Winnipeg, then at the Business School, had provided a list of Mennonites teaching at Harvard, among them J. Lawrence Burkholder. When I went to the office of Harvard Divinity School and asked for Burkholder, one of the secretaries made a quick assessment of me and my story and suggested I visit Connie (Mrs. Leonard) Wheeler, a Cambridge City Councillor. She was looking for a house-sitter for a month at an address on Coolidge Hill Road. When I went there I was offered the key to the house. She trusted me wholly from the first meeting, refusing the suggestion of references. A recommendation from Burkholder's secretary was enough! Justina and the children could come to stay with me and we would have the run of the place. It was only a ten minute-walk and bus ride into Harvard Yard.

The story of Connie Wheeler's generosity in the use of her house in 1967, even when Len Wheeler was at home, now seems hard to believe. The back-and-forth to Sackville and to Ontario to meet my academic committee, and the many family guests who came cannot be detailed. Someone actually dubbed it "Peter's Hotel." While Connie was at their cottage at Chocorua, New Hampshire, I often served up breakfast which Len and I ate outside.

Once in Boston, I went to see the Boston Red Sox and did the "Freedom Trail." As meaningful as this was, I wanted to get home to Sackville to celebrate **Canada's Centennial Day**, July 1, 1967. This was the occasion when, according to pictures, Robert and Ruth dressed up for the Sackville parade, Robert as a shepherd pushing a bicycle, and Ruth as a little lady of an earlier period, pushing her doll carriage.

After that, Justina and the children came with me for three weeks; we visited some of America's history: Lexington and Concord, as well as Plymouth Rock where the *Mayflower* unloaded its 'Pilgrim' passengers in 1620. We enjoyed getting to know members of the Boston Mennonite Fellowship. Besides the professors who attended, there were graduate students such as John E. and Eleanor (Wall) Toews, Winnipeg. John E., son of MBBC's John A. Toews, my former professor, was reading history under E. Stuart Hughes at Harvard, supported by a renewable $4,000 history scholarship.

Before leaving that summer I wrote a letter of thanks to Connie and Leonard Wheeler who, so down to earth and friendly, were listed in the New England equivalent of *Burke's Peerage*.

The Summer Months of 1968 in London, England

Even though I did not fit the image of a student who desperately needed an international home I was allowed to stay at the **Mennonite Centre, Highgate.** In 1953, the Mennonite Board of Missions, Elkhart, Indiana, purchased 14, Shepherds Hill where Quintus and Miriam Leatherman took leadership in establishing a Centre for Mennonite Fellowship and a home for students from abroad. My photo collection has reminded me of the activities and company at Highgate, and the rose garden cared for by Richard Kwan (and his wife Mae) from South East Asia. There I got to know Alan and Eleanor Kreider, Goshen College graduates, who provided leadership among the student residents.

Alan has told how the Leathermans "established the Centre and its characteristic ethos, ...functioning as parents to generations of students from all over the world who felt displaced from their families and cultures. Miriam cooked countless meals for students – she also presided properly at tea-time, which became another Centre institution." The London Mennonite Fellowship (LMF) met weekly under Quintus' leadership, providing a chaplaincy to students.

Though Highgate was actually far from the heart of London where most of my libraries were situated, that ride did not take long on the Northern Line of the "Tube." The bottom of the escalator was very deep underground, so when one exited at the top into the greenery of Shepherd's Hill, it was always a refreshing experience.

On May 23rd I wrote Justina about my walking tours and of my first interviews with various well-known scholars at the School of Oriental and African Studies (SOAS). This brought me to the University of London and the British Museum, situated in Bloomsbury, where I was making progress in research. I also had prospects of going to Edinburgh for research.

Norman Marsh and the Clapham Common

During this summer devoted to research, before Justina came to join me, my most unforgettable experience occurred on the Clapham Common. On Saturday August 10, 1968, I took the Underground south about five stops from Waterloo Station to see what historical remains I could find of members of the so-called Clapham Sect, whose leader long ago had been William Wilberforce.

I saw this man on the Common, walking his Newfoundland dog. Of all the people on the Common he was the first person to whom I directed my query. He replied: "Is it not interesting that you should ask me that question, because I am one of only a few people who could help. Come with me, I live right over there in Number 13, and I can give you a book which will help you." He seemed so excited to find a stranger who was interested in the Clapham Sect that he took me right into his living room at 13 North Side before I had a chance to introduce myself. Then he called "Christel, Christel, there's a Canadian here interested in the Clapham Sect."

How could this happen to me? This was Norman Marsh, QC, former fellow of University College, Oxford, then working on the Lords' Law Commission to reform the Divorce Law of England! His wife Christel was then serving as secretary to Amnesty International. He recognized me as a Canadian from my accent. It was not American or European, he said. Norman Marsh, upper middle class Anglican, serving English Intelligence in Germany, met Christel, from East Germany, and they married just in time to get out of Hitler's domain in 1938. We soon learned that they had four children, Bridget, Lawrence, Elizabeth, and Henry. The last-mentioned, Henry, is

Norman, Christel, and Henry Marsh, 13, North Side, Clapham Common, London, 1968

shown here with Norman and Christel and the Dog. Henry is famous today as a leading brain surgeon and for his 2014 book *Do No Harm: Stories of Life, Death, and Brain Surgery.*

The Marsh family lived on the North Side of the Common in a Queen Anne House built about 1713. Following an interesting walking tour, using one of Norman's books as guide, I was invited back for tea at four o'clock, and for dinner the next day, Sunday. That friendship lasted until his very last years!

As witness I have a thick file of correspondence and contacts over the years, including their visit to us in Sackville in 1981. Years later, before she died, Christel wrote her story entitled *Ends and Beginnings, An Autobiography* (2004) and we were sent a copy. When he died in 2008 at age 95 his daughter Bridget sent us an obituary notice as well as copy of a tribute she gave at his funeral in St. John's Church on the Common. In it she mentioned this incident with the 'Canadian' because her father had spoken of it to all and sundry during his working life and in retirement.

Unforgettable indeed.

One of the things that cemented the relationship during this first sabbatical year was the considerate attention this family gave to Justina, Robert, and Ruth during my four-month absence in India, November 1972 to February 1973, inclusive. During that time Justina took the children by bus to Clapham on December 10, 1972. Bridget and her husband, John Cherry, and daughter Eleanor were also there. Christel and Justina became good friends and Christel came to Richmond to do some shopping with Justina on George Street. Justina and the children were invited for Boxing Day, December 26.

From that time over the years we had a number of occasions where we could visit them again, and Norman and Christel visited us in New Brunswick, as told in another place. Our correspondence, at first formal, became less so, and we never failed to exchange letters during the Advent season. Christel's letters to Justina by the mid-seventies were often four page letters, full of news – splendid sharing. Both seemed to enjoy good health and Norman was especially fit from his much walking to and from the Underground. He retired from the Law Commission in 1977.

Oxford and Edinburgh

Most amazing was my visit to Derek Hum at Oxford. He, a New Brunswick Chinese, was Mount Allison's Rhodes Scholar for 1967. Though much junior to me, we got on well and became close friends. As a result of my visit I had the privilege of finding overnight accommodation in Lincoln College, the college of John and Charles Wesley. He showed me Magdalen, Christ Church, and Oriel Colleges. He came to stay at Highgate for part of July and all of August, 1968. Not only did he almost become an Anabaptist, he met his future wife there! All this I explained to wide-eyed Justina in Sackville who could hardly wait to get underway.

After that we kept in touch with Derek. He got a teaching position at the University of Manitoba. In April 1970 he showed up in Sackville unexpectedly. His sixteen-year old sister had been killed in a car accident in Bathurst. He told us he was engaged to Mary Mow, from Lae, New Guinea. They met in Highgate when Mary was there as a guest of Richard and May Kwan. The wedding to which I was invited was scheduled to take place in Timothy Eaton Memorial Church, Toronto, on September 30, 1970.

In Edinburgh I was able to stay with Marina and Walter Unger, whom I had first learned to know in Winnipeg. I spent sixteen days (fourteen days of sunshine!) exploring the *Muniments* of Lord Dalhousie, Governor-General (G–G) of India, 1848–56, in the Scottish National Library. The Ungers took me on a car trip to Loch Lomond north of Glasgow, and I did a side trip to visit the David Livingstone Memorial at Blantyre.

Justina Came to London

Justina was able to join me for three weeks during the summer of 1968. But first she had to drive with Robert and Ruth from Sackville in south-eastern New Brunswick to St. Catharines, Ontario, where they would stay with their grandparents, the Janzens.

Once Justina arrived, one of the first things we did was a planned outing with Erica Jantzen to the little village of Kersey, where we got 'tea in bed at eight o'clock' and I even slept between pink sheets [I hate pink] in a 300-year old house. Justina and I went to see Lady Hardinge in Kent County and she welcomed me to come to her estate to look at the papers of her husband's forbear, Sir Henry Hardinge, G-G of India from 1844 to 1848.

With the help of John Coffman at the Centre I was able to plan a trip to the Netherlands for Justina and me, with the particular object of visiting Witmarsum, the site of Menno Simon's activity in the 1530s. This was as close as we were going to get to the virgin soil of Menno's Anabaptism and the source of a Mennonite migration eastward to Prussia, and then Russia. Our planned trip took us to famed Utrecht, to Leeuwarden where we looked up the Mennonite church pastor, then to Haarlingen with its water canals, and on to Witmarsum in Friesland. There we got off the bus to find a half dozen wooden-shoed Dutchmen sitting, just waiting to answer our question: where is the Menno Simons Church?

At the church there was a sign: *"De Schletel es bee Numma Dre"* (the key is at # 3). At that house we were pleasantly greeted by Mrs. Burma who showed us inside the church and the register of all the guests who had come for the Mennonite World Conference of the previous year in Amsterdam. About 1,400 delegates had converged on Witmarsum. That we could exclaim about a lot of familiar names gave us Mennonite credibility! She gladly walked across the field with us to see and photograph the Menno Simons monument. What we found remarkable is that we could easily understand each other as she spoke her Fries dialect and we spoke our Low German.

The Summer Months of 1969

During the summer of 1969 Justina, Robert and Ruth joined me at the London Mennonite Centre for several weeks. On our first venture together Justina wanted to do Oxford Street for shopping. While that took in our first Thursday, on Friday we did the tourist things, like visit Westminster Abbey, Parliament Buildings, Whitehall, Trafalgar Square, and the National Gallery. Saturday we took in the Trooping of the Colour, India Office Library, for dinner at the Centre, and then south again to Queen Elizabeth Hall for the London Orpheus Choir.

Monday and Tuesday (June 16–17) were taken up with our interesting trip to Glastonbury, Somerset, to visit the Hugh C. Gould family related to James Thomason, my potential dissertation subject, one I was exploring seriously. Major General C. Thomason Beckett, Commander at Malta during the War, had been helpful in putting me in touch with Clifford Gould, a nephew, who made arrangements for us all to go Glastonbury, Somerset. We took the train to Bath, and then used a rented car to get to their home. They treated us like special guests, or so it seemed to us, to lunch, afternoon tea, dinner, tea in bed next morning, and a full breakfast. Back in London next day, we took in 'Oliver' in Leicester Square. Then followed visits to the Madame Tussaud Wax Museum, and the Victoria and Albert Museum.

Though I had several months of research left, I was able to take my family on a highly recommended bus tour to Scotland. This took us up the west side of England, to Chester and Lake Country to Edinburgh, Scotland. On Monday, June 23, we did the 'Golden Mile' from the Edinburgh Castle to Holyrood Palace, and the National Gallery. I showed the children the David Livingstone, Walter Scott, and James Ramsay (Dalhousie) statues, and we felt we had done some of the sights and sounds of Scotland.We came back to London on the Flying Scot on Tuesday.

We travelled home together, having thus ended my six months in London (four months in 1968 and two months in 1969). From there I went back to Cambridge, Massachusetts, to work on my thesis.

John Company's India Civil Service, Mid-19th Century

Hardly anyone could have expected me, a Canadian Mennonite, to take up a study of the English Civil Service that ruled India and was made up of persons from upper middle class families from the British Isles. Yet that is what I began to do, starting modestly.

In brief, my doctoral dissertation fell into nineteenth century British India when the East India Company ruled until 1858. This huge empire had three Services: Civil, Military, and Political. Focussing on the Civil made me look first at the former East India College, Haileybury, where prospective civilians appointed by patronage attended classes for two years. I soon discovered that Haileybury had been done, but what did its graduates do in India? In 1968 I was

East India College, Haileybury, Hertfordshire, c. 1810

able to visit this College, now a Public School, about twenty kilometers north of London. I was entertained by headmaster Tony Melville and his wife. That is where I acquired two attractive prints, dated 1813, of that institution when it was the East India College.

As told earlier, my research in 1967 took me first to the Widener Library at Harvard with its seven million volumes. There I expanded my theme, with permission of my thesis supervisor C.M. Johnstone, into an exploration of the role of Haileybury's 'graduates' in pre–Mutiny India. They were a select group from mostly Church of England evangelical homes who became 'Collectors' and Commissioners in upcountry jobs in India. They were in fact schooled by **James Thomason** who became their Lieutenant-Governor in the North-West Provinces during a crucial period of implementation. I argued that this topic met the criterion of originality, the availability of primary sources (in England and India), and the creation of something new about the East India Company.

This first effort covered the period from the 1820s to 1853, a period that saw five significant personages in the Governor-General's position in Calcutta and whose papers I researched with reference to James Thomason and his 'disciples' in the NWP and the Punjab: Lord Bentinck's in Nottingham, Lord Auckland's in the British Museum (BM); Sir Henry Hardinge's, at Lady Hardinge's, Penshurst, Kent County; Lord Ellenborough's at the old Public Record Office, Chancery Lane; and the Lord Dalhousie papers in Edinburgh's National Library.

Lady Hardinge, Kent County

Having the opportunity to go to Lady Hardinge's was special. She was a granddaughter of Lord Salisbury, Prime Minister during the latter part of Queen Victoria's reign. She lived in Kent County on an estate called South Park, once the country estate of Sir Henry Hardinge. She welcomed me to look at the Hardinge papers which she had in her house. In front of her place the visitor was met by a colossal statue of Hardinge on his charger. He and his two sons were present in the First Sikh War in 1845, a story I would tell briefly in my biography of Robert Needham Cust.

Lady Hardinge was most gracious and helpful. Though the papers were not as productive as those of Governors-General Auckland, Ellenborough, and Dalhousie for my purposes, I enjoyed that research visit very much. Inside, the house was chalk full of history – mementoes, curios, books, and paintings by Hardinge's sons. All she charged was a 'tip' to the servants. The Hardinges had been strong supporters of the monarchy and she never forgave Edward VIII for his abdication. The Dowager Lady Hardinge's husband Alec had been principal private secretary to Edward. She wrote her husband's story under the title *Sir Alex Hardinge, Loyal to Three Kings*.

Charles Murray Johnstone and the Final Stretch, 1969-70

All of this led to the first clarification of a dissertation title "the Thomason School in Northern India, 1822-1853" for the register of dissertations in progress and which Johnstone and others at McMaster accepted. I received Johnstone's support all along the way, including the application for a renewal of the Canada Council scholarship for 1969 which I would use to split my time between London and Cambridge, Massachussets. By March I was projecting the completion of my dissertation by the fall of 1970. This would be six years – the full time limit – since I started the PhD program. He and I met in Toronto in April 1970 at the Royal York Hotel in order to make one final review of the whole dissertation. I considered myself fortunate in having such a good writing historian as my chief advisor.

**James Thomason,
Lieutenant-Governor,
Agra, India, 1843-1853**

The final draft of the dissertation, "The James Thomason School in Northern India, 1822-1953, a Biographical and Administrative Study," was typed by Justina at home in July 1970 and the master copy was sent to McMaster University for duplicating into the required number of copies by end of July. Johnstone wrote that copies were in the hands of the examiners and the oral examination was set for October 5th.

That final examination turned out to be something special. I went to Hamilton the night before and presented myself at 9 o'clock for the oral examination. Professor Geit from Classics chaired this examination made up of my four professors Johnstone, McCready, French, and Beame, Fritz from History also, Robertson from Religious Studies, and Dale from English, as well as a few observers. Following my brief preliminary statement Johnstone fielded the most questions, French had some, while Beame and McCready declared themselves satisfied. Fritz was both commendable and critical, while Dale had what he called some 'quibbles', and Robertson left some criticisms.

After the oral I was asked to withdraw but when I was called back after a few minutes, they were all standing to offer congratulation. It was all over except the typos. The strange thing was that after the quibbles of eight professional people had been collated, I still found some typos no one else had caught. Johnstone took his whole group over to the bar, then to a buffet dinner. I was McMaster's second successful PhD in History.

We then decided after all this time, effort, and money, to celebrate by going to Convocation. Many members of Justina's and my family came for Convocation on November 20, 1970 when I was invested with the Doctor of Philosophy Degree, the Chancellor, President, and Deans **standing**. [The candidate for a BA degree kneels before the Chancellor, stands for a Masters, while for a Doctorate, both the candidate and the Chancellor stand, signifying academic equality.] The Johnstones both came, confessing that this was one of the few times they had been to Convocation. We were then invited to their home for refreshments.

When I was advised by Cyril Poole to buy the McMaster academic gown at once on the grounds that I would never have money for it again, I did, and purchased the University's Oxford–style gown in wine and white that everyone liked very much. This proved to be sound advice because I discovered later that the price of these gowns rose substantially. It looked rather good for my job of parade marshall at Convocation at Mount Allison.

The Reception of My Enlarged Topic

By the time I finished with the PhD I was convinced that for publication purposes I would need to enlarge my research into the implementation of the Land Settlement Act of 1833. When Charles Johnstone heard of this plan, he called Holden Furber, his former thesis supervisor at University of Pennsylvania, about my desire to broaden my focus to include Robert Merttins Bird who was senior to Thomason and, what is more, extending it into the post-Mutiny period. Furber assured Johnstone that I was onto something and should be encouraged.

During my sabbatical of 1972-73, the subject of my next chapter, I went back to the great sources: to the India Office Library and Records housed in Orbit House, Blackfriars Road, and to the British Library, housed then in the British Museum, located in Bloomsbury, next to the School of African and Oriental Studies.

This activity enabled me to cover the reach of the land settlement into the Punjab, annexed by Lord Dalhousie in 1849. It seemed that leading historians from London and Chicago misunderstood me because **they** had not conceived of the possibility of my topic, and how was it possible that an unknown Canadian from a school like McMaster, not known for Asian Studies, would try that? So I **was** doing something original and significant! Fortunately I found a better reception from Eric Stokes, St. Catharines College, Cambridge, who became almost a friend. He invited me to his digs and to the head table in this College. Stokes, the author of the seminal book *The Utilitarians and India*, really was very helpful.

What was of consequence was the eventual completion and publication in 1986 of what I consider my magnum opus: *The Patronage Bureaucracy in North India: The Robert M. Bird and James Thomason School, 1820-1870.*

If undervalued in North America, this book was (is) appreciated in India where it was put forward as the best source on the work of Bird and Thomason. One Dr. R.S. Tolia, an official in the Government of Uttaranchal, northern India, giving the Raja Todar Mal Memorial Lecture for XXth INCA International Congress told cartography delegates this:

> Peter Penner, a Canadian Historian, has very lucidly recounted the great contribution made by [Robert] Merttins Bird and his disciples, in **his eminently readable book, the Patronage Bureaucracy.** To the historians

amongst those present here, I strongly recommend this piece of work.

.....If I am asked to name an eminent successor to the great Raja Todar Mal, at least for the region to which we are referring, I would unhesitatingly name ... Bird first and, of course, equally James Thomason. Bird and Thomason improved the land settlement system of a region, Oudh, which was the birth-place of Raja Todar Mal. ...

My Publication Did Not Shield the British

I was not happy that I had to go to India for publication of *The Patronage Bureaucracy in North India*, but I found resistance to my efforts among the major university presses. This was comparable to the resistance I discovered at the School of Oriental and African Studies when I appeared to be developing theses which would have been squashed in London. Since Independence under Jawaharlal Nehru in 1947, Indian scholars had exposed the British Government and Services in India as exploitive and somewhat responsible for the Indian Mutiny/Rebellion in 1857. In fact, in the revaluation of that horrendous event, there were English critics who blamed evangelical-ism for the levelling down approach of this 'school' developed by Bird and Thomason which I had explored in detail, from beginning to end.

Chapter Six

Incredible First Sabbatical

1972-73

While my research subject was all important to me, the year 1972-73 was of supreme importance to the whole family. Within that sabbatical I had carved out four months in India, absolutely essential for my progress in research. Both our first sabbatical year and my four months in India had a special meaning, neither of which could be duplicated even though they hung together in significant ways. I knew I needed to enlarge my topic to make a viable publication. There were many very useful documents in London but, as I learned, many more in Allahabad, Uttar Pradesh, India.

By 1972, it was most satisfactory to learn that my total salary for my first sabbatical would be more than my annual salary would have been. This included the sabbatical year salary at 80 %, a Canada Council grant, some money from the Marjorie Young Bell Faculty Fund, as well as a senior short term Shastri Indo-Canadian Fellowship, covering travel and four months of research in India, to be paid only in rupees.[11]

---

11 This Institute, named after Lal Bahadur Shastri, the second Prime Minister of India, 1964-1966, was first worked out at McGill University, making possible the awarding of fellowships to worthy applicants to be paid in rupees.

The First Three Months in Richmond-on-Thames

Equally important as finding affordable housing, we needed to find schools for our children. We were fortunate to find Peter Burroughs and Judith Fingard, historians at Dalhousie University, Halifax, who had a house at 11, Rosemont Road, Richmond-on-Thames, actually a former worker's cottage dating from the 1830s. Peter, British himself, had acquired this little gem of a place for his frequent research trips and their own sabbaticals and summers, but would rent to friends and colleagues. Once referred to them, we finalised arrangements to take up residence early in September 1972. Though tiny, there were five rooms and a bath and a half, a small garage, many flowers outside for Justina, and central heating. The location was wonderful, as these arrangements go, because we could and did walk in three directions:

down to the Thames River through a gorgeous Terrace Hill flower garden, into Richmond Park to see the Queen's deer, and down to Richmond proper, a rather famous shopping area in its own right. We were able to move in on September 3rd when Peter and Judith returned to Halifax, Nova Scotia.

Our home on Rosemont Road, Richmond, # 11, 1972-73, 1979-1980

Though we might have made other arrangements, Norman and Christel Marsh of Clapham Common permitted us to house-sit # 13, North Side, Clapham Common, while they went to their Wales cottage. Besides, we would be out of the house for our 'five capitals' tour' on the continent. We arrived at Heathrow on July 30th in the morning, and headed for this early Queen Anne house. The place was immense, with five-foot width staircases, ten-foot halls lined with books. We had rooms on third and fourth floors, and had our own bathroom which I painted while we were there. This became the 'Canadian' bathroom. We especially appreciated BBC/TV programming, far superior in many ways.

Once settled on Rosemont Road, we gravitated toward Kew Road Methodist Church. We tried Richmond Duke Street Baptist, exporter of famous preachers like Alan Redpath to the USA, but these Baptists seemed less friendly. Robert liked the young people at Kew, even though the programme was quite unstructured. Besides, we discovered three Kew Road families on Rosemont Road: Judge John and Joy Baker, the daughter of a famous India missionary, and Roy and Audrey Smith. John and Eileen Smith lived on Vineyard path on the way down to George Street. So we soon had friends and Justina had some company to turn to while I was away in India for four months. Because Peter Burroughs let me use his car, an Austin, occasionally we would drive to 14, Shepherd's Hill, Highgate, to the London Mennonite Centre (LMC), but that took more than a half hour around the western ring road.

As to other friends and activities, we linked up with Indrani Khanna, whom Justina had met on previous visits. She was the one who made arrangements for me to stay with her sister in New Delhi for the period of Diwali once I got to India, and for which I was thankful.

During those first months, we tried to do as much sight-seeing as possible, within London and round about: Greenwich, Bournemouth (where we heard the Vienna Choir Boys), and Guildford Cathedral. Justina was much more interested in this than the children. As they were old enough to stay alone, we did quite a number of things, using the underground, by ourselves. One of these was to explore the City and particularly Leadenhall Street, the former site of the East India Company.

The Children in School and Robert's Violin Lessons

Nearly everyone in Sackville was excited about our going to England for a whole year, though we had colleagues who said they would never similarly place their children in English schools. But ours were up to the challenge and we hoped for the best as Robert turned sixteen during that summer, and Ruth was thirteen. Though we investigated several schools recommended to us, in the end we were able to place Robert in Twickenham Valley Grammar School (TVGS), easily reachable by bus. We placed Ruth in Putney Park School, a private girls' school. As it turned out, this was a mistake. Ruth came home completely disillusioned with this school on her first full day there, September 14th. There was overcrowding, lack of facilities, pretentiousness, and we took her out on 17 October. Fortunately for us, we had qualified and helpful neighbours on Rosemont Road willing and able to help in the 'disengagement' with that school: John Baker, a judge, as well as Lt. Col. Harston, an expert on schools. They recommended that we enrol Ruth in St. Mary Magdalene Secondary School. She was much happier there, found friends, was the only Canadian, hence a celebrity of sorts, and could walk to school.

Robert found French challenging at TVGS on Fifth Cross Road, Twickenham, but the music program was very good, and he was reasonably happy. He acquired quite a strong accent, and was very good at imitating the English. On his sixteenth birthday, I noted that Robert "is our pride and joy, so understanding as to be unreal." Ruth had her nose in Louise Alcott, Winston Churchill, and Mazo de la Roche (the Jalna series).

On the eve of my departure for India on November 2, Robert and I had a good chat. I confessed to some shortcomings in handling ongoing family irritations, and told him he would now have to carry some of the family burdens in my absence. This sixteen-year old encouraged me by suggesting that I was too pessimistic about this particular sabbatical, and then said that "all would be worth it for the love of a son for his father."

His violin lessons with Frederick Grinke, Ealing (formerly of Winnipeg, Manitoba), cost six pounds sterling, but they were worth it. Grinke taught for the Jehudi Menuhin Academy of Music and had once taught Rodney McLeod, with whom Robert had started in Sackville. It soon became obvious that if Robert was to make progress in violin, he needed more than Grinke. He also needed a new violin. With Frederick Grinke's assistance we bought one from Hill's, made about 1780, and well-priced. Much later, Robert had this violin redesigned and gut-strung for Baroque music.

Overwhelming Research Material

Given all this activity and the responsibilities of settling the family securely before I left for India, I found it difficult, at times, to do what I came to do, to extend my research into the James Thomason 'school' of settlement officers. I was already familiar with the British Library, then still housed under the dome of the British Museum. At Clapham I learned about the Thornton family famous in England and India. The Church Missionary Society (CMS) archives on Waterloo Road (then) were also immense.

As to Robert Needham Cust who became the subject of a full-scale biography, I found his journals in the Manuscripts Division of the British Museum; also many of his letters in the Royal Commonwealth Society Library, near Trafalgar Square (where I discovered the Sherlock Holmes pub). Most importantly, I found Pandora Dewhurst, great granddaughter of Cust, living in Barnes, not far from Richmond. She showed me everything they had in terms of books, especially Cust's eight volume series entitled *Linguistic and Oriental Essays*, and pictures. She made arrangements for us to visit her mother in Cambridge, Mrs. Oldfield, Cust's only granddaughter. There we met Pandora's other sister from New Zealand (Albinia Oldfield Willis). We were warmly welcomed, given coffee, a full lunch, and tea. I was allowed to see all the heirlooms, and to take away books for my use, even to take them with me to Canada.[12] More than that, I was able to visit Christopher I.V. Cust, a grandnephew of Cust, who invited me to his flat at Earl's Court. He was descended from Cust's brother Edward with whom my subject had fundamental family differences.

---

12 In 2001, out of the blue, came a letter from a 14-year old great great grandson of Cust, living in Robin Hood country, England, asking: where are those Cust books and can we have them back? The archivist at Mount Allison University, where they were housed, agreed to release them and young Anthony got his wish!

Justina in Richmond-on-Thames

I was naturally concerned about Justina alone with the children in Richmond. She was however encouraged by the general happiness of Robert and Ruth in their situations. Robert found a good friend, Margaret Mohlstadt, from Wooster, Ohio, the only other foreign student at his school. She was also a violinist. Ruth eventually found a friend in her school named Johnny C. As always, Justina made new friends around her, especially among students attending classes at an American school for third year students doing a year abroad. This was housed in the old (Methodist) Richmond College just around the corner. Justina particularly liked Maryjo Adams from Michigan whose parents came to visit in November. Norman and Christel Marsh as well as Justina's neighbours invited her, also Pandora Dewhurst in nearby Barnes. She had a few correspondents such as Mabel Croft who kept her in touch with events and life in Sackville.

Meanwhile, once I was in India for my stint, as told in the next section, Justina liked the description of my situation in Allahabad with Mike and Elaine Lapka as company in the Presbyterian bungalow. She was quite overwhelmed at my fascinating experiences. By the middle of February Justina had received seventy-five of my aerograms.

Four Months in India, November 1972 to February 1973

Most unique for me, naturally, was anticipation of those four months in the strange land of India. I had obtained considerable advice on life and health in India, not least from a retired Baptist missionary. She wrote that I must keep three dietary rules: cooked food, peeled fruit, and boiled water.

I journalized those months in eighty-five numbered aerograms to Justina, as well as in my tiny and very legible handwriting in my daybook. She wrote forty-four letters in return. The following are mere highlights.

My decision to fly to India via Moscow, using Aeroflot, proved to be more adventuresome than anticipated. We were late in departing for

Moscow, and when we got there on Thursday November 2nd, we had missed the connecting flight to Delhi, and were told we would have to wait in Moscow until the 6th. Well, the South Asians with British passports, some of them well-placed, going to India for weekend weddings, were not willing to wait and were able to move Aeroflot to give us all passage on a larger airliner (SU 535), leaving Friday late. Even then, we had to stay in the Aeroflot hotel for one night and got a bus tour of Moscow on the Friday. Not having been in Moscow before, I thought the whole experience rather exciting. As it was, we got to Palam Airport in New Delhi on Saturday, November 4th close to nine o'clock in the morning.

First Ten Days in India

Shanti and Urmila Ratna, daughters Jaishree, Ameeta, Sangeeta, Rajkika, and one son, Rajneesh, Haus Khaz, New Delhi, November, 1972

Once Mr. Malik, the India executive officer of Shastri Indo-Canadian Institute in New Delhi, had met me at Palam and taken me to this Institute in Golf Links where he had his office, I was picked up by Urmila (Khanna) Ratna and her Sikh driver. This invitation to the Ratna home was made possible by her sister Indrani Khanna whom I learned to know as a scholar doing research in London. Urmila took me to their home in Hauz Khas, a suburb south of Connaught Circle, not far from the Qutub Minar. I was now obviously in another world. It was Diwali, Festival of Lights, for Hindus the equivalent of Christmas, I suppose.

This Punjabi family consisted of Urmila, Shanti (the husband, a lawyer), and four daughters and one son Jaishree, Ameeta, Sangeeta,

Radkika, and Rajneesh. All names have pleasant meanings. They welcomed me warmly and treated me extremely generously. The gap between the poor and the well-to-do such as my hosts who have live-in servants in their 3,000 square foot house was everywhere in evidence. In one of my letters I described Delhi traffic in some detail, utterly fascinating in its variety.

Once the driver had taken the children to their private (Catholic) school, and deposited lawyer Shanti at his office, Urmila then directed the driver to take me wherever I wanted or had to go for business or shopping (or to register at the Canadian High Commission). With Malik's assistance I had two meetings with James Draper, the Resident Director of Shastri in India. With their help I was able to make plans for a trip to Agra to see the Taj Mahal on Friday.

That trip was unforgettable. Not only was I impressed with the fascinating Mughal architecture of Fatehpur Sikri, the Red Fort, and the Taj, I realised that this was the seat of the James Thomason government and this the place where his successor John Colvin died in the midst of the Mutiny of 1857. The whole experience here was simply awesome.

I stayed with the Ratna family until November 10 when I had a flight booked to Allahabad, four hundred miles downriver from Delhi.

With the Harpers in Allahabad, Uttar Pradesh

The flight to Allahabad was for me spectacular, in a turbo-prop Fokker Friendship plane. It took me over the Ganges Canal, the Grand Trunk road and the areas I would be researching in Allahabad's Uttar Pradesh (UP) State Archives. Once landed, I had several options for accommodation. Most promising was the offer from Erica and Ed Harper, American Presbyterians, who occupied the old missionary bungalow on Ewing Christian College campus. They had planned to be away for several months at the International Christian Woodstock School at the hill station Mussoorie, founded in 1854, but I would have

Michael and Elaine Lapka from Wooster, Ohio, there. The American Presbyterians had first come to Allahabad in the 1830s.

There was no hesitation in accepting the Harper's offer. The campus was on the banks of the Jumuna river, had students, was within cycling distance of the State Archives. The bungalow was fenced-in, had a versatile cook trained by missionaries, named Umar, and I had the Lapkas for company. As long as the Harpers were present they took me to meet high Allahabad society: their Rotary friends, P.K. Nehru, a cousin to Jawaharlal Nehru and former ambassador to China at a very expensive wedding, also the district magistrate. These all seemed quite glad to know that I was Canadian. Actually, whereas the Lapkas had to have a visa and report travel plans, at that time, all because of the Commonwealth connection, I had a mere Canadian passport and was free to travel where I wanted.

By the third week of November I was quite used to Allahabad life though I did not particularly like the working conditions in the State Archives. After November 20th I had Umar, the cook, all to myself, and entirely at my bidding. He called me 'sahib!' Only occasionally did I have meals with the Lapkas. The Harpers had also introduced me to the principal of Ewing Christian College, Dr. Job, who had a son named Simon who loved to play badminton competitively. I had my first game on November 21, on a clay court on a windless evening, beside the Jumuna river. These happy situations kept me going to my otherwise wild and confusing archival scenario.

Allahabad Culture

Allahabad provided an amazing experience. The temperature was wonderful, ranging from 65 to 80 degrees Fahrenheit for the ten weeks I was there. We had one good rain, and several gentle ones. The grapefruit out of the Presbyterian compound garden were excellent, and tempting to the children living just over the dike protecting us from the Jumuna River.

My experience at the UP **Archives** was something else. A video would have shown "four bell-ringers, three bundlelifters, an indeterminate number of scholars and technical assistants between that range." It was hard to say how much scholarly activity actually went on, though I persisted and sometimes even complained of the incredible nuisance scenarios that developed at times. I wrote: "Then there were the chaprassies, the chowkidars and sweepers, all in a row – employed only when the bell rings. Then there are the visitors, and telephone users, the whoopers, whisperers, burpers, yawners, and the talkers. What boredom they must undergo." If it had not been for the incredibly interesting material on the land settlement officers I was researching, I would have been very unhappy. For some days I managed to find a seat in a more private place in the archives.

The Land Settlement Act of 1833

In spite of these distractions I found most valuable materials on how the Land Settlement Act of 1833 was actually implemented, first in the North-Western Provinces (NWP) and then extended to the Punjab following its conquest in 1849, and then applied to the huge principality of Oudh in 1856.

This implementation, a radical intervention into the political and social fabric of the Northwest Provinces, stretching from Benares (Varanasi) upstream beyond Delhi, was made possible under the authority of the British Parliament. Pitt's India Act of 1784 set up a Board of Control which held ultimate authority over the East India Company. The Act stated that the Board would henceforth "superintend, direct and control" the acts and operations of the three divisions which operated under the Company: the civil, political, and military. The Governor-General seated in Calcutta had his powers in matters of war, revenue and diplomacy greatly strengthened. Land settlement matters and revenue collection was authorized in the Land Settlement Act of 1833, known as Regulation IX, whereby the Company greatly increased its revenues.

What did this implementation mean? Briefly, the *taluqdars* who were a holdover from the former Mughal emperors were dispossessed of their landholding and taxing powers for the purpose of settling the lands with various lower grades of tenants. The men chosen to execute the directives given by authority figures like Robert Mertins Bird at the central revenue office and James Thomason, elevated to the position of Lieutenant-Governor of the NWP, were all men who had studied at the East India College. They were bonded civil servants, covenanted not to embezzle the finances in India as their predecessors were accused of doing. Once in India they studied languages at Fort William College in Calcutta before being offered lower-ranked positions up country (the *mofussil*). When they advanced to the position of Collector of a District, they were paid, for that day, much larger salaries than their counterparts at home in England.

It was this subject in all its manifestations that I explored. The material in Allahabad was immensely valuable in that it filled out for me large areas of understanding how the great task was undertaken and completed and with what results. Exploring the details here is of course not possible. For me, however, it was totally satisfying to be able to complete *The Patronage Bureaucracy in North India: the Robert M. Bird and James Thomason School, 1820-1870* and have it published in 1986.

My New Toy and My Guests

One of the great things I did was to purchase my own bicycle, thus obviating the daily haggling about fare with rickshaw drivers who could not be expected to know any English. Doctor Job asked a chemistry professor named V.M. John to take me to the Sind Cycle Shop where technicians assembled the bike while I waited. My new toy, a standard Evans bicycle, cost 230 rupees. This gave me independence and exercise. With this bike, my first ever new one! I rode all over Allahabad every morning before 1030 hours sight-seeing, stopping to shop in Civil Lines, the former English site, and having coffee with

Major Chopra of Cozy Nook. When he introduced me to his charming wife, I asked her to help me buy a Benares silk sari for Justina. Trying to decide for myself in one of the many sari shops was simply too bewildering.

I wrote an extensive article about these experiences and observations, "Wheeling and Dealing in Allahabad," for the readers of the *Sackville Tribune Post*. I found some good book shops in the city, and proprietors were prepared to wrap them for shipping to Canada. When I arrived home from the year-long sabbatical, I had about 150 books waiting to be unwrapped. Some packages were underway for months.

Among my guests were the Ernie Arloffs who supervised the work of the Oriental Missionary Society, housed on the grounds of the former Zenana Bible and Medical Mission, much of it built by Lieutenant-Governor William and Lady Muir in the 1860s. The Arloffs helped me plan my trip to Benares (by train) and from there to Calcutta (by DC-9 Jet service). They invited me to attend one of their services as well as for a meal on Sunday in early December. Because Umar was quite willing to cook dinners, I also entertained guests. I once had the British Council officer, Roger Bower and his wife over during the week. As a result of my visit to Professor Ishwiri Prasad, the author of four books on the Mughal period, I invited him with Burneshar Singh Gahlaut, the son of the City manager, whom I met at the archives, for dinner. Prasad was then 91 years of age. This was significant because people of his kind did not readily enter a white man's house or accept his offer of a meal. I had become *Sahib Penner!*

Benares and Calcutta

In December I ventured to Benares (Varanasi) and Calcutta (Kolkata). In the former so-called holy city of the Hindus I had a good hotel experience, and a good guide. He showed me the brasses, silks, and arranged for a boatman to show me the bathing and burning ghats along the holy Ganga. I also persuaded him to show me the Sanskrit college at which my chief research subject, James Thomason, had made his one recorded speech in early 1853. My stay in Benares was all too short, but I made more time for Calcutta where I stayed five days.

This was great fun, all told, beginning with the flight in a brilliant sky from which to see Mount Everest on the way to Dum Dum airport in Calcutta. On Wednesday December 13 I took a guide who showed me various temples, though I was keen to visit the famous William Carey Church and the Old Mission Church. Most significant of all was the visit to the Victoria Memorial Museum built by Lord Curzon around 1900. I also wanted the experience of the Grand Hotel on Chowringhee, which was once part of the Maidan [a large green area with a track for horse riding] for the East India Company grandees and the incoming civilians.

Not least was my appreciation for the invitation to stay three days with the Mennonite Central Committee [a relief organization] workers in residence, **Neil and Herta Janzen** from Winnipeg. They showed me the source of many of the articles that were being sold in Canada under the program "Self-Help" [later 10,000 Villages] and were also willing to hear of my experiences.

While waiting at the Dum Dum airport for a plane to arrive from Patna, I had the bonus of meeting Frau Julika Roller. She and three other German tourists, two of them doctors, were going on to Benares and then home. I spoke German to them, and she was so pleased that she invited Justina and me to visit her after I got back to London. Not only did I act as interpreter for them in meeting a guru with his devotees, I complained to the airport manager for leaving us in uncertainty until late in the afternoon. The result of all this was a friendship with the Roller family which lasted beyond Julika's death.

The Somewhat Frantic Last Weeks

I cannot of course mention everything that took place in India. My time in Allahabad was running out, and I was frantic to cover all the records I needed to read before January 24. "Time marches on, even in idling India," I wrote. I also wanted to finish off some articles, witness a Hindu *mela* [where the Ganga and Jumuna rivers meet at Allahabad] and go to Banda where Robert Needham Cust held forth as Collector 120 years earlier. Harper's secretary did a lot of typing for me and as a result I was able to organize my notes as well as send off some articles as the record shows. By this time I was also making plans to go to Hyderabad and Mahbubnagar in south central India to visit the Mennonite Brethren mission field and its last workers "in station."

Gahlaut, who some days worked elbow to elbow with me at the Archives, was prepared to accompany me to Banda because, as he said, he had an uncle there, and it would be unsafe for me to travel alone. He was serious, you must not go alone! The distance was more than 100 kilometers, through Jute country no less, and that by third class bus only. But first I had to meet his father to make sure I was *pukkah* (*bona fide*).

My trip to Banda was a highlight, utterly fascinating, taking me through jute country with literally hundreds of oxcarts laden with jute drawn by oxen. Space prevents me from including the details I wrote to Justina in London. I was everywhere treated with respect and gracious Indian hospitality.

Joint Household, Banda, NWP, India, Gahlaut, my friend, second
from the right; his lawyer uncle in the Nehru coat on the left

Christmas and New Year's in Allahabad

I did enjoy Christmas, though I missed my family in Richmond, and they missed me. Together with Mike and Elaine Lapka from Wooster we had the Job family and friends in on December 23. More guests came, mostly Indian (among them the eminent Professor Prasad and my friend Gahlaut), and our servants, on Christmas Eve, complete with the scrawny-looking turkeys which the servants had tried to fatten in the compound. Umar our cook read the Christmas story from Luke's Gospel, and explained it very well to the other servants. Christmas Day started with an exchange of gifts. Justina received a wonderful tablecloth from Mike and Elaine. Later we went to St. Peter's Cathedral for morning worship, and I went to the Arloffs where I had Christmas dinner with Kerala Christians.

Meanwhile, having met Professor Razivi, a Muslim, I planned to spend some time with him on New Year's Day. We had bicycles and were able to cover much ground: the Grand Trunk Road, a quick ride through the Chowk (downtown!), and the nearby 'red light' district. On the second day we rode to Minto Park, the pillar along the Jumuna River commemorating the Queen's Proclamation of 1858, and looked in the Christian burial ground for the headstone for Robert N. Cust's second wife. After that I attended a year's end party at the home of Bower, the British Council representative, featuring various friends of theirs and mine.

I was able to sell my bicycle for a reasonable amount (160 rupees) to one of the secretaries at the Archives, said goodbye to Umar, the other servants, and to Mike and Elaine Lapka, and rode the train to Lucknow, UP, on January 24. In Lucknow I rented an old bike and pedalled around that famous city, the scene of the famous "siege of Lucknow" where Henry Montgomery Lawrence died on July 4, 1857.

Last Weeks in New Delhi

My destination now was New Delhi and the Republic Day parade of the more than one hundred exhibitions down Rajpath to the India

Gate. As to a residence, I had a choice between returning to the Ratna family in the Haus Khaz suburb, or staying with James Draper in Golf Links headquarters of the Shastri Institute. It was cold in Delhi at this time, the temperature going down to about five degrees Celsius, and people without homes and blankets were dying from exposure. Though I stayed with the Ratnas until after my trip to Hyderabad, I eventually chose the Shastri house, especially when James and I developed a good rapport. I realized I would see more of India by doing things with him, like getting to Aligarh and the Muslim university there, and meeting a Shastri scholar from Australia. The Ratna children were disappointed, but understanding of my decision. Urmila took me to witness the Hindu service in a private house wedding, a very interesting experience.

My Visit with MB Missionaries

Early February saw me flying south to visit the Mennonite Brethren missionaries at Mahbubnagar about sixty miles south of Hyderabad City [not knowing that two decades later I would be spending more than six years researching and writing the MB 'Mission among Telugus']. Once I arrived in Mahbubnagar by bus, an English-speaking young man whom I met put the rickshaw driver and me in the right direction to the home of Henry and Amanda Poetker. Because I was expected and the Poetkers were having their siesta, a servant showed me to a bed where I could have a rest. When I awoke, we enjoyed our first tea and conversation. The Poetkers were from Hepburn, Saskatchewan, and the others I was expected to meet were also Canadian. One day was set aside for a picnic under an enormous banyan tree where I met Dan and Helen Nickel, George and Anne Froese, the two other couples who, along with the Poetkers, were among the last to serve ``in station.``

I cannot here recite all I saw and experienced with **Dan Nickel**, "that splendid human being`` on February 3, 1973. In one twelve-hour day he showed me distant mission stations such as Gadwal and

Wanaparty. It was a time of terrible drought, and I saw hungry people, a mother and child, who found us having our lunch at noonday. M.B. John, pastor of the Mahbubnagar Church, asked me to give a brief sermon on Sunday morning when R.R.K. Murthy would be my interpreter. All of this was grist for the mill of my mind when I came to researching and writing the whole story, beginning in 1988. The Henry Poetkers gave me generous hospitality and took me back to the Hyderabad airport.

In New Delhi I was able to meet with Anne L. Ediger (from Winnipeg, 1920–1981) who had been seconded by the MB Mission to the Far Eastern Broadcasting Association. Like me, she was a graduate of MB Bible College, and had worked her way into the radio ministry of the Mission. She introduced me to some of her friends, took me to an afternoon meeting, and then allowed me to entertain her at the Asoka Hotel, where we had tandoori chicken in the Peacock room. *When again will Sackville/London and Winnipeg meet in New Delhi?*

The Last Five Months in London, March to July 1973

I was warmly welcomed back by my family and all of the Richmond friends, as we saw them one by one: Roy and Audrey Smith and other Kew Road Methodist Church people, and Norman and Christel Marsh. Among outside-of-London guests we had David and Eunice Warkentin from Agincourt, Ontario. It was balm to my heart to hear him say that he still thought of me as his pastor. In memory of their son Bruce who was killed in late 1965, Robert gave a Haydn recital for them and they were pleased.

There were reports for the Shastri Institute and articles to write, and sorting out of papers. More importantly, the India research experience, having helped to focus the investigation, urgently drew me back to the India Office Records, as quickly as back-to-routine would allow. I worked out an understanding with Justina. She was willing to help me transcribe the Robert Needham Cust letters in the Royal

Commonwealth Library, Trafagar Square, but she wanted to have Sundays with me.

Julika Roller, Groszsachsenheim, Stuttgart

One of the interesting events of April was our visit to *Groszsachsenheim*, Wuertemburg, West Germany, to see *Frau Julika Roller*. My meeting with her and her friends at the Dum Dum airport in Calcutta during my India sojourn, as it turned out, led to a long-standing relationship. Even before I got back to Richmond, Justina already had repeated invitations for us to visit her in Stuttgart. She was a great traveller and loved to drive long distances, alone if necessary. So she wanted to squeeze us into her timetable early in April, something we managed.

This was quite a unique experience for us, to be welcomed so warmly into German society. We were wined and dined, feted by all those *Buergermeisters*, the peers of Paul Roller, the Mayor of *Groszsachsenheim*. Among other things, together with the Rollers we visited the Canadian Forces Base at Lahr and were entertained by Alex and Jan Morrison, he a graduate of Mount Allison University. Julika and Paul took us to the home of one of the doctors we met in Calcutta, and I had champagne for my forty-eighth birthday!

The correspondence with this remarkably energetic Wuertembuerger continued until her death. When we were anticipating a sabbatical year in 1979-80, we kept her fully informed, and we visited her during our trip to see *Aussiedler* relations. When she died in May 1990 her daughter Brigitte Roller Fliegauf sent us the death notice: "*Unsere liebe, treusorgende Mutter und Oma Julie Roller (geb. Rapp) ist uns heute im Tode vorangegangen [1903-1990]* (Our dear Mother has gone before us in death). I wrote Brigitte that we would never forget Tante Julika, as we called her. The friendship had been continuous from 1973 to 1990, and after that with Brigitte.

The First Aussiedler

That visit to Germany in 1973 gave us an opportunity to go to Westphalia to meet the first of the Janzen clan to come to Germany as *Aussiedler* (resettlers). On Sunday April 8 we flew to Duesseldorf, took the train via Dortmund to Lage an der Lippe, near Detmold, Westphalia, where we were met at the train station by Abram and Helena (Wiebe) Janzen. Neither knew the other, but given the circumstances, it was not hard to recognize Abram because he looked like a Janzen on Justina's father's side and was in fact Justina's first cousin.

This was only the first; by 1992 Justina had sixteen first cousins and all their families living in and around Bielefeld and Paderborn, Westphalia, and other parts of Germany. Thus began the unfolding of the stories of these people who had been in Joseph Stalin's *Gulag* for a minimum of ten years. All were reticent to talk, as though they had come home [*Heimkehrer*] from a terrible war which had scarred their souls. What amazed us from the beginning was how generously West Germany was treating these 'landed immigrants' with temporary and then permanent housing, according to generous standards, jobs, and schooling in the German language.

By way of explanation, these *Aussiedler* were descendants of the German-speakers who went to Russia by invitation 200 years earlier. Between 1972 and the mid-90s, Germany took in as *Heimkehrer* (returnees) more than 1.5 million *Ruszlanddeutsche* (Russian Germans), of which about 250-300 thousand called themselves Baptists or Mennonites.[13]

Trips and Guests

After our Germany trip, we took up Judge John Baker's offer of the use of his Morris for short trips. His only concern was having the vehicle off the street in our garage, and taking care that the water

---

13 Jim Coggins interview with Missionary-to-Mennonites in Germany John N. Klassen, Abbotsford, in *MB Herald*, December 20, 1996

level in the radiator was maintained. During April we did Hatfield House, St. Albans with Allen and Ellen Kreider. Then followed Salisbury Cathedral, Horningsham Meeting Place (1566), and the Cotswolds, Lechlade, where I had been in 1968, as well as Oxford and Blenheim Palace. Before the end of the month, we also managed to visit Lady Hardinge in Kent County. She thought I was onto a good thing with my discovery of Robert Needham Cust, as his biography reflected the entire Victorian era. I also managed some research in the usual libraries.

Though the children did not necessarily relish riding with us, we did more ambitious trips in May to Rugby and Birmingham where we visited Matthew and Ann Graham who had served St. Paul's Anglican in Sackville, NB. We also headed north to Grantham, Lincolnshire, where we did Belton House, a Christopher Wren house, home of the Brownlow/Cust family since the seventeenth century. Norman and Christel Marsh took us as guests to their annual Justice Ball at the Savoy Hotel. This fell on Friday, June 8, 1973. For this Justina was stunningly dressed in her India silk garnet and gold gown which she had sewed from the Benares silk I had brought home, and I had to rent a tuxedo.

For some time we had anticipated the arrival of Vern and Frieda Heinrichs. Once arrived on June 6, we had a wonderful time getting caught up. They actually stayed with us in our small cottage. We went to Royal Festival Hall and saw the "Mousetrap" which had been running for about twenty years. We hired a car to drive with Vern and Frieda to the north, Doncaster, to visit some friends. On the way home I showed them Haileybury College, located north of London. Frieda and Justina spent more than a few days together, including a visit to the famous Silver Vaults and the antique shops of Richmond. Frieda seemed to need that time with Justina, and when she left for home on July 1, she gave us all specialised gifts.

Kew Road and Last Events in Richmond

Both Justina and I had opportunities at Kew Road Methodist and at the London Mennonite Centre, Highgate to give talks about Canada and India, respectively. During this sabbatical year we had not been to Highgate very often because of distance and Justina's having been alone for four months. The Kew Road and Rosemont Road people had proved quite a wonderful substitute.

As we neared the end of our sabbatical year Justina, and sometimes Robert, who was writing exams and practicing for his last lessons with Frederick Grinke, went with me to the India Office Records on Blackfriars Road to help transcribe materials. While there, only ten days before our departure in July I met Robert Eric Frykenberg, University of Wisconsin, Madison, an India specialist who had an impressive number of PhD candidates. In retrospect, it would have been good to have had more time together. What was important, this meeting seemed to cement a scholarly relationship that lasted for many years. He seemed pleased to know that somewhere there was another intellectual interested in British India who is also a "brother."

Ruth ended her school year on a high note when an English Chinese boy named Johnny Lee, from her class, took an affectionate interest in her, and asked to walk her to school. On the second occasion of his doing this, he brought her a rose. We were watching from the upstairs casement window! Ruth the Canadian topped her class in English!

Our last events of significance involved our friends the Marshes, the Smiths, Pandora Dewhurst, and the Kreiders from Highgate. With the latter we did some sentimental walks around the West End and Richmond Park.

The furlough was not really over until we were home in Sackville and settled in our home again. Betsy and Robert Shorthouse, my replacement for the year, had left our house spotless. Our Robert was getting ready to join the New Brunswick Youth Orchestra for their trip to Scotland, and a concert in London. We were warmly welcomed back by everyone at the University and the Church, as well as by the people of Sackville.

"Research and a 'Ramble' in India"

Several months after getting back to Sackville from the altogether fascinating sabbatical and my term in India, on a Monday evening in November, I finally had a chance to give my faculty seminar entitled "Research and a Ramble in India". This was an illustrated talk about my four months in India. The suggestion of a "Ramble" made people ask whether I had done any work while in India. I explained that this referred to my favourite open air restaurant in Connaught Circus, New Delhi, during late January and early February. In the noon sun it was quite pleasant; at night the temperature was going down to 40 degrees Fahrenheit (6 degrees Celsius).

There was a large attendance in the Manning Room of the Chapel and the presentation was well received. The South Asian members on the Mount Allison faculty present were quite impressed that I had not dwelt on the poverty and dirt of India but rather on the positive things I had found, much beauty, and the possibility of friendships wherever I went.

Chapter Seven

Two Decades of the
Greatest Job in the World
1973 to 1992

Undoubtedly, I had one of the neatest situations: a secure position teaching in a great but small university; able to devote much time to research and writing, actually my first love; living within walking distance of our department; and working at a leisured pace with congenial colleagues. We were not without some tensions and differences in Faculty Council and Senate. Some presidents had more difficulty serving their mandate under a Board of Regents than others. While there are glimpses of our privileged lives in other chapters, here I want to share some highlights of our experience at Mount Allison University. The annual *Maclean's* University Rankings were still two decades away, so I will leave that discussion to coincide more or less with my retirement.

What Was I Expected to Do?

Once I arrived for what was my first visit to the History Department, I was hired to do an introductory survey course, one English history and one European history at the third year level. When President L.H. Cragg (1962-1974) confirmed the appointment, he hoped this contract could be renewed by "mutual consent," and explained that

University appointments ran from July 1 to June 30, that is, one was paid on a 12-month basis.

When I compared this with what I knew about other schools and the workloads at some American universities, I asked: is this my workload, three courses only, and perhaps supervising one or two honours theses? Some of my friends who knew nothing or little about the university as a place of work, were disbelieving. Is that what you get paid for?

That was it, whether these courses were at the second year level, or the third or the fourth. Once I was established I usually had two third year courses and one fourth year seminar (with small enrolments) and one or two honours theses to supervise and judge.

Were we expected to publish? Was there a 'publish or perish' push, that is, did advancement, or early promotion depend on publications? No, this was not part of the contract, or the understanding in my early years, but certain professors in some fields chose to work hard at research and publications and, being successful, put pressure on others to do likewise. I know of cases where in my later years some colleagues were not promoted to full professor because of lack of such work.

Briefly, at Mount Allison it was not all about teaching and publishing or producing in music, art, or science projects that were given a lot of money. Two other things were considered for advancement: service to the University in committee work, for example, and participation in and support of the community of Sackville. I was able to be active in all areas.

Curriculum Drafting Committee

In 1972 (as one of my contributions outside the classroom) I was asked to chair the "curriculum drafting committee." This was an attempt to implement an earlier Senate initiative on the need for a curriculum overhaul. Central to it was the requirement of six core courses and seven related cognates to make up an "area of concentration."

The other seven courses required for graduation could be electives. Though there were subsequent attempts to rewrite the curriculum, ours held up for about twenty years.

Besides sitting on several other major committees, this was also the year when I was making plans for my first sabbatical. Among these were writing for grants, for permission to see papers in the British libraries, and finding a suitable couple to occupy our house while we were gone. Occasionally I had to introduce new courses to accommodate changes in history faculty. Within my British Empire interests I developed 19th century British India. Much later I also introduced an omnibus Russian history course to the department's offerings.

Some Troubled Years

In Chapter Five I had occasion to touch on the issue of **censure** from the Canadian Association of University Teachers (CAUT) in connection with the suspension of a music teacher for alleged incompetence. Even though she was given an appropriate severance package, the case was used by a supportive group with which to attack the President. Hence during the years 1970 to 1973 President Cragg came under fierce criticism in many Faculty Council meetings. At the height of this struggle some of us used to gather off campus to caucus in anticipation of moves the opposition might be planning for Council debates. The speaker for our viewpoint was the late Gordon Treash, a good parliamentarian able to think on his feet. Though I thought this counter activity was necessary then, the affair divided faculty politically for many years. In fact there were colleagues I did not talk to for about three years. Later I vowed never again to become politicised in that way.

All of this had some implications for Convocation. At the 1973 Convocation the Sunday-evening Baccalaureate speaker, a prominent United Church of Canada person, and the student Valedictorian next day openly voiced criticism of the administration's handling of this affair. We were away on that very satisfying sabbatical, 1972–73, when a graduate named Steve was voted to give the valedictory address by a handful of his buddies in the senior class. He took the occasion to openly attack Wallace McCain of McCain Foods who was on the platform getting an honorary doctorate. President Cragg intervened and asked Steve to step down on the grounds that McCain was not in a position to defend on that occasion. Following that debacle the senior class was asked to bring nominations for valedictorian to a subcommittee of the Convocation Committee, namely to David Fensom and myself.

Fensom was a Biologist who was hired by Mount Allison with a mere Honours BSc degree. He was already famous in faraway places as plant physiologist at Ridley College, St. Catharines. He was also a water colorist and known in the area for his ink sketches of old buildings to preserve their memory. For me, more immediately, he became a friend and my mentor in Convocation Committee matters. He inducted me into the old Mount Allison tradition of the dignified convocation parade. In consequence I was involved with Convocation concerns and marshalling for about a decade.

Following this embarrassment to Convocation, I helped in the fall of 1973 to marshal the graduating students into Convocation Hall. Until then a mere forty had stayed for Convocation. A few years later nearly everyone stayed, up to 400.

In 1990, already retired, but still teaching one course, David Fensom staged an art show. It was very well attended. Justina had already bought me his *Red Fort of Delhi* which was hanging on his office wall. His paintings had enormously increased in value. On December 9, 1990, in the upstairs gallery of Owens Art Gallery, Peter McNally of Montreal gave a fascinating paper on David Fensom, his travels, the mythic (out-and-about) character, his techniques, the "unique embodiment of two cultures: scientist and humanist combined in one person."

Margaret McCain, Chancellor and Friend

One of the friends that came into our lives was Margaret McCain, wife of Wallace McCain of Florenceville, New Brunswick. She became Chancellor of the University in the mid-'eighties. From the beginning I found it very easy as chair of the Convocation Committee to relate to her. She wanted me to 'teach' her the intricacies of getting honored guests, graduates, and faculty into and out of Convocation Hall with dignity and efficiency. By that time (1985) I had prepared a Convocation Handbook which President Guy MacLean endorsed. A decade later she was the Honorable Margaret McCain, having been appointed Lieutenant-Governor of New Brunswick.

In 1988 I had a long chat with Margaret about the research I was doing on the Fawcett family for my book on Sackville Methodist/ United Church. She was riveted because she, a Norrie, stems from the Fawcetts. She told how when young she had loved to roam around the Fawcett property where our daughter Ruth was living. So I suggested she might one day want to come to tea at Ruth's. When I told Ruth this, she nearly had kittens!

In 1988 we had a convocation made glittering by earth-shakers in the ranks of the honorary doctoral candidates: Archbishop Desmond Tutu of South Africa, Stephen Lewis from the prominent New Democratic Party family, and Lois Wilson, outspoken Moderator of the United Church of Canada. That was the year sniff-dogs were sent through Convocation Hall before the event.

My History Colleagues during These Decades

For the most part I had dedicated hard-working colleagues, almost wholly devoted to history – especially to teaching. William Godfrey produced many reviews and articles in Colonial history in these decades. Other long-lasting colleagues were less active in research and writing. Following my sabbatical when I got back on track in terms of writing reviews, articles short and long, I saw the appearance in 1983–1984 of two books I had edited. It was a fact, little known to my colleagues, that I was far more active in research and writing activity than all of them together. Though much of that was non-academic, my academic writings exceeded them all, with student assistants, as I will show in later sections.

My History colleagues, standing, Bill Godfrey, John Stanton, Mark Davis, Gene Goodrich, David Beatty; seated, myself (Head), Glenara Anderson, secretary, Graham Adams Jr., 1990

When it came to applying in 1983 for a full professorship, as one had to do, I needed five references, four from outside the University. One of my referees was able to show how productive I had been in that world outside the University. This work in another sphere which was part of our Anabaptist witness impressed the relevant committee. My hyperactivity began with the 1974 series on "Mennonites in the Maritimes" published in the *Mennonite Reporter,* based in Waterloo, Ontario. These and other pieces were readily accepted by editors and appreciated by readers. Yet all this time I was re-working my dissertation to include what I had gained during that amazingly productive research sabbatical in London and India.

Health and Wellness

Preparation for a sabbatical overseas brought up the issue of fitness. I need not have worried because the daily regimen of getting to a library or archive in Metropolitan London, using train and underground ("the Tube"), demanded much more walking than getting to work in Sackville. Nevertheless, in preparation I had started a fitness program with Laird McLennan, basketball coach, in 1972. Wanting to lose weight, we decided on noon-day warm-up 5BX "Air Force" exercises, followed by two games of badminton (a game he taught me), and perhaps a swim. As a result, within two months, I came down to a trim 182 pounds (82.7 kilograms) from 196 at New Year's. This was my success story of the year.

Our friendship and badminton court fellowship lasted until he left the University in 1977. Laird got a teaching position, first at Plaster Rock, then near Fredericton, where his wife Carole, one of my history students, was taking Law and articling with a Fredericton firm. My appreciation for Laird (1933-2015) and Carole continued and we met again at Convocation in 2010.

The Drama on the Badminton Court

My other close friend and partner in badminton was Jack Drover, the hockey and soccer coach. Rarely could I defeat him or Laird, yet I managed an average of perhaps eight points. Later I played many times with members of the athletic staff, Janet Robinson and Sue Seaborne, most often when we had a foursome. From staff and faculty there was my good friend Bill Evans (whom I loved to tease) who took over the University's mail service, and David Stewart, who became Vice President, Administration.

Occasionally faculty such as Rainer Hempel of the German Department came to play badminton. He boasted to Justina in the Department that he could get by with cheap floor shoes. When I ran him back and forth and side to side, chasing my 'birdie,' suddenly one of his new shoes burst, as though made of paper mache, what a howl! George Evelyn from Music was another who was determined to perfect his game at my expense. What fun we had over the noon hours.

This activity kept my weight in check. I tended to record my fitness activities and weight. In November of 1974 I was about 177 pounds. Once I had started running seriously, I worked up to five, to seven, kilometres by the summer of 1979 when I was 54. When we in Sackville organized a **First Terry Fox Run** in September 1980 I was able to do ten kilometres in 52 minutes. This fitness program completely changed my day-time habits and I was able to increase my scholarly output with less tiredness. I began to come home at four o'clock, have a glass of sherry with Justina, then a short sleep while she prepared supper, and then work at home or in the office until about eleven o'clock at night.

When Justina's job as organiser of the Circulation Department in the Library ended, she planned to be at home for a change. But in 1976 she was offered the secretary's position in the Department of German. She took the job on condition it involved mornings only, allowed flexibility for necessary family-related travel and other interests, and required her for the University year only – and paid extra money for her language ability.

The Flood of Publications, 1983 to 1987

The climax of my work on British India came during the years 1983 to 1987. They were not without anxiety as I was denied publication by a number of the presses I would have preferred. It came home to me, as suggested here and there, that it is important to attend the right university and have advisors from a prestigious department. I had this, but McMaster University was not known as an Asian Studies school and my advisor told me right away that I would be on my own when it came to getting things published. Had I done my British India studies under Robert Eric Frykenberg at Wisconsin, my publications lot might have been quite different.

This publication spree created some excitement among my colleagues, family, and friends. But I had grown tired of the British India topic and the search for publishers and I turned henceforth more or less to various aspects of the Mennonite experience, including the Germans-from-Russia research. But just as I was getting ready to move to Calgary, I was asked to contribute from my expertise in British Indian personnel to three dictionaries, among them a new edition of the prestigious *Dictionary of National Biography* of the United Kingdom.

Unforgettable Friends

Like David Ewert (1922–2010), an early mentor for my historical writing, I wrote at length only about those I liked. In this paragraph I can only mention those I admired. Besides those in Athletics, in English it was Peter Mitcham (who died in 2010), in Music George Evelyn, in Chemistry Richard Langler, and among staff members our secretary Carolyn Smith and the President's secretary, Linda Wheaton.

Then there was Gloria of the cleaning staff who gave a glimpse of her positive attitude toward service. She told an interviewer:

> "Working in the buildings that I'm responsible for – Canadian Studies, the Black House, Rectory Lane, Bermuda House, Cuthbertson House and Convocation Hall – is like doing my own house work. The only difference is that there are people in all of the buildings, except Convocation Hall, who brighten my day. They're all lovely people and I enjoy what I do for them." (*Campus Notebook*, December 1995, 3)

In Fine Arts my admiration and affection grew for the engraver, superb artist, **David Silverberg,** especially after we had gotten over the delirium of 1970. He was from a Jewish family in Montreal, a consummate artist, engraver. During the censure issue, David and I were on opposite sides. Only during the latter part of the 1980s did we become friends, partly because Justina and Yvette, his French wife, found each other. Unfortunately, during Bill Crawford's presidency the Dean's office hired on a new crew in Fine Arts. They were a different set by comparison with Lauren Harris, Edward Pulford, not to mention the consummate artist Alex Colville who retired as early as 1960 and eventually moved to Wolfville, Nova Scotia. When David felt isolated as an artist as well as socially, he asked the Administration to find another studio for his engraving equipment. They gave him space above the Biology laboratory in the Flemington Building. There he toiled, launched forth on endless trips with his sketch book, built his reputation, and sold his art, like my favorite 'Siberian Iris' which we bought.

In my Department of History there was **David Pearce Beatty** from Michigan (1933-2015). David had a farm-boy mind-set. In Michigan he had belonged to the Grange where he won speaking contests in his district, and once declaimed from the platform of the Grange head-quarters just off Michigan Avenue in Chicago. He always looked up a bit as though he was speaking to the gallery, would raise his voice, and gesticulate demonstratively. Quite easily he could fill the lecture hour with several stories. And, as all of us could remember, he could be heard far and wide while lecturing in the Avard/Dixon Building. **He was a "Performer."**

Every 'jock' who came to Mount Allison wanted to take his courses in American and Canadian foreign policy. As Eugene Goodrich put it, students did not 'take' Beatty, they "experienced" him. He gave of his time generously. Students would line up waiting to see him to get an earthy story and some help with a paper. He recruited for students in provincial high schools; he followed the Mount Allison Mounties football team around to nearly all the games on their circuit for all those years.

He was always a reliable friend.

Though he had difficulty meeting the standard for a professor-ship, he eventually received that recognition for his publication of the diaries of two World War One soldiers: Private V.E. Goodwin and Lieutenant Stanley Edgett, (co-edited by Dr. Tom Edgett). He was also awarded the Herbert and Leota Tucker Award for Excellence in Teaching.

To the very last year he was overloaded with students in each of his three courses. To the end he stayed with his specialty thus coming to fulfill the old adage: a specialist is one who knows more and more about less and less. He never changed courses, and he never varied his exercising program, running about six miles (10 kilometres) a day with a big leaping stride. During rainy days he never tried another kind of activity on the gymnasium floor. When he retired after thirty-three years in 1999 many came from far and wide to his fare-well party!

Satisfaction

I began this chapter on a note of satisfaction, and I want to finish in that mode. Over the years I have received the normal promotions, in 1967, 1975, and 1983. Promotions are important, if not for one's ego, but also for one's family and reputation, as well as for retirement. There are stories about giving tenure in order to protect those who should really be turfed. There was some truth to that. Failure to be promoted to the associate level might be a signal to try for another job.

As I indicated above, my research took me abroad. My focus was British India, and that meant libraries in London, Nottingham, Edinburgh, and also in India. I had three very rewarding sabbatical years: two in England, 1972-73, 1979-80, and one in Fresno, California, 1988-9. Together with summers in England, Massachusetts, and western Canada, I was away from Sackville a total of more than five years. These excursions have always focused on some project of research and, as stated, produced six publications, and led to travels, sometimes including the family, the meeting of interesting people, and the making of lasting friendships.

Teaching at a small university which allows for such freedom to benefit from sabbatical leaves must be considered one of the very best situations in the world of work. Many people think such a system is often abused. I did not abuse my privileges while at this great University. I have been and remain thankful for the opportunities given me by Mount Allison.

Research has been most rewarding for me. After a while I realized I was fairly good at it, and that I could ultimately write a readable, fairly lucid, and understandable narrative. So I developed a passion to accomplish certain projects which interest me and which others were neglecting. As a result I came full circle, back to people of my background, and also back in 1988 to the subject of India when I began to research and write *Russians, North Americans, and Telugus: The Mennonite Brethren Mission in India, 1885-1975*, the story of the India mission I had visited in 1973.

Some Recollections of Mount Allison University

I arrived at Mount Allison in 1965 and retired in 1992 just as *Macleans* was beginning to make comparisons to help students with parents decide where to seek their fulfillment at the undergraduate level. Mount Allison has been rated **Number One** by *Maclean's* magazine a record eighteen times in twenty-four years, never placing lower than second. It has about 2,250 students, with highly accessible faculty committed to excellence in undergraduate education. The University's degree is highly valued in the "business of life after university" and has an excellent record of graduates who are later accepted by post-graduate and professional schools. Fifty-three Rhodes Scholars have graduated from Mount Allison University to date, 2014, and also some winners of Rotary International Scholarships.

Without going to great lengths here, *Maclean's* places universities in one of three categories: comprehensive, medical-doctoral, and primarily undergraduate. It recognizes the differences in types of institutions, levels of research funding, diversity of offerings, and breadth and depth of graduate and professional programs. *Maclean's* then ranks universities in six broad areas based on twelve performance indicators, allocating a weight to each indicator. Primarily Undergraduate universities are largely focused on undergraduate education, with relatively few graduate programs and graduate students.

The Maritime Provinces have for many years presented at least six small universities. Mount Allison began Methodist; Acadia University, Wolfville, Baptist; St. Francis Xavier, Antigonish, Gaelic; St. Mary's, Mount St. Vincent, Halifax, and St. Thomas, Fredericton, had Irish Catholic origins, to my knowledge. Of seventeen smaller undergraduate schools in Canada, it has not been surprising to see the first three listed here at or very close to the top of these ratings each year.

Mount Allison University's Deserved Position

I am not going to write about those who were presidents when I was teaching. I liked them all: Laurence Cragg, William Crawford, Guy

MacLean, Donald Wells, and Sheila A. Brown, but knew them personally more as familiar colleagues than as persons who had to defend their positions politically. President Cragg's showdown with faculty has been discussed. I was on his side. For the rest of the time I was too busy doing my job than to talk about or work at politics. In fact, I had resolved that after the fight about the music teacher's dismissal in 1970 was over, I would not allow politics to estrange me from my colleagues, though there were faculty in all divisions who had only politics in their hearts and minds and thus prevented friendships from being formed.

Here the focus is on Ian Newbould who came to Mount Allison from Lethbridge. He was appointed as Mount Allison University's eleventh president and was the first president in twenty years to be granted a second term. Newbould had no sooner arrived in 1991 when there was an air of tension and it was not long after giving his opening remarks in Faculty Council that some members began to criticize him. They had supposedly done some research through whatever channels (of no consequence here) and totally pre-judged him on administrative issues sure to be brought up. No welcome – there was no honeymoon period!

Though I retired from that scene in 1992, I followed Newbould's career closely for some time. He was hired by the Board of Regents to reach certain goals. He was determined to do so and became somewhat irritated with the surliness of the anti-establishment members of the Faculty Council. As became evident, Newbould was not deterred, could and did stare down that Council more than once, and proceeded with Administration`s plans for the positive development of Mount Allison.

Ironic as it was, just as the faculty began to rage against Newbould, *MacLeans* was beginning its annual survey of Canadian universities and found Mount Allison University to be Number One in the undergraduate division. I don't know how the Mount may have fared comparatively if the media had transfixed it with the same dozen or so questions under Wells or MacLean. But here is what Newbould thought in 1992:

"In the United States schools like these are regarded as the best ones to attend," he says. "If our students were going there, they would have to spend $15,000 to $20,000 a year to receive the same attention." In other words, Mount Allison was offering students the kind of education that few countries outside Canada could afford. Harvey Gilmour, the university's director of development at that time, contended that Mount Allison was unique even in its class because it was located in Sackville, a town of about 6,000 where students confront none of the distractions of big-city institutions. *MacLeans* in 1992 realized what an uphill battle Newbould faced:

> "Even so, maintaining Mount Allison's precious intimacy has been a challenge for Newbould. When the rangy, sandy-haired historian became president on July 1, 1991 – after 16 years of teaching at the University of Lethbridge, Mount Allison's 1991-1992 deficit was heading for $2.3 million on an operating budget of $22 million. Its long-term debt stood at $2 million. Newbould's program to reduce spending, which included reinstating mandatory retirement and asking the 130-member Mount Allison Faculty Association to accept a pay cut, sparked a bitter strike that opened deep rifts on campus. Newbould, however, has no apologies. "My priority as president is to pursue financial integrity," he declares, "but not at the expense of academic integrity."

In a speech to the Rotary Club in June 1992, just before my retirement, I made some remarks about the strike that cut into my last two days of classes, threatened the examination-writing of all the students, and the holding of Convocation. Mount Allison had given me a new lease on life, a new career at forty, and many enjoyable years with students and colleagues. Hence I grieved about these threats.

> "The issues that led to a strike", I said, "were not black and white. Good people chose different sides. Witness the different approach between my esteemed colleague and fellow Rotarian, Charlie Scobie, and me [he was

present in the meeting!]. His convictions, his perception of the issues, his attempt at mediation behind the scenes, and perhaps his theology permitted him, nay, told him, to strike. On the other hand, I decided years ago that I would not be on the picket line in case of a strike. I had written the Mount Allison Faculty Association leadership as much. My decision was by and large accepted by them."

Should Mount Allison worry about slippage? There were record numbers of applications from students, and its endowment fund stood at $30 million, a huge sum for such a small institution. John Demont in 1992 told *Macleans* that "the enduring affection of many of the school's alumni, who include famed realist painter Alex Colville; the late Wallace McCain of McCain Foods Ltd; and the late Purdy Crawford, chairman of consumer products giant Imasco Ltd. Newfoundland painter Christopher Pratt, who met his artist wife, Mary, while attending Mount Allison in the 1950s, recalls that the university's small-town camaraderie and its mix of undergraduate programs "rounded out the experience in a way which many other schools could not."

How We Learned to Know the Newboulds

Christmas came around in 1991 and faculty, staff and administration gathered for the Christmas dinner and dance. We sat down at a table and we noticed Ian and Carla Newbould sitting two tables away from us. Whereas in most years faculty would be eager to sit near the President, now no one was doing that. So we went over and invited the Newboulds to sit across from us.

We learned that he had been Vice-President at the University of Lethbridge, so they were familiar with Alberta people and weather. What we had in common was his PhD in British history, University of London. Then we discovered that Ian had a twin brother in Ottawa, a lawyer, and this lawyer's wife was the sister of the Member of

Parliament from Kitchener, John Warkentin. John was a member of First Mennonite Brethren Church in that city, a family we knew. So, the joke was that we were very nearly related through the Mennonite connection! Needless to say, there was no tension between Ian and me. Ian was given a five-year renewal in 1995 and stayed ten years over much opposition and strike action from faculty.

As to **Carla Newbould**, we learned to know her a bit later as *'the Hostess with the Mostess.'* While Ian spoke from the Mount, Carla 'fed the five thousand!' We became friends before she built up that reputation. She joined Rotary before we moved away, and when we did she had a Rotary Club farewell for us at Cranewood. When we went back two years later in 1996 she, having heard we were in town, asked us to Cranewood and insisted that Ian leave his office for one hour to visit with us. On that occasion she presented each of us with a Mount Allison-faced watch.

Cranewood, built as a Georgian style house in 1834, used until recently as the President's home, lent itself to large gatherings. And Carla, who had a budget for entertaining, had slowly gotten into a routine of serving large numbers by hiring students and some staff like Gloria Beal to help her in preparation and presentation and guided tours of the house.

Sometime after 1994 Carla began to invite groups like the merchants for an evening in Cranewood. Few Sackville town people over the years had ever been inside that Georgian House. They had been kept out by the earlier 'town and gown' feelings. Cranewood had been pretty much closed to them. Now, however, in season, Carla invited every recognizable group over to Cranewood, much to the delight of the town residents and to the buildup of good feelings for the University.

Following his ten years at Mount Allison, Ian took the presidency of a similar size University in North Carolina for five years and, then surprising to us, the presidency of the American International University in London. This school was housed in the old Richmond Methodist College located just over the fence from the house we had occupied in Rosemont Road.

My Student Assistants and Friends

Myself returning home from Convocation, carrying my gown and hood, 1990

In previous chapters I have written much about my teaching and research years and hardly anything about my students. But this is a memoir and what I write about or leave out is my choice. In this chapter I want to present some students important to me, my assistants and friends.

It was uncommon for students in the Arts in an undergraduate university to have the chance to do sustained and rewarding research for their professors. When in the early 1980s I had as many as four books on the go, nearing completion, I had assistants anxious to be engaged in research, several of whom were paid something for their work. Most notable was Richard Dale MacLean; another was Rhianna Watt, and a third Kim Evans who already had a Masters. Each helped significantly to get publications done and each benefitted in terms of research experience.

All were duly recognized and thanked in the Preface of the relevant books, as were the librarians of the Ralph Pickard Bell Library and departmental secretaries, the late Glenara Anderson and Carolyn Smith who on occasion did huge amounts of typing.

Richard Dale MacLean, who has been teaching journalism at Holland College, Summerside, Prince Edward Island, wrote in June, 2006, in something he called a "rant:"

> "... I was wrapping up my final year when I decided I should have been an honours student, which required a

thesis. Professor Peter Penner laughed when I plopped down on a chair in his office. I thought you'd never figure it out, he smiled. He had a project and $500 a month for the summer for someone to do..... "Those were wonderful years that I still look back at fondly, particularly the two summers spent working on *Rebel Bureaucrat,* probably boring my kids with stories when they'll listen."

Rick became very interested in my South Asian stuff, and was willing to tackle a big project that eluded me, and that was to research the life of Frederick John Shore (1799-1837), a critic of British India even though his father had been a former Governor-General of India. The task was to make his two volumes of writings published in 1837 into some manageable length for moderns. He worked on this as my research assistant during the summers of 1979 and 1980. He even went to London to research the India Office Records.

After doing some work at Carleton University, Ottawa, and passing the Foreign Service examination, he joined the Diplomatic Corps for two years. After that, in 1984, he earned a Master of Arts in Journalism from the University of Western Ontario. He then became editor of the twice-weekly *Miramichi Leader* and stayed with that paper until 1996. Though winning awards for best paper in Atlantic Canada a record seven times was important, that was not the most exciting part.

He captured the country's attention with the 1989 manhunt for serial killer Allan Legere. He wrote:

"I co-wrote two books on that case. *Terror,* published in 1990, was written in 20 days and was a bestseller in Canada, selling about 50,000 copies. It looked at what the community went through during the period from May-November while Legere was killing people in the area. *Terror's End,* published in 1992 was a detailed look at the Legere case, based in part on the trial transcript – Legere was convicted of four counts of first-degree murder. ...I could not have written either of those books without the skills I learned as a history student at Mount Allison ... to get that work done in record time."

Kim Evans of Moncton, New Brunswick, a 1975 Honours History graduate of Mount Allison University, and holder of an M.A. degree from Queens College, assisted me with *The Patronage Bureaucracy* about 1983-4, especially at the reorganization and drafting stage. As both typist and critical reader his assistance was inestimable and I even found some money for him. His wife Linda and my daughter Ruth persevered as typists of the finished work.

Rhianna Edwards (Godfrey) had just graduated from Mount Allison University with Honours in History when she accepted my offer of assisting with research for *The Chignecto 'Connexion': the History of Sackville Methodist/ United Church, 1770-1990.* Through the mediation of Charles Scobie of the Department of Religious Studies we were able to obtain funds to engage her for the summer months of 1987. She explored and researched records in the Mount Allison Archives and I worked farther afield. This book was published in 1990.[14]

Bryant Fairley, honours history and political science student, persevered in the difficult Journals of Robert Needham Cust which I had on microfilm in the Mount Allison Library. This was for my biography of *Robert Needham Cust, 1821-1909.* In time, following graduate school work, he got a teaching position at Queen's University in Kingston, Ontario. In London, Justina and Robert, my son, had helped transcribe some of the Cust Letters in the Royal Commonwealth Library. They had been bound so tightly as to make copying impossible.

---

14 Sadly, this UCC building, Sackville, was torn down in September, 2015. See *Sackville Tribune Post.*

Some Student Friends

Geraldine Rossiter who hailed from Dublin used her BA in English and History from Mount Allison University to earn a MA in International Relations from the University of Dublin. While this was not what she had originally intended, she eventually went to work for Hewlett Packard in Houston, TX, where she did exceptionally well in a period of eighteen years in the "creative application of technology and services." While in Houston she managed to find time for some volunteer work in several local community organizations.

In May 2010 she made a surprise visit to see us in Calgary. She was in the midst of moving to Toronto with her family, husband Cliff and loveable daughter Sarah. She planned to further her graduate education by taking courses in literature and creative writing by long distance from Houston.

Who can forget the Newfoundland boy, **Kevin Bowering** – budding journalist? He had barely arrived and he entered the local journalist's territory by writing startlingly good reviews of Varsity hockey games for the *Argosy Weekly*. He soon published articles about David Beatty and me. I noted that he "could be a pain at times," a reference to his too frequent visits to our offices. As son of a United Church of Canada minister, Kevin naturally had a strong interest in the UCC. In March 1991 he wrote a magnanimous review of my *The Chignecto 'Connexion'* and sent it to the *Sackville Tribune Post*.

Among students were the **odd ones out.** I was asked to work with a **dyslexic** and I saw him get his coveted BA. I had a student who wanted to pass history without learning to spell! 'Who will do your correspondence when you have your own business?' Oh, I will leave that to my secretary. 'But who will check on the secretary?' I hope he has his bread and butter. And then there were those who paid others to write perfect-looking essays, obviously not their own.

An Exceptional Scholarship

There are some people who accomplish more than most of us could ever imagine. **Tim Baycroft** came to Mount Allison as a descendant of the first President Pickford, and was often at our place, even if he never took my courses. His several scholarships took him first to Flemish-speaking Belgium; his second to Wolfson College, Cambridge. He might have liked to return to Canada but when he married Christine who is French, it was simpler for both to take an opening in 1996 in Sheffield, England, where he is Senior Lecturer in History. In twenty years he has done much in terms of teaching, research, and publishing modern French history. He supervises research students in several areas of modern French and European History. He has published three books, nine articles since 1996, and had five doctoral students in 2010.

The Baycrofts had three children ranging in age from 14 to 8. Tim likes to joke that as a specialist in the fields of Modern French history and nationalism, his children are French and Canadian, but not French-Canadian.

Chapter Eight

Revisiting Mennonites during University Years

Our departure from Ontario to the Maritimes in 1965 did not remove us from contacts with Mennonites. We had lived our first forty years among Mennonite Brethren, as told, and worked in three provinces with and for them. Now, job mobility had removed us to a location where they were few and far between. Nevertheless, over the years we maintained contact through our friends, and whenever we met any of the leadership, especially those of my generation at MB Bible College, we were warmly glad-handed. This certainly was the case in 1982 when we did a four-month research tour from Quebec to British Columbia for the book *No Longer at Arm's Length*.

We also stayed in contact through the pages of the new *Mennonite Reporter (MRep)* which succeeded the *Canadian Mennonite* in 1971. I was fortunate to be invited to represent the Mennonites of the Atlantic Provinces on the board of the *Reporter* for the years 1981 to 1990. During much the same time period, with the help of family members, I was able to collect all forty years of the *Mennonite Brethren Herald*.

Pastor Isaac Tiessen in Toronto, a friend and supporter, knew of course that I would continue writing while in New Brunswick and wished only that I would not try "to correct the past, particularly with respect to those who may have hurt us." The reader will have to judge whether my writings have been too negative. They were not meant to be, but I was now writing from a different platform and with a different *Weltanschauung* from what I had when I experienced all those things in my first forty years – fundamentalism, ignorance, and my own shortcomings.

Visitor on a Mission, J.J. Toews

To better understand the following story, my readers need to know the organizational setup. There were five provincial conferences from BC to Ontario, the Prairie Provinces in between, and an overriding Canadian Conference of Mennonite Brethren churches. Quebec and the Maritimes were the main outliers, the focus of outreach of the Conference to be undertaken by an Evangelism office in Winnipeg.

In the 1960s the MB Conference decided to extend their evangelistic outreach to the Maritimes. Evidence of this was the visit from Winnipeg of Jacob J. Toews. He and his wife stopped in Sackville to see Justina in 1967. I was away in Cambridge, Mass. He was now the 'evangelism secretary' for the Canadian Conference. We knew him as one, back in the 1950s, who had declared the Lawrence Heights subsidised housing complex as the most suitable mission field for outreach in Toronto. Justina soon turned the discussion to what we had read about the Conference having declared the Maritimes a 'mission field.' At the time we thought this was preposterous, since these provinces were dotted with a variety of Baptist churches and Bible schools more attuned to the traditional approach to such activity.

Justina also cleared up any misconceptions he had about our 'withdrawal of membership' and all that. We did not move to the Maritimes to get away from anything. I had found a teaching position at Mount Allison and we both liked what we were doing. Actually, Justina enjoyed their visit and they sent me warm greetings.

Later in my series on "Mennonites in the Maritimes" I would express my views on MB arrogance in declaring the Maritimes a mission field. I was convinced that if Mennonite Brethren were coming only as another evangelical church, they should leave the work to the various Baptist churches. If however they were coming as Anabaptist/Mennonites, they would be welcome and might even do good work. The image MBs were presenting did not come close to matching what we were trying to do: interpenetrating the University and Church communities with Anabaptist views of Christianity.

Mennonites in the Atlantic Provinces (MAP)

In 1968 we discovered other Mennonite Brethren families in the Maritimes. Dan with his wife, Nan (Enns) Doerksen, had come to Fredericton to teach English at the University of New Brunswick. Dan came from the Doerksen family in North End MB church, Winnipeg. Nan's sister Gertrude was living in Sydney, Nova Scotoa, where her husband John Froese, well known as a teacher at Fort Simpson, BC, in the 1950s, was now the educator at Canada's Coast Guard Training School.

In that year Peter and Nancy Rahn from Abbotsford came to Sackville, Peter to teach Classics and Nancy to teach piano. They had several children. A year later Abner and Shirley Martin (Ontario Mennonite Church) with their four children came to Sackville. Abner joined the Music Department, and Shirley was an experienced director of children's choirs. Because our children resisted Sunday school in Sackville United Church, and the Rahns and Martins seemed prepared to have our own time together before church, we met at our house to sing Mennonite hymns together with our children. This led to having our own Sunday school, so to speak, and then we would join in the United Church service at eleven o'clock.

In 1974, as a result of searching for other Mennonite professionals working in the Maritimes, a number of them suggested we become acquainted. A meeting at our home during the summer of 1975 became the first meeting of 'Mennonites in the Atlantic Provinces (MAP).' Whereas the first two annual get-togethers were "entirely social and ethnic," and geared to professionals, the subsequent annual retreats, held on a weekend from Friday evening to Sunday noon, focussed on some historical or inspirational theme and always had an Anabaptist/ Mennonite emphasis, and everyone was made welcome.

We met in various locations. The first meetings were in private homes; three meetings were accommodated by the Dartmouth MB church under various pastors; five were held at Mount Allison University's Chapel and Manning Room (where we could get meals in the University's dining room); some were held at Petitcodiac Mennonite Church; and finally we settled on the Baptist's Wildwood camp near Moncton/Shediac as the best location, and on the last weekend of September as the best time. Over the years we had such speakers as John Howard Yoder and Dan Zehr from the (Old) Mennonite branch, and F.C. Peters and John Redekop from the Mennonite Brethren. At our last MAP meeting in Dartmouth, with Ewald Unruh as host pastor, Redekop gave us a remarkable presentation on his vision for Evangelical Anabaptism.

Our most memorable MAP meeting was with John Howard Yoder from Goshen, Indiana. He came by car for a four-day visit with his whole family: wife Annie, Daniel, Elizabeth, Esther, and John David. We took this occasion at John and Sophie Esau's in August 1977 to have a communion service out under the trees led by Baptist J.K. Zeman, Wolfville. After that the Yoders came to Sackville to visit with us and the Charles Scobie family.

In 1981 I did a second survey asking "Who Are the Maritime Mennonites?" and also had it published in the *Mennonite Brethren Herald*. By 1981 the Mennonites in these provinces had become diversified by the influx of the *Kleinegemeinde* from Belize and the Church of God in Christ, Mennonite (*Holdemaner*) from Manitoba.

Two programs sponsored by MCC, Maritimes, were especially significant, touching the lives of many people. One was job creation through MCC's Employment program in the Maritimes, led by Al Reimer from Landmark, Manitoba; the other was Self-Help, transformed into Ten Thousand Villages.[15] Justina and I helped the sponsoring church, Petitcodiac Mennonite, to bring the sale of multiple crafts annually to Mount Allison University. Eventually shops were opened in Saint John, Halifax, and Hawkesbury, Cape Breton Island, and Charlottetown.

After we had moved to Calgary in 1994, MAP continued for the next five years without our presence on the steering committee. We were invited to the twenty-fifth anniversary in September 2000 and I

---

15 Ten Thousand Villages, a program sponsored by the Mennonite Central Committee (MCC) was designed to provide employment for people in developing countries by marketing handicraft items these people can make but are unable to sell locally. First it was called the "Needlework Program," then in the 1970s "MCC Self Help Program."

gave three talks as requested: who we were, who we are, and who we aspire to be as Anabaptists. After that, MAP decided to emphasize the MCC theme at this annual retreat. MCC and its related service programs have probably had a more influential impact in the Maritimes than has Church Growth as applied by the Task Forces of the MB Evangelism office.

My Generation in Home Missions

At the MAP meeting at the Esau's farm in 1977 we discovered that Henry Brucks, then Evangelism Secretary in Winnipeg, was present also. When I told him about a suggestion that I should update my history of church planting in BC, Henry thought I should do MB church planting (or home missions) in the whole country. He was most anxious to have the Quebec story told in which he had been involved. This bigger project could only be made understandable by placing it into the context of the total effort. Though living in New Brunswick, far from the MB epicentre of Winnipeg, I became motivated to tell the story of my generation in home missions, renamed church planting.

In 1981 I began research into MB church planting in Canada. Encouraged by the Evangelism office, we took four summer months in 1982 to travel all of Canada looking over home mission sites and interviewing as many church planters as we could. Actually, the project took four years to research and write. It was not a history of the Conference as such, but of its outreach at national and provincial levels, including particularly Quebec. The result was *No Longer at Arm's Length: MB Church Planting in Canada (1883 to 1983)*, the first book about the Mennonite Brethren in Canada to cover the story 'from sea to shining sea,' published by Winnipeg's Kindred Press in 1987.

During the early part of 1985 Ewald (Wally) Unruh asked me to write "a history of the Dartmouth MB Church" [later called Cornerstone Community Church]. That congregation had experienced serious ups and downs between 1967 and 1980. Under Hartley Smith

(1975–1980) the attendance swelled and then nearly collapsed because of a split over the charismatic emphasis. Henry M. Willems from Hepburn, SK, was called to bring some order to the church. George and Ruth Wiens who hailed from Linden, Alberta, served well, as did Wally Unruh who began in 1985. Until Wally came with his young family and stayed seven years, I believe, the pastoral tenure had been too short for Maritime conditions, one of which was high mobility in a new church.

In 1986 Herb Kopp as editor of the *MBH* came as MAP's speaker and did a "cover story" on the Mennonites in the Maritimes in order *to examine the eastern vision.* My requested article was entitled: "What flag will MBs fly and who will unfurl it?" Again I suggested that unless they 'unfurl' an Anabaptist/Mennonite flag, they have little that is distinct to offer. I recommended that church planters have part of their education at the university and seminary level in Maritime schools and they commit themselves to a long tenure, or send Maritime potential planters to MB schools in western Canada or Fresno, CA.

Ken and Carolee Neufeld from Winnipeg could have made the kind of impact that was possible if they had stayed longer than one year. When they came to Moncton, however, they brought four grown children – James, Paul, Mark, and Jennifer – in 1993–94. What a remarkable thing to do. These siblings were willing to leave friends at school and church and adapt to another culture, if only for one year. During their stay, being more profoundly Mennonite within the MB conference than most church planters to come to the Maritimes, they found that their parishioners were prepared to carry the name Mennonite Brethren. What a change in attitude.

'Tis a pity, they could only stay one year.

Why Should We Be Concerned?

Already in 1965 when we moved to the Maritimes, there was growing concern among many that the Mennonite Brethren were losing what they called their 'distinctives,' but also any Anabaptist persuasion they may have had. After 1970 these were shunted aside in favour of transforming MB congregations into community churches without the Mennonite name. For some time John H. Redekop tried hard to convince MBs to adopt the name 'Anabaptist Mennonite,' but without success [more of this below]. Other people began to take notice and one writer in the *Mennonite Mirror* in 1990 wrote that the MBs were getting set "to jettison their embarrassing name."

Here is what transpired in the Greendale, Fraser Valley, MB church. As explained by Peter Harder, the new worship style had taken priority over classical hymnody and preaching.

> "Our church is undergoing numerous changes. Our Sunday School is now Childrens' Ministries. Our worship services are now called Celebrations. The pulpit is gone and organ music and harmony are out. Instead we have an open stage which is used from end to end by the pastor [in shirtsleeves] and the music is accompanied by guitars and drums. Just where all this will take us we are not sure but we trust the essential ingredient of our faith will survive. Sometimes the words of King Solomon come to mind when he says, 'This too will pass'."

Famous last words! Greendale went the way of all those 'community churches' in BC that have dropped the Mennonite name. By the year 2001 some members were attempting to use their local constitution and democratic procedures to reclaim the Greendale congregation, to wrest it from the control of the Pastor and his Elders. They were having a measure of success.

The MBH, 1962-2015
Reflector of Changes in the MB Conference

For me the *Mennonite Brethren Herald* (MBH) (and the papers that preceded it) had been a wonderful resource for those books of mine which featured "my generation," those born between 1915 and 1935. It played a strong role in my interpretation of the MB Conference in *No Longer at Arm's Length: MB Church Planting in Canada* (1987); and *Russians, North Americans, and Telugus: The MB Mission in India, 1885-1975* (1997). We of that generation spent many years in Bible school or/and MBBC. We asked ourselves, seriously, in the decades following World War Two, whether or not we should take an assignment in mission at home or abroad. The *MBH* helped us.

The *Mennonite Brethren Herald (MBH)* was a reflector of the changes in the MB Church and Conference since 1962. Nothing else could match this run of fifty years. Researching the *Herald* for my books on the Mennonite Brethren brought home to me that the first half of the 1980s were watershed years to a considerable degree. Four related questions – **identity, Church Growth, music changes, and ethnicity** – all surfaced strongly. It was less a cause for celebration that MBs had been derailed into something other than what they were during those decision-making years coincident with my first forty. Various persons such as John Rempel, Harry Loewen, Jake H. Quiring, Walter Kroeker, and Jacob A. Loewen in his *The Sword and the Spirit* (1997) have shared my concern about where and when the MB derailment took place. Since I cared deeply for many years about the issues raised I offer this brief review.

Rudy H. Wiebe as First Editor

Rudy Wiebe was working towards a Master's degree in Literature at the University of Alberta, Edmonton, when he was invited to become the first editor of the *Mennonite Brethren Herald (MBH)*. Many thought he had launched a great paper, full of news, thoughtful editorials, helpful and provocative series, coverage of missions, home and foreign. He however came to be perceived as too critical of the church body. The "biblical frankness," the use of honesty and openness, as stated in his first editorial (January 19, 1962), was not what the publication committee had in mind.

Rudy was asked to resign largely because of the furor that resulted from the publication of his *Peace Shall Destroy Many*. It was clear to me then that the distance from a university English department to the psyche of the average Mennonite church paper reader was quite a quantum leap at that time. Who of the *Russlaender* of that day was reading novels such as Rudy's?

Once Rudy was gone from the editor's chair, and Peter Klassen, music professor at MBBC, had been given the interim position in July 1963, the *MBH* went along very well for most people. During this year I did my series for university students, as well as some other themes such as "glossolalia" (speaking in tongues). One decision Klassen made had far-reaching consequences. He brought John H. Redekop in as a columnist. It seemed that he was free to select his own themes, decide what is timely and relevant. When Harold Jantz became editor in 1964 he was often courageous in calling a spade a spade, though his editorials seldom got letters in response. When he changed the format and put Redekop's "Personal Opinion" on page ten opposite the editorial, the letters increased, but they were mostly in response or reaction to John, not Harold.

Harold Jantz, 1964-1985

Nevertheless, the next two decades belonged to Harold Jantz. He seemed safer to a broad spectrum in the readership as well as leadership. After some years, in March 1979, Jantz orchestrated a *Herald* issue in which he tried to bring out again what the MB church is and strives to do and thus inadvertently triggered the **identity** question. Though he tried to bring forward Anabaptism, it was Evangelicalism, not Anabaptism, which seemed to be the chosen guiding light. While John Redekop tried to be balanced, calling for the acceptance of a new identity based not on history and heritage but on the centrality of faith in Christ, he began to develop what he called 'evangelical Anabaptism.' He was anxious about the integrity of the MB. He deplored the fact that many congregations no longer used the hymnbook, did not teach the whole Confession of Faith in membership classes, including non-resistance, and were little interested in Conference priorities in mission, or anything else.

By 1984 Jantz recognized the growing ambivalence, and perhaps indifference, among Mennonite Brethren leaders. He was a bit exasperated: "We need a secure identity for the sake of the nation, for the sake of Mennonites in Mennonite World Conference, and for the sake of the historic faith. Not to take this position is to separate." Fortunately, thoughtful persons in responsible institutional positions like James Pankratz entered the debate on "Mennonite identity" very effectively: "The only people we ever found to be offended by Mennonite ethnicity were Mennonites, not our neighbors and our professional colleagues."

This was also our experience during our years in the Maritimes!

Herb Kopp (1985-1989) and Church Growth

When Harold Jantz resigned after twenty-one years in the editorial chair, Herb Kopp succeeded. Whereas Kopp saw his assignment as editor to 'keep the thoroughbreds all running in the same direction,' two issues reached critical proportions during his tenure: the Church Growth Movement (CGM) and music styles. Even though many warned against buying into church growth, the lay moderator, first David E. Redekop, and then John H. Redekop, seemed as concerned about numbers as about maturity. Statistics must improve! Church growth – setting goals – became the official line of the Evangelism Secretary James Nikkel who learned from C. Peter Wagner associated with Fuller Seminary, Pasadena, CA. Wagner was invited to expound the philosophy of CGM at the Disciple-Making conference in 1985. Fortunately, Myron Augsburger from Eastern Mennonite Seminary, Virginia, was also there to counter this with his Anabaptist version of discipleship. While Nikkel hoped the Canadian Mennonite Brethren could "double" by the year 2000, my own book, *No Longer at Arm's Length*, demonstrated clearly that the prospects were not good.

The Quebec Conference, recently minted, bore this out. It was quite embarrassing by 1989 to have to admit that this effort, the outgrowth of the application of Church Growth and the vision of former missionaries from Zaire, was experiencing considerable 'growing pains.' It was finally admitted that the goal to have forty churches by 1992 was totally unrealistic. The consultation at Richmond, BC, in 1991 to discuss the value of CGM in light of the repeated very slight increase in membership became tension-filled. James Nikkel's 'vision' was challenged by John E. Toews, Fresno theologian, who called it into question based on MB theology and tradition. Herb Kopp tried to bring forward some positive features of CGM, while Nick Dyck, Abbotsford, thought that converts resulting from 'church growth' would go through three stages – pioneering, transitional, and fully integrative – before the cultural differences would disappear.

In the Maritimes, in 1990 James Nikkel had projected ten churches by 2000. However, as shown, after trying for thirty-five years, the Dartmouth Church (Cornerstone Community) closed its doors.

The Music Issue

The other big issue was music in the Conference and congregations. In 1985 Kopp had brought out a special music issue in which Irmgard Baerg, the pianist in Victor Davies' 1975 *Mennonite Piano Concerto*, had the lead article. While she tried, like others, to answer the question: what is good music for worship, something that Christine Konrad Longhurst and Peter Letkemann of Winnipeg had made clear earlier, Bill Klassen, music minister at Willingdon Church, Burnaby, BC, was by then persuaded that choruses, simple songs such as "Majesty," "I Love You, Lord," "Glorify Thy Name," sung repetitively, led by a worship team supported by guitar and drums, usually standing for about twenty minutes, best exemplified the biblical standard of "spiritual songs."

Three years later Jim Coggins opened up the debate once again and even questioned the need for the new *Hymnbook* projected for 1994.

Did the Conference even have a mandate for this? The model of the great church music seminars in 1989 with Helmut Rilling as conductor, and Edith Wiens as soloist, notwithstanding, selling the new hymnbook was an uphill battle, and substituting something for the worship teams seemingly impossible. It was therefore wonderful to be present May 27, 2001 when the Mennonite Historical Society of BC successfully staged the 'Celebration of Yesterday's Music Makers' in Abbotsford. The focus was on "the musical heritage of Mennonites in the Fraser Valley" and featured the life and contribution of conductors George Reimer, Henry P. Neufeldt, Franz C. Thiessen, and Cornelius D. Toews, violin maker Heinrich Friesen, and music teachers Menno and Walter Neufeld. Of these only Neufeldt and the Neufeld brothers were still alive and thankfully able to be present.

When all was said and sung, Tony Funk came close to saying to all in attendance, 'just think about what we seem to have lost' in our circles to **music from another culture**. He did not rub it in, though he might have been justified in doing so. That this event was sponsored entirely by a historical society, not by a conference or church, was a coup of historic proportions! The capacity crowd in Central Heights church raised about $7,700 for the Mennonite Historical Society of BC.

Redekop and the Ethnicity Debate

In 1987 John H. Redekop brought forward his publication *A People Apart, Ethnicity and the Mennonite Brethren.* While the Board of Spiritual and Social Concerns (BSSC) had asked him to study the question: why are new church-plants not using the Mennonite Brethren name in their billboards and bulletins, he brought out this ambitious full-scale sociological survey which contained interviews with a curious public media. The subsequent discussion in that year was considered to be very damaging to the MB witness.

Most delegates at the conference that summer recognized the obvious. Redekop as Moderator of the Conference was in a 'conflict-of-interest' position. No one pointed this out as clearly as J.H. Quiring, a former Moderator and Bible College President. In an open letter to the conference Quiring scoffed at Redekop's proposal to change the name to Evangelical Anabaptist, and argued that such a momentous study should not have been assigned to the moderator, whatever his ability. Another critic, Walter Kroeker, Winnipeg, in April 1987 wrote an obituary for the death of the MB Church in Canada. This was published in the *MBH* one week after Quiring's statement. Kroeker thought that the achievement of the destruction of the old MB church would not "bring acclaim to Dr. Redekop from his associates.... Left to mourn ... are many faithful adherents....".

The debate raged on, but the name chosen by Redekop, "Conference of Evangelical Anabaptists (MB)" was not adopted. Fortunately, as predicted by Kroeker and criticized by Harry Loewen and others, the new Board of Faith and Life had second thoughts about Redekop's book on ethnicity. It had injected a "dissonant chord" into the MB constituency. This leading board, Isaac Block stated, "had difficulty naming the problem that the book is intended to address." Six persons were appointed to study Redekop's report and each found 'shortcomings in the field survey.' There was more to the 'presumed objective data.' A broader base needed to be found.

All this was of intense interest to me because I was in the midst of researching major projects of the Mennonite Brethren – church planting within Canada, and overseas mission – and the *Mennonite Brethren Herald* continued to be a chief reflector of how this branch of the Mennonite people seemed to have changed, hopefully not irreversibly.

My Last Mennonite Brethren Project, 1988-89

That aside, during the period of researching and writing *No Longer at Arm's Length* (1980–84), I was approached officially about doing the Mennonite Brethren mission story, world-wide. In response I proposed a modest budget for a visit to each of the mission sites (Europe, Japan, Republic of Congo, Latin American countries) to initiate this during a sabbatical year. This was turned down by a new general secretary who felt he could not authorize the spending of mission money to write history. So I elected to do solo research, with University support, on the project that first engaged the Mennonite Brethren in Russia and North America: the mission to the Telugu-speaking people of Andhra Pradesh, India. This project brought me to the main archive of the General Conference of MB churches located in Fresno on the campus of the Mennonite Brethren Biblical Seminary (MBBS) and the Fresno Pacific College (now University). These two schools shared the Cornelius Hiebert Library which housed the Centre for MB Studies.

This proposal in 1988 was readily accepted by my Dean at Mount Allison University. Getting permission to access the papers of the India Mission in Fresno's Centre for MB Studies was also easy. Paul Toews, Director, and his brother John E. Toews, then serving as Dean of MBBS, not to mention their father, the venerable J.B. Toews (JB), were thrilled to think that someone was taking a sabbatical to work in the archives in Fresno. I would be most welcome. As the year went by we were, in some ways, given the red carpet treatment. I was in effect an Adjunct Professor, the first Visiting Scholar there on a J-Visa. The person who handled much of the correspondence was Valerie Rempel, then acting as Director of Admissions.

What did all this mean for us? This was our last opportunity for total immersion among Mennonite Brethren, this time in Fresno, California. No one asked questions about our previous relations with the Mennonite Brethren church and I could do my research with complete freedom and support. For her part, Justina could develop a whole set of new relationships, especially with the MCC quilters in nearby Reedley. While this project would reach into and engross many hours of further research and writing, during retirement, this was our last sabbatical from which we would be returning to Sackville.

Chapter Nine

Family Story from Sackville to Calgary

Purchasing Our First House

Having lived in rented quarters for five years, we began to look for a house in 1970. We needed a home for our family, uncluttered by others around us, long before the children grew up and out of the local schools. Another was the need for privacy for our children's music-making and distance from the

Abram and Justina Janzen visiting, with Ruth, Justina, and Robert, 1973

music-making in the flat below us on Bridge Street.

Though we looked at other houses within walking distance of work, at the suggestion of Mabel Croft, Justina's friend, we bought the house at 28 Lansdowne Street, with its five dormers, from Greg and Katie Ross. It was built by George S. Wry for his family in 1909. This was located three houses up from the curling rink, and only five minutes-walk into the University campus. We bought a number of items from the Ross family such as the high quality Fawcett propane cooking stove with two ovens; and four blue hand-braided rugs made in St. Andrews, New Brunswick, which everyone just loved.

This purchase pleased Justina's parents who visited in 1971. With their financial help we managed in the next few years to pay out the purchase price with increasingly inflated dollars, and eventually sold it after 24 years in a market deflated by the recent sale and removal of Atlantic Wholesalers from Sackville to Halifax. Another factor in this decline in the real estate value was the gradual encroachment of university students into residential areas.

Celebration of the Twenty-Fifth

While still on sabbatical in London in May 1973 we began to think of how we could celebrate our twenty-fifth wedding anniversary. If Robert and Ruth were prepared to travel with us, we might do a cross-country trip by car in the summer of 1974.

Once back from London, we had an 'open house' in Sackville for about fifty invited guests, mostly from the Church and University. No one declined. What we did not expect is that a well-meaning neighbor would beg Ruth for the guest list and then go round to twenty-five households and obtain signatures on a card for the gift of a large size Family Bible (about 1,500 pages in all!) and incorporating the Authorized Version.

Our dear Baptist neighbor, Mrs. Sharpe, dry-humoured the event by saying: 'I am so glad you got a Bible [like that], now you don't have to come over to borrow ours!'

In total, the Twenty-Fifth (1974) was fun. Because Robert and Ruth at 17 (almost 18) and 15 were willing to travel with us, we took our trusty 1972 Impala Chevrolet – what a big car it was! – and drove right across to Mile Zero in Victoria visiting various friends going and coming. Primary among these were Peter and Katie Harder in Chilliwack who had planned a number of enjoyable things for all of us to do. Altogether it was a great trip.

Going home, we left the Harders behind right after supper and drove through the mountains at night in order to avoid the slow-moving campers and trucks of that time, stopped once to sleep a bit, and had breakfast in Strathmore, east of Calgary. The Harders of course thought we were crazy. After stopping briefly in Morden and Steinbach, Manitoba, we drove into southern Ontario only because we were anticipating a garden party at the Heinrichs, a celebration for the Neufelds and us. When we got there we discovered that Ruth Neufeld was *too ill to attend!* Everyone was disappointed but we could easily agree that we needed to postpone this event indefinitely.

The 'Menno Travel' Year, 1978

Whenever Mennonite World Conference (MWC) came within road-reach we had the urge to go. 1962 was such a year, in Kitchener, ON; 1978 was such a year when the tenth MWC was coming to Wichita, Kansas. It was a long road for us, but John and Cathy Lerch (my sister) lived about half-way in Wooster, Ohio, and they had a vehicle with air conditioning. "Our Menno Travel year" turned out to be hot, hot! Assured of that combination, on the way we took in Akron and Scottdale, PA, two Mennonite Meccas. Akron was the headquarters of Mennonite Central Committee for world-wide relief service, and Scottdale was the home of Mennonite publishing for many decades. We stopped at the small town of Hillsboro, Kansas, which was for many decades the site of the chief institutions of the Mennonite Brethren: Tabor College, for a long time the only Mennonite Brethren school for arts and sciences, the MB Publishing House, and the office of the Foreign Mission Board. Nearby North Newton was the site of Bethel College of the General Conference with its similar institutions.

The 1978 return trip, via the Niagara Peninsula, allowed us to take in the celebration of Dad Janzen's seventy-eighth birthday in their new home, the Scott Street Church apartment. Justina was given articles to take home, as their small apartment could not hold every-thing Mother Janzen could not bear to part with. We also took in the church service at Toronto MB on Ranee Avenue, where we met some of our members from 1962-1964. Next day Peter and Sue Langeman took us to Klineburg to see the McMichael Collection. With Shirley and Abner Martin in Waterloo County we took in St. Jacobs and Old Order Mennonite country. What a summer! We got home in time for Robert's twenty-second birthday in August.

The Sabbatical of 1979-80

During my next sabbatical, the last extended stay in London, we left early in September and took up residence again at # 11, Rosemont Road, Richmond-on-Thames, where Vern and Frieda Heinrichs were the first to call. They were staying at Claridge's, in Mayfair, no less. We were invited to dinner there with John Dick, Denver, Colorado, Frieda's brother, just when European Royalty and Burkes Peerage people descended on Mayfair for the funeral of the assassinated Lord Mountbatten.

We reconnected with our London friends, as well as with Alan and Eleanor Kreider at Highgate. There was now a new center of social gravity for Mennonites at St. John's Wood with the residence in London of Jake and Else Koop, Nepean, Ontario. He had been posted to London by Canada's Department of External Affairs. We enjoyed several parties at the Koop's, among them one on New Year's Day, 1980, when Fred and Nettie Enns, Edmonton, on sabbatical from the University of Alberta, and Marlene and Alex Redekop, with the United Nations in Geneva, were present.

We entertained also, by giving a party at the end of 1979. We had invited a mixture of London friends, among them Norman and Christel Marsh, Roy and Audrey Smith, and North American friends Alex and Marlene Redekop and Jake and Else Koop. London was like that, where else could we meet such an array of friends?

When Judith Lynn (Kehler) Siebert, came to London from Winnipeg to do a concert in Leighton House, Holland Park, I took Judge John and Joy Baker, our near neighbors in Richmond, to hear this good Mennonite pianist on March 28, 1980, and wrote an article for the *Mennonite Reporter*. Elsa Koop had a reception for Judith at her house for all the Mennonite folk from Highgate and around, as well as many others. Sixty percent of the guests at the concert were associated with London Mennonite Fellowship.

For anyone who has ever been touched by the London Mennonite Centre, Highgate, they will be grateful for Alan Kreider's historical account of the first fifty years of the Centre, an article readily accessible on the Internet or in *Anabaptism Today* (Issue 32, 2003), published by the Anabaptist Network.

Westmorland Historical Society

We joined this county historical society soon after our move to Sackville in 1965. Having been a member since 1966 and served as a Director, I was elected President of the WHS in May 1975 in succession to Ray Mabee. This meant that during the next two years I became involved in the annual openings of Keillor House which dated from 1813. This was the Centennial Project of the Westmoreland Historical Society. At my first meeting as president of the WHS our Board decided to purchase the Hickman House (dating from around 1790) which, when fully restored, later became the **Bell Inn.** This held some attractive flats for rent but more importantly allowed for a restaurant to be developed by David and Wayne, providing Maritime meals 'to die for.'

We became less active in this Society as I was almost consumed with publications. But we were always invited to the Christmas festivity at Keillor House, and occasionally I was asked to speak at one of their functions. Before we left Sackville, we took out a Life Membership of WHS, an enjoyable 29-year association.

Visit of Norman and Christel Marsh, June 1981

I have told how I met them in the summer of 1968 and how this friendship blossomed. Since they had never once made us feel that we were colonials (as some Brits tended to do), we had urged them to return the visit. They wanted to come for three weeks and Justina rightly wondered what we could do with them in the Martimes for so many days. It turned out to be much easier than we thought. Norman and Christel were interested in everything. We picked them up in Halifax International on May 31 and they were with us for nearly three weeks when they rented a car and did Nova Scotia on their own at the end of their Canadian stay.

During the first week, naturally, we showed the sites near at hand: the University, the Town, and Fort Beausejour, each of which has a significant history. We did Murray Corner on the Northumberland Straits where we bought scallops from the fishermen and had the use of our neighbor's cottage for several days. On Thursday Norman spoke to the Rotary Club on the Law Commission of the House of Lords of which he was a member. Two days were taken up by the annual Shiretown Festival at Dorchester. The mayor took them to the Town Hall for a ceremonial signing of the register and they were inside Yeoman's 1834 house called Rocklyn twice for receptions. There was the usual parade and the opening of Keillor House. Nothing could quite top one of John Carter's auctions on Saturday morning over at Point de Bute. All in all, everyone thought these guests were special. In the evenings we played Scrabble.

During the second week we went farther afield: the Rocks at Hopewell Cape, Fundy National Park, where we had a picnic lunch, something they enjoyed. Then followed Saint John, the Reversing Falls, the Museum (where we saw Alex Colville's Wartime Collection) and on to a Fredericton motel for the night. Tuesday we did Kings's Landing, north of Fredericton, a replica of life in the 1860s, and then we hurried back to meet our Member of the Legislative Assembly at 1400 hours.

Lloyd Folkins from Sackville was waiting for us on the steps of the Legislative Building in Fredericton. He had arranged everything for what were considered special guests: a tour of the Legislative Building, a brief moment inside the Chamber where the 'estimates' were being debated, and then, what proved to be the highlight of the week, twenty minutes with Premier Richard Hatfield in his office. He thought a visit from a Law Commissioner for the Lords in London was special (with the Penners, no less!). Richard showed off his Audubon Bird books and asked questions about Norman's work.

We then visited the Cathedral (Anglican), next to the Beaverbrook Gallery, and then to Moncton where they were willing to try a Ponderosa Restaurant dinner! The next few days were a bit rainy and overcast, but we did the University Library and Justina took Christel to Moncton shopping. Friday was given over to Prince Edward Island and Charlottetown. This of course meant a ferry ride and a tour of some of the most famous sites, including Anne of Green Gables. Sunday was given over to the Amherst, Nova Scotia area, including the rocks at Nappan and also Springhill, the site of the tragic mine disaster of the 1950s. Moreover, on Sunday evening Lloyd and Hilda Folkins took us all to the Shediac area for a lobster dinner.

Well, we still had not yet tried to confound our guests with **Magnetic Hill, Moncton, where the water runs uphill,** the only place in the world! They were totally confounded. While the Bell Inn, Dorchester, had proved a special treat, they asked for Ponderosa again! Wednesday evening found us at the Marshlands Inn for dinner, and on Friday Justina planned a party at our house. We had Ned and Gertrude Belliveau, a well-known publicist, Lloyd and Hilda Folkins, Wendell and Dorothy Meldrum (former MLA elevated to a judgeship), our neighbour Ralph Sharpe and his daugther Phyllis, David and Yvette Silverberg, artist. A few others could not come.

And we had wondered what we would do with these celebrities and how we could give our guests (as well as readers) a tour of New Brunswick and Prince Edward Island!

Staying Healthy on the Job

My commitment to badminton and running paid off remarkably in terms of greater stamina and physical well-being. This activity added to my sense of wellbeing as I rose in the ranks and influence in my Department. Following two sabbaticals and twenty years of teaching and research activity, I was deemed worthy of a promotion to Professor of History in 1983 and then given the Headship for two three-year terms in 1985. By then I was in the midst of publishing as told in conjunction with my student assistants.

Actually, I had high hopes of greater longevity because between age 45 and 60 I was in great shape. I played badminton in the school months and ran during the spring and summer months. As the summer extended into fall, beginning in 1980, I would prepare for the Terry Fox Run that fell during mid-September. When my feet gave me more pain than the joy of badminton and running was giving me, I gave up both and turned to cycling and walking. I continued participation in the Terry Fox Run annually, completing the 20-year certificate in Calgary.

There Is a Time to Die!

It was sad to learn of my mother's stroke at age 75. She lived to be 84, but her last nine years were bereft of quality and usefulness. Her career as skilled seamstress was shortened by almost a decade. We had offered to have her come to live with us in New Brunswick, but she would have been away from so many familiar things: her church, her sewing clients, her family. She might have suffered severe culture shock, given her background and experiences, by attending a strange church and adjusting to Maritime custom. Could it have been home for her?

However, one may also speculate that coming to the Maritimes may have helped prevent such a stroke. The interest of the whole family might have shifted eastward! Just think of that?

As it was, in 1976 she was admitted to Tabor Manor, St. Catharines, a home operated by the Ontario MB Conference. While she received what was called quality care, Mother Penner's condition worsened and she became an unhappy camper until she died in late December 1984. My brother Corney looked after her finances and reported to the rest of the family as needed.

An Untimely Death

The family near at hand knew Mother was slipping away. But what took them by surprise was the sudden death in Manitoba of her oldest son-in-law, Abe Friesen, on December 17 at Carman, Manitoba. We had gone off to London, England, for a short trip, engrossing December 7 to 17. When we got back the telephone was ringing off the hook. Abe had died of a heart attack while out using his snow blower. Mother died five days later.

While two sisters Cathy and Thelma decided to go to Carman to be with Erna, we made a hurried decision to drive to Vineland from Sackville. We arrived at Tallman's Funeral Home in Vineland, ON, on December 23, just in time to see Mother Penner in her coffin. "Everyone was relieved that she had at last been released from this …seemingly interminable lingering vegetable existence." So I wrote.

Next day, Christmas Eve, we were most fortunate to find Pastor Gerry Ediger of Vineland MB Church and a congregation that still thought of all of us as being in a way part of them! There we were on Christmas Eve, finding people to cater, to remember a life well lived (until 1975). Relatives and friends came from around the area. Only Erna was missing, grieving her double loss: a husband and a mother! This event of course meant that our Christmas was completely different, plans altered by the intervention of death.

The passing of Abe Friesen who was eleven years older than Erna, and of Mother Penner meant, in a sense, the end of an era. Where was 'home' now? Though Justina's Mother lived until 1991, for me the Penner home was lost even though we passed through the Niagara Peninsula many times in subsequent years. On numerous occasions we drove down Tufford Road to look at the old house with the stone verandah. On one further occasion, we discovered that it been destroyed in a fire. That was the end.

While a complete medical history need not be given, neither of us were immune from short-term illnesses. While Justina generally enjoyed good health and an active life, she developed angina, something that her Mother had also, though she lived to be 92. Justina's angina was brought under control medically during the late 1980s.

After our second trip to Fresno, 1992-93, Justina was not alone with her heart condition. Edwin Wiens, Fresno, internist, told me that a cardiogram showed that at some point I had had a 'silent' heart attack. That was news to me. It was not until we moved to Calgary that I was thoroughly examined by a cardiology team, something that never happened in New Brunswick. Dr. Donald Meldrum confirmed that I had suffered a mild heart attack sometime in the past, but when? Upon searching my Daybook, I surmised that I had the attack in 1966 when we moved to the upstairs apartment at 74 Bridge Street, Sackville. I had a second examination in 2006 and another six years later.

Two German Funerals

In late summer of 1985 I received an urgent request to arrange for a German-language funeral for Herr Alfred Fassauer, the head of a new family from Germany. Eldon Hay, then living next door to this family in Point de Bute, told Sackville Undertaker David Jones that I was the only person around who could possibly do such a funeral in German. This was quite a challenge, since I had not done many funerals. Actually, it worked out well for everyone. Eldon Hay as the United Church person presided, James Stark of the Music Department offered a solo number in German, Justina read the Scripture, while I did the eulogy. This funeral brought together some of the German community, the Germans at the University, and neighbors. We then became welcome friends of Erika, and her children Hannelore and her husband Alvin, who opened a new restaurant at Aulac in due course.

About fifteen months later, in November 1986, another German family head died. This organic farmer who came over with his family in 1982 lost his life in a shooting accident while out hunting. Apparently his wife had heard of my doing the Fassauer funeral from other German families and asked for me. When David Jones phoned, I went to see Anne-Marie to explain that I was willing but it would be a Christian funeral. She consented to that although she allowed that they were humanist. She requested that the service be conducted in two languages, German and English. It was, and the spiritual impact can only be guessed. Another organic farmer, well known to us, told me he had not felt such a spiritual awakening of his senses for a long time. The funeral service was held in Jones' Funeral Home in Port Elgin, a spacious and rather elegant old house. The place was packed in all rooms downstairs, also the staircase going up. There were many emotions and tears. Sandy and Wendy Burnett joined us in singing as a mixed quartet.

Justina as Volunteer and Friend in Sackville

Justina has had a remarkable run as a volunteer. She has done things I could never do, and has excelled many others who had far more education than she has.

All her voluntary contributions were made while employed part-time at Mount Allison. First she gave seven years to setting up the "course reserve" in the Library and then took the secretarial position in the German Department. Her German always was quite good and she quickly adapted to the more academic German.

Justina in IODE

Even if the idea of giving a loyalty voice to women did not originate in New Brunswick, the first chapter of IODE (Imperial Order of the Daughters of the Empire), was formed in Fredericton, NB. The Empire built up under Queen Victoria (who died in 1901) was under threat and Canada was preparing to send troops to fight in the War against the Boers of South Africa. While there is a lot of history intervening, the acronym IODE was officially adopted in the 1970s to signify the change to a not-for-profit charitable organization devoted in New Brunswick to giving aid to the education of children. Justina was invited to join the Lord Sackville Chapter of IODE a half dozen years before I was invited into Rotary in 1978. By January 1974 she had committed herself to becoming Regent and served in that capacity for two years. The major money-raiser for this Chapter was an annual gigantic book sale, held in the parlors of Sackville United Church.

While Justina enjoyed the fellowship, unwanted cliques and politics occasionally entered into the equation. However, undeterred, and having won many IODE friends throughout the Province, she was welcomed into the Shepody Chapter, Dorchester, in 1987 and remained a member there until we moved to Calgary.

Justina's Contribution to the United Church

Concomitantly, Justina got involved with United Church Women (UCW). In October 1977 she was elected President of Chignecto Presbyterial of the UCW. Her itinerary read like a *Reiseprediger* (itinerant preacher). She had about sixty units in her Presbyterial district, from Rexton, north of Moncton, to south of Amherst and round to The Shore (Northumberland Strait). She tried, unlike almost anyone else, to visit them all. She found this very gratifying because those who had never been visited (for example, Spencer Island, where the ill-fated *Mary Celeste* was built during the early days of sailing ships) really appreci-

Justina leaving for a United Church Women's event, 1977

ated the concern expressed by such a well-spoken person.

In 1978 she was appointed to the Executive of the Maritime Conference of the UCC. One of her notable speeches was to give a vote of thanks to Dr. J. Perkin of Acadia University for his address to Maritime Conference. Occasionally she would ask me for help, but she got better at giving homilies as time went on. These were given at World Prayer Day services where she once had the privilege of speaking from the pulpit of the Catholic Church in Amherst, said to have been the first non-Catholic to do so.

In February 1980 while on sabbatical in London, Justina gave a talk to a women's group at Kew Road Methodist entitled: "On being a Mennonite and a Methodist in Canada." In this talk she told them about Canada, Mennonites in Canada, and about the United Church of Canada, and her work in this Canadian church with its Methodist background.

Beginning in 1979, Justina was elected to the Board of the UCC Home for Senior Citizens, popularly called the Drew Nursing Home, named after one Carl Drew. She was co-opted as a result of her work in Presbyterial and Maritime Conference, and joined the Spiritual and Social Committee shortly after returning from sabbatical in 1980. In May 1979 Justina's good friend Polly Ervin was elected the first woman moderator of the Maritime Conference of UCC. Justina and Polly remained good friends, and have kept in touch by phone and letter until the latter died early in 2015.

One of the cherished experiences during her years with the Drew Board was the friendships she made, especially with Ann Johnson, Administrator, Sandra Hounsel, Jean Scobie, and many others. They were a 'fun bunch' but also dedicated workers. As a result of this association she was frequently together with these women at province-wide meetings concerning senior citizen's homes.

International Students

After we got home from our second sabbatical in 1980, Justina and I were approached by the Dean of Students to play an active role in the orientation of students from abroad. In a word, we were asked to be Advisors to International Students, a designation which came to include Canadians and Americans. For this reason the name was changed to Society for All Nations (SAN). We planned several days of activities to help such students feel welcome and find answers to their questions, this alongside the orientation that was part of registration for first year students.

We interpreted our role as one of trying to provide a home away from home as much as possible. Our house was only a short distance from campus. All Internationals could easily find it. So Justina began to think of preparing food for special occasions and over the five years, we often had up to thirty young people in the house for a party and food. One year, with the help of students and use of the University's kitchen, she baked *paska* for about 200 people anticipated at the International Dinner and Fashion Show. Students had been coming to the house for Easter for several years and fell in love with this Russian Easter bread. Justina usually baked *paska* in cans and let them mushroom over the top.

Among Justina's favorites were the four Botswanians who came for four years of pre-engineering before going on to Nova Scotia Institute of Technology. They would drop in for tea and a new game for them, crokinole, because they knew the door was open if Justina was at home. Geraldine Rossiter from Dublin became a long-time friend, also Felicity Riding from Bermuda. And then there was the Bailey family from Trinidad-Tobago, all four of them in turn, Albert, Alison, and the twins Alma and Alline.

Justina's Travels in the '80s

Not all of her trips can be recorded. We have mentioned meeting the first Janzen family at Lage, Germany, in 1973. During the very hot summer of 1976 while I was researching in London, Justina travelled with Ruth on an Eurail pass. They looked up "Aussiedler" cousins, but also Julika Roller, Groszsachsenheim, near Stuttgart, and her daughter Brigitte Fliegauf, Karlsruhe, and did Copenhagen, Venice, Salzburg among others. I knew where they were when they phoned me in Richmond-on-Thames.

Justina planned a five – week trip to Europe in the summer of 1984. Robert and Ruth were not surprised when their Mother showed her independence and determination by going alone. I was determined to complete the manuscript for *No Longer at Arm's Length* for Kindred Press. She naturally thought of visiting her cousins and friends in Germany. She flew to London where she stopped over in Rosemont Road, Richmond, with Roy and Audrey Smith. Then, by ferry and train, she met up with a Menno Travel Tour for a planned trip to the Dolomites, Venice, and Lucerne and much else. She then went to the Passion Play at *Oberammergau* whose people were staging a special 350th anniversary production. Mennonite World Conference, meeting in Strasbourg, France, was however the main attraction. There she met our Toronto friends, the Heinrichs, and heard the well-known singers Edith Wiens and Bill Reimer in concert.

She loved to visit with our English friends. However, once she had met the first members of her dad's family, the children of Heinrich and Tina Janzen, Germany ranked higher as a destination. There were two older brothers of Justina's father who, with their large families were released from Gulag conditions in 1956 and allowed to move to warmer climates, such as Kirghizia. Justina's father had been separated from his siblings in 1902. In the 1980s his relations left the Soviet Union one by one until there were sixteen first cousins taking up residence in Bielefeld and Paderborn, Westphalia, and Frankenthal, Phalz. Justina, the only relative who took the trouble to visit them, went over repeatedly because she found these visits most rewarding.

In June 1987 she took off for another trip to Germany to do some research on these families and to attend the wedding of Peter Wiebe in Leopoldshoehe, outside Bielefeld. While she had some success in research, it was not until we were with a Fresno-based tour to the Soviet Union in 1989 that she was able to establish herself as the **missing link** between the children of Heinrich and Peter Janzen (her dad's older brothers, all sons of Peter and Susanna Wiebe Janzen), and all those Wiebes related to Jean (Wiebe) Janzen of Fresno, the poet, and Leona (Wiebe) Gislason of Toronto. Exciting indeed!

House Renovation and Redecoration, 1985-1990

Justina and I both agreed in the mid-1980s that we had 'camped' long enough at 28 Lansdowne. First we replaced storm windows of wood with vinyl. Then we took advantage of a government program to have the house insulated in August 1979. Next came the re-shingling of the roof. Having completed much of the outside work, in 1985 we began inside by renovating the kitchen completely, from floor to ceiling, in the modern European style, off white pressed wood with beautiful oak trim. We used a local contractor who bought the cupboards made in Shediac. All told, we were very pleased with the results and Justina got her red kitchen sink that became the talk of the town. Justina often met folks while walking round to the Post Office and they would invariably arrive at this question, "And is it true you have a **red kitchen sink?**"

The kitchen was followed in due course by complete rewiring and installation of electrical baseboard heaters upstairs. Then we did the downstairs bathroom. In the fall of 1987 dear old Fred Estabrooks made sure we got a new furnace from all the insurance money we had paid for seventeen years. He had a sense of fairness in that way. In 1989 we had the chimney repaired, topped up, and a stainless steel liner put in from the top down to the furnace.

Last, but not least, in 1990, with retirement in Sackville in mind, we renovated the entire downstairs: floors, ceilings, and walls (refinishing the living room hardwood floors, and carpeting the rest). It was 'some job,' as they say there, but we had help. On the advice of our neighbor we chose Acadian tradesmen to do all the dry walling, nine-foot ceilings walking on stilts, plastering, and floors, where necessary, as well as Acadian furniture makers. We chose local carpet people. Guided by an interior decorator, we did all the painting and papering ourselves with the expert help of our hardworking and skillful neighbor Stewart Martin, as well as Ruth and a friend. Five of us working in sequence on the papering made us experts by the time we got to the dining room. The job looked professional.

When it was all done, it was clear that we could stay in that house, in that town, for the next twenty retirement years, because the house looked inviting. Upstairs we did the ceilings and walls, leaving the old pine flooring. In 1991 I tore away the old deck and built a new one, more or less by myself, for more deck space. During the next summer, with the help of a cousin from Germany, I built an eighty-foot fence, around the two maple trees on the east side, and then twenty-four feet into the lawn to create some privacy.

Our Celebration of the Fortieth

By the time of the fortieth anniversary (1989), we felt we wanted to say thanks to God for forty years, give a witness of who we were, and to express appreciation to the community of Sackville in which we had been privileged to live and work for a quarter century. While we were planning a 'Mennonite' service in the Mount Allison Chapel for Sackville and area people to take place on Sunday, Ruth, supported by Robert and Angie, living in Calgary, had invited special guests from far and near for dinner at the Marshlands Inn on Saturday. Frieda and Vern Heinrichs, Ed and Thelma Reimer and Susie had come from Ontario, while Siegfried and Margaret Janzen, Bruce and Ann Johnson, and Bob and Jean Seely were from nearby.

This anniversary celebration is the only one that resembled a church service. It had an 'order of service' with hymns, scripture readings, and a sermon. There was also a recital, a reception for invited guests. Though the invitation said the Chapel event would be in the form of a 'more traditional Mennonite Service,' the prayers and sermon were given by United Church and Presbyterian preachers. We had asked Dr. Charles Scobie of the University's Religious Studies Department to give a "meditation," but he told us that Presbyterians don't meditate, they **preach**. So he took as his text Deuteronomy 8:2 to remind us to think of how the Lord had led the children of Israel through all those forty years. They were not really years of 'wandering in the wilderness,' but years of learning. He saw the forty years as a metaphor for life with its "ups and downs, successes and failures, satisfactions and disappointments, good times and bad." Most meaningful to us,

Charles went on to express his appreciation for what our witness in Sackville had meant since 1965:

> "We in Sackville have been blessed over the years by having the Penners as representatives of the Mennonite tradition. The Mennonites have made a distinctive contribution to Canadian society, a contribution which Peter himself has helped to chronicle.
>
> "In particular the Mennonite tradition constantly challenges us to take the biblical precepts seriously. They have the disturbing notion that when Jesus said 'turn the other cheek,' or 'give your coat away,' or 'love your enemies' that he really meant it, and these precepts are not only binding on those who call themselves Christians, but really the only hope for the world in which we live. ...
>
> "And, if I may say so, in a time when marriage and the family are under pressure as never before, Peter and Justina in their forty years of marriage have given their own form of example and witness to God's precepts...."

Even if very few remembered those appreciative words about our life in Sackville, what they talked about in town for days were two things: 1) our ability to get together a pickup choir of eleven voices who could sing the words *"Wehrlos u. verlassen"* in harmony *a capella* to the tune well known as the second movement of the Mennonite Symphony Orchestra; and 2) Robert's half-hour violin recital in our honour accompanied on the Chapel Casavant organ by University organist Willis Noble. Overall, our guest list for the Sunday afternoon (service and reception) read in part like a 'who's who' of Sackville society, though we did not forget friends who would not make it into such a list.

Justina's Retirement in 1991

Her retirement from the German Department was mandated by staff regulations. Ruth and I managed a surprise birthday party at the Bell Inn, Dorchester. On April 29, 1991, the day of her sixty-fifth birthday David McAllister's second dining room was completely filled with her friends who corresponded with me through the History Department secretary. Thilo and Uta Joerger of the German Department also managed to surprise her with a party in the Department's foyer. All the people from the third floor of the Crabtree Building, other friends, and Peter McRae, photographer for the Mount Allison *Record*, were there.

Retirement from Sackville United Church

We had been members of Sackville United Church since 1967, and I had written its 225 year history, published in 1990 as *The Chignecto 'Connexion:' The History of Sackville Methodist/United Church, 1772-1990*. Even then, we were finding worship less and less satisfactory, so in the spring of 1991 we decided to approach Siegfried Janzen and his Petitcodiac Mennonite Church about full membership. We had attended this fellowship off and on since the core group came from Ontario a decade earlier. Seen in retrospect, however, joining Petitcodiac was not a very satisfying move. While the Janzens welcomed our supportive membership very much, we never felt as welcome as members as we had felt as guests. After about a year we tended to drive there about once a month. When at Petitcodiac church we were an hour from home, but no one ever invited us to come home to dinner, except Ada and Peter Bunnett (once). When a Burkholder daughter married the son of a Bunnett, we of all the members were not invited. Occasionally, therefore, we would attend the Presbyterian service in Sackville, because we liked Herbert Hilder's sermons and knew most members of the congregation.

Highlights of My Rotary Membership

As a result of my neighbour Ralph Sharpe's invitation and his proposal to the Rotary Club of Sackville, I was inducted as a member in
December 1978. It was the beginning of a significant new dimension
to my life though I had to request a leave of absence from the Club for
my second sabbatical 1979–80. In 1987–1988 I served as President of
the Club whose Charter extended back to 1931. I had served as bulletin
editor for many years, had been secretary for several years. This was
the period when Rotary Clubs worldwide joined the effort to do away
with polio in the world. The Polio-Plus program caught on and millions were raised for the program launched in 1987 and many more
millions with United Nations help since.

Back in 1993, Ray Kelly, a Scotiabank manager from Calgary, came
to our club for a makeup (a way of receiving credit for attendance).
He was visiting family in Hampton, New Brunswick. Once in Calgary,
he and George Seaborn, father of Susan on the Athletic staff at Mount
Allison, agreed to sponsor me, and this made it possible for me to join
the Rotary Club of Calgary South on Thursday, February 16, 1995 at
age 69.

Moderator of Constituency Political Debates

In 1991 Wayne Harper of the Rotary Club, and Chair of the Chamber
of Commerce, asked me twice to chair the panel of local political
candidates. One of these occasions came during the provincial New
Brunswick election of September 1991. Marilyn Trenholme, later
appointed the Lieutenant-Governor of NB, and then a Member of
Parliament, won that election handily. I wish only to record here that
the editor of the Sackville paper at the time wrote on Wednesday,
September 25, 1991: "Dr. Peter Penner turned out to be a great moderator. He kept the debate under control, while at the same time
injecting some good humor throughout the proceedings." Though we
had the opportunity to become members of the Liberal Party when

Frank McKenna was leader, I never felt comfortable with the idea of making such a political commitment.

A Shifting Sense of Home

Even though we had agreed in 1990 that the whole house should be redecorated for our retirement years, when I retired at age 67 in 1992, Justina joined me in rethinking plans for the future. Justina's mother died in Tabor Manor, St. Catharines, on November 18, 1991, at age 92. Though Ruth was still living in the Sackville area, Robert and Angie had been in Calgary since 1983, and were now talking family. Justin David was born October 8, 1992. All of this made it easier to think that we needed to establish a new locale where we might be the centre of our family, and not just a peripheral consideration.

By consulting my daybooks it would be possible to count up the number of times over the years we went by car to Ontario, whether from the West or the East, to visit family and friends, during the summer or at Christmas, or Justina by air to visit her mother, or myself by air to visit, sometimes in conjunction with business or board meetings.

Travelling to Investigate Calgary

We went to Calgary for Christmas 1983. It was bitterly cold for those two weeks; the temperature went down to minus 30 degrees Celsius. But we managed to have Christmas dinner with various friends such as John and Leonora Pauls whom we had known previously. I was the guest at the Rotary Club of Calgary, meeting in the Palliser Hotel. I even managed to visit Kay de la Ronde, Executive Secretary of the Shastri Indo – Canadian Institute which had supported me in 1972–73 in India, but whose office had moved from McGill, Montreal, to the University of Calgary.

Our move to Calgary and Alberta, where we had never lived before, proved startling to some. But in June 1993 we made the long trip, including a stop at nephew Victor Janzen's in Deep River, ON, another at Steinbach, MB, and Coaldale, AB. We found Robert, Angie, and little Justin in Calgary. They lived in the district of Rundle, part of the so-called Properties in the Northeast of a City which then had about 700,000 people. There we looked at houses for a whole day with Alexis whom we liked very much. She showed us various properties in the North East from Pineridge to Rundle to Beddington.

At Easter 1994 Justina went to BC to visit a friend. We met in Calgary where Grant took us around and showed us, among others, a house in Rundlelawn Close, North East. A few days after we arrived back in Sackville, we had an acceptable offer on our house. By FAX and phone in April we bought this much-preferred house in Calgary, about five minutes-walk from Robert and Angie who had since moved to a larger house.

Most people understood the draw of a grandchild. Jean Seely in Sackville was the first to suggest she would do a farewell party. Others, such as Carla Newbould, wife of the University President, had a farewell party for us at Cranewood, and even a second one when we were delayed in selling. She was a wonderful hostess and for this second party she invited the Rotarians.

Never East of Winnipeg!

Once we had actually sold in Sackville in the spring of 1994, had our yard sale, and saw our 8,000 pounds of goods loaded and taken away, and enjoyed the last farewells, four in total arranged by neighbours and friends, we got into our 1989 Cutlass Supreme and drove west. We told everyone, including friends and family, that henceforth our travelling orbit would be Calgary to the Fraser Valley westward, and never east of Winnipeg!

Actually, first we went to Ruth's in Aboushagan Road to rest up and spend some days with her. Because we had agreed to vacate on June

22nd, but would not be able to take possession of our Calgary home until about mid-July, we had time to stop in everywhere to say farewell, beginning with Henry and Vera Janzen in Kingston. Following two more stops in southern Ontario we drove on via north-shore Lake Superior and stopped to visit with Wally and Nettie Dyck at their cottage on Rice Lake. In Manitoba we visited my sister Erna and her family, living near Carman, as well as Jack and Ruth Neufeld, then living at Roland. From there we went to Winnipeg to visit friends and to take in all the places where Justina had once lived, in Niverville and Steinbach, as well as the Inter-Lake area where Justina lived from age four to ten. It was a nostalgic trip.

An invitation to stop in Saskatoon with our friends Ted and Sylvia Regehr meant taking the 'Yellowhead' road west. We finally arrived in Calgary at 29 degrees Celsius (84 Fahrenheit) on July 8, 1994. Robert and Angie and Justin received us joyously and took us to Boston Pizza where our only grandchild Justin David was a favourite. We had arrived in Calgary, our new environment.

Chapter Ten

Paths our Children Took

It is not for me to attempt a detailed account of our two children. If in future they wish to write their stories that will be up to them.

The reader may remember that Justina and I were surprised that officers of Children's Aid Societies would give us children to adopt even when we were relatively poor. One's economic scale however was considered not as important as the willingness to let a child, given into our care, develop along spiritual lines of their own choosing. Would we try to coerce them into our belief system?

Well, we did not, though Robert and Ruth, adopted and brought up by us initially while we were in the ministry, had opportunities to choose our path within, first, the Mennonite Brethren milieu, and then within our independent position as Anabaptist-Mennonites within the United Church of Canada and on a University campus. We however never sent them to Christian schools where they might receive a solid education in Christian beliefs and become familiar with our Anabaptist persuasion. What they learned and adopted from our example was hopefully sufficient.

The reader will come across Robert`s appreciative toast to us at our 60th anniversary. It is only just to say that Robert found his spirituality in Shamanism and Ruth, who kept a large library, was turned off by evangelicals as will become evident, and read widely in New Age. That is, both sought spirituality outside the formal church.

Robert's Career

Robert was nine when we arrived in Sackville. He came under the influence of the United Church through to age 18. This included Sunday School, youth choir, catechism classes, and Scouts. He was not baptized, though Rev. Bill Beach offered such services, even to the extent of going to another church to baptize by immersion, if that is what was desired.

At age 16-17 he attended Thames Valley Grammar School, Twickenham, London, which had Christian influences, and Kew Road Methodist church, and he mixed with Christian youth in an Anglican church for some time. That was not the only break in the Sackville scenario. From age 10 to 19 Robert was a member of the NB Youth Orchestra, chaperoned during the concert season. This took him away from church and from us almost every other weekend, though we knew he was in good company with a well-known chaperone couple and conductor, and with wholesome young people from Woodstock to Fredericton, Moncton, and Sackville.

Robert, dressed for NBYO event, our 1972 Impala in background, 1974

Robert's Orchestral Stepping Stones

Robert began his violin career in 1965 by joining a Susuki class conducted by Rodney McLeod of the University's Music Department. By spring Robert was helping Rodney tune violins for others in the class. At age ten Robert joined the New Brunswick Youth Orchestra conducted by Stanley Saunders of the same department. Saunders once told Justina: "Take care of Robert, he's a terrific boy you have there."

Saunders wanted us to make certain that Robert developed his considerable talent in music.

During our first sabbatical in 1972–73 Robert had a gratifying year, given the strong music program at Thames Valley Grammar School. Robert and an American student from Wooster, OH, the two best violinists in the school orchestra, helped that program to succeed.

As told in Chapter Six, in London Robert was fortunate to be able to study with Frederick Grinke, Ealing, a violin teacher who came from Winnipeg, Manitoba, and who taught for the Jehudi Menuhin Academy of Music. Certainly this experience in London was a turning point for Robert. While Justina and I were not gifted in music, we did encourage our children to excel and participate musically to the level of which they were capable. There was in our family a long standing appreciation and participation in musical activities, mostly at the church level, as mentioned in another section.

Robert had his last NB Youth Orchestra concert on March 16, 1975. During the summer of 1975, before going off to Brandon University, he was able, on the basis of an audition, to join the **National Youth Orchestra** for an unforgettable and rewarding summer. He soon realized that he was in a different league, but he measured up.

Robert, dressed for NYO event, summer 1975

Robert had a good start at Brandon, enjoying particularly English and History. He even went to the Mennonite Brethren church, having become acquainted with Professor Peter Klassen whom we knew. While the orchestra at Brandon was not much better than his Thames Valley Grammar School experience, he benefitted immensely from his violin teacher, Francis Chaplin, recommended to us by Ben Horch, our friend since Bible College days. Chaplin had been a child prodigy from northern New Brunswick and his music degree was taken at Mount Allison University. As a result of this reinforcement of his ultimate goal in music, Robert in 1978 wanted to study with Gamalien, a famous violin teacher, at Meadowmount music camp in Elizabethtown, NY. We managed to take him there in conjunction with our trip to Ontario that year.

Eventually Robert became a professional. Following his marriage to Angela Parkes in the summer of 1979, he played first in the Regina Symphony as Assistant Concertmaster, beginning early in 1979, actually half-way through his last year at Brandon. When Robert got this appointment, friends of ours there wrote in 1980 to say how much Robert was the envy of other students for his placement in Regina. He was the leader of the baker's dozen who made up the professional core in that Symphony.

Robert's Marriage

Sometime after our first sabbatical, Robert met a brilliant young woman from Dartmouth, Nova Scotia, at a mock United Nations Seminar at Mount Allison. She played the role of Israel, and Robert represented Poland. Angela Ora was the daughter of Victor L. and Lea Parkes. He was Maltese and Roman Catholic, a marine engineer and she was a German Jewess who fled Nazi Germany in time.

Angela, born when Victor and Lea lived in England, was baptized in the Church of England. For their wedding she chose Woodlawn United Church, Dartmouth, and they chose August 25, 1979. We would have preferred to have them wait for one year, but no, they wanted to be married before we left on our second sabbatical in London. Angela was still a student at Queens and Robert still had to finish at Brandon University. It was three days after Robert's twenty-third birthday. The engagement was announced about August 6 and, as was expected, we were responsible for the rehearsal dinner, at La Scala's, Halifax. Doctor Beveridge, the minister of Woodlawn United Church, did the service. Justina liked to tell how they used the Jewish custom to walk down the aisle together with Robert, as did Victor and Lea with Angie. It was all very lovely.

Robert and Angie moved to Regina when Robert was appointed concertmaster to the Regina Symphony Orchestra. While Robert moonlighted with Health and Welfare, Angie learned the nuts and bolts – and their serial numbers – at Robertson Machinery Company.

Angela has been supportive of Robert and they have been married for more than three decades. She has taught their two boys Justin and Jonathan both Christianity and Judaism. The family seldom came to our church, hence our two grandsons have no youth or worship experience in our Presbyterian congregation, though they were interested in going along to Mexico to help build houses for the poor.

With this in mind it is astonishing that Jonathan, the younger grandson, would find a Mennonite girl–friend in Lester Pearson High School in North East Calgary. Elizabeth Block's influence on him was strong enough to make him want to attend a Mennonite church in Vancouver while attending Film School there. He agreed to baptism classes and was baptized as an Anabaptist Mennonite in August 2015, and married Elizabeth in October. She came from a Mennonite Brethren family that was attending Abbeydale Christian Fellowship, Calgary SE. The wedding ceremony took place in the sanctuary of Grace Presbyterian Church on Saturday October 24, 2015.

Robert and the Calgary Philharmonic Orchestra

Robert auditioned for a string position with the Calgary Philharmonic Orchestra on April 11, 1983, and got the job in the second violin section. This meant that he and Angie Parkes moved to Calgary where in the next year he auditioned successfully for a place in the first violin section. In the CPO Robert played under the direction of such luminaries as Mario Bernardi (1984-1992) and Hans Graf (1995-2003).

Over the years in Calgary Robert had made himself into a computer expert and a website creator. For ten years he developed and wrote the website for the CPO. He also served on a CPO members committee representing its union interests for a number of years. He received his 25-year pin in 2008, and Robert was elected to the CPO Board and served for several years. Robert has taught violin to many persons since moving here. In the year 2014 Robert had completed thirty-one years with the CPO.

In 1998 Robert was invited by Craig Hutchenreuther, second violin, to join with Arthur Bachmann, viola, and Thomas Megee, cello, all long term members of the Calgary Philharmonic Orchestra, to form what was named the **Zabaglioni Quartet.** They performed for private gatherings and school children. For example, in 2010 they made a special trip to Grande Prairie for this purpose in order to entertain as well as to encourage youth to take up classical music.

What made them attractive was the easy combination of musical excellence and a sense of humour. They share a passion for chamber music. This has made them a great favorite with small specialty audiences and has provided opportunities for 'gigs' and also the occasional concert in Calgary and in rural Alberta. Zabaglione's programs aim to present great music excellently played with humorous moments well presented.

Robert has also had many weekend gigs in Banff where he combined with a cellist and pianist to form a trio. On many occasions for intimate house parties and dinners Robert has been asked to play solo, whatever he thinks suitable for the occasion.

Ruth's Different Voyage

Ruth's early years have been told in conjunction with the life of our family. Ruth Catherine Jeanette Penner was born on May 3, 1959 in Vancouver. We adopted her while we were in Abbotsford and I was teaching at the Mennonite Collegiate Institute (MEI). She was barely a year old when we decided to return to Ontario. In 1965 she found herself in Sackville, New Brunswick where I took a teaching job at Mount Allison University and she started in Grade One.

Her story can be roughly divided into three parts: New Brunswick, Ontario, and Nevada, though not without some back and forth between Ontario and New Brunswick.

Ruth in New Brunswick

Once we were settled in Sackville, Ruth at age six began to sing in choirs, in music festivals, the church junior choir, and did Brownies. This is a program which encourages girls to develop their own identity and positive relationships with others. She had both her elementary schooling and high school in Sackville. She responded well to most teachers, was challenged in music by teachers like Mary Junjek. She wrote her first letters at age nine. Ruth seemed to like expressing herself in writing and received letters from friends and aunts at an early age. Her first big and impressive project was a researched essay entitled "A Journey Across Canada". She was in grade six at the time.

Somewhat amusing to everyone was the fact that Robert and Ruth in 1968 wanted to go to the famous Marshlands Inn, just across Bridge Street, **alone,** to have 'dinner'. When Justina talked it over with Herb Read, the proprietor, he warmly encouraged it. All dressed

up for dinner they were quite a sight seated at the big table in the corner, and when some older women stopped by to ask, 'do you ever quarrel?' Ruth at age nine replied, 'no, we're not allowed to.'

Ruth had her first overseas travel in the summer of 1969 when Justina brought her and Robert over to the Mennonite Centre in Highgate. Many children in Sackville were envious of this and the expectation of a whole school year in London in 1972-73. In Mary Magdalene School she was the only Canadian in the school and did better in English than all her grade eight native classmates. During the summer of 1976, she traveled with Justina all over Europe, from Copenhagen to Vienna and around to Munich and Stuttgart. Because we lived in several provinces and were away from the larger family in Ontario (which was considered 'home'), our two children did not have many opportunities to mix with the Clairmont, Reimer, and Lerch children, let alone their other cousins, the Friesens, Unraus, and Wiebes, nor their Coombs cousins from Justina's side. Ruth was too young to benefit from those relations during our Ontario years, 1960–1965. After that, in Sackville, we had to do the driving. Half of the families came to visit, but half never did. Ruth found herself distanced from them for this reason.

Seeking a Career

After graduation from Sackville's Tantramar Regional High School in 1978, Ruth went to Dalhousie University, enrolling in the theater course for the year 1978-79. She had done well in drama at TRHS under the direction of Anne Manson. We were quite amazed at how well she performed in the lead role in *Our Town* by Thornton Wilder. At Dalhousie Ruth enjoyed Russian history and English literature courses, but found those enrolled in theater courses somewhat strange.

Her next year overlapped with my second sabbatical in England. She was prepared to transfer to Mount Allison, live in the house and help pay for the upkeep by renting rooms to students who would share the kitchen, the cooking, cleaning, and expenses. Those were the arrangements, signed and sealed. This turned out to be a mistake, because the three female students, while professing evangelical faith, all failed to live up to their promises. One of them kept bringing her boyfriend up to her room, ignoring meals that Ruth made, making her own and not sharing. Following Ruth's visit to London for Christmas, things went awry and Justina went home in March and, with the Dean's support, evicted this student before the year was up. These experiences turned Ruth off from confessing 'Christian' students and to some extent from Mount Allison.

During the spring of 1980 she decided to try for a career in travel agency work. Classes at Westervelt Business School in London, ON, seemed to go along well and she became certified as a travel agent in 1981. She preferred to be in or near Moncton where she had three brief encounters with travel agencies. Sky Lark went broke, Johnson's used her for summer months only and her experience with Atcan Travel in Moncton was not any better. Though not without fault, Ruth lost interest in travel agency work in 1983.

Dramatic Talent

In spite of this disappointment, she managed to participate meaningfully in drama. In late 1982, encouraged and supported by her mother, Ruth joined Curtain Call Theater, Moncton, as an actress and stage manager. During the winter of 1983-1984 she undertook to do the play, *"Whose Life is it Anyway?"* by Brian Clark. She directed it and was persuasive enough to draw in Professor Alex Fancy of Mount Allison's French Department. He had a strong reputation as a drama expert, playwright, director, and actor. Her lead actor was David Ridley of Moncton. This was a very successful production and brought her some recognition locally

She also planned and carried out some astonishing things. Just as her Mother was returning from her 1984 trip to Europe, Ruth took the overnight bus from Moncton to Manhattan, New York, where she stayed in a modest hotel for five days until her money ran out. Having done her homework, she walked the streets of New York, in her broad brimmed hat looking as though she belonged.

As early as 1985 Ruth had several interesting incentives for moving to Kingston, Ontario. She lived on Colborne Street with her cats, next to downtown, for two years while trying to make a living wage. While here, for the one and only time, Ruth's cousins: Mark, Stephen, and David Coombs came from Toronto to visit. Henry and Vera Janzen, her aunt and uncle, were good to Ruth as long as she was in Kingston, also their son Gordon.

For some part of this Kingston foray, Ruth got a job at Central Airways, Kingston, as Flight Coordinator. She did very well at this but the company was small, private, the owners split up, and the business was taken to Toronto Island. Ruth wanted to keep that job but could not face trying to manage in Toronto, commuting to and from the Island location, on $18,000.

Mountview Road, Sackville

Where Robert had entered into marriage and a music career, Ruth moved into a life alone and eventual cinema management. She had a strong desire to live in her own place, in the country, away from the hustle and bustle of Sackville, where the stars were visible, and she would be alone. In 1987 she discovered that half of a huge house built on Mountview Road by the Yorkshire Fawcett family long ago was available. Her accumulated furnishings fit in very well. There was a big yard between her and the road, a garden plot, and the property abutted on Silver Lake. Ruth was 'some happy', as they say there, as were her cats Montmorency and Cordelia.

During Ruth's residence in the Fawcett house, she turned to collecting antique pieces of furniture. She wanted a piece in which to display her doll collection, up to about fifty by this time; she needed space for her growing library, and she began seriously to do 'cross-stitch' (needle craft) of very high quality. Her mother encouraged her at every turn. She was painstaking and her work was much admired, and she sold some pieces. She kept this up, partly with a former classmate's help, until they took their pieces to the big Moncton craft fair in 1989 where they bought space and decorated a Christmas tree fully with their crafts.

When we went to Fresno, CA, for a sabbatical in September 1988, Ruth had her first introduction to California, a land that seemed to excite many minds. She managed to fly from New Brunswick, while

Robert and Angie came for a California Christmas from Calgary. We had been asked to house-sit the home of the president of the seminary in whose library and archives I was working. Ruth stayed on long enough to see Disneyland and Universal Studios in Anaheim and Hollywood.

During the summer of 1990 Ruth helped her parents to redecorate the entire downstairs at 28 Lansdowne Street, as explained above. With respect to papering, we used the following sequence: Justina did the cutting, Ruth the soaking, Peter the hanging, and two willing and gifted helpers the finishing of the wall-paper process. The finished product looked quite professional. For Justina's 65th birthday, as told, Ruth helped me plan a surprise party at the Bell Inn, Dorchester for twenty invited guests.

Robbie Reid

Ruth and Robert were school friends of Robert (Robbie) Barnes Reid, the youngest son of the former owners of Marshlands Inn. The two Roberts lived across the street from each other and played in the NB Youth Orchestra. When Robbie went away for some time, rumors floated that he was 'gay.' When he came home in the late 'eighties, legally blind, walking around town with a white cane, perhaps after dark, I could alert him to my presence by calling out: Robbie. He knew my voice.

Robbie died on May 1, 1991 as a result of 'gay bashing'. Young men, some of whom we knew, beat him, left him lying on Bridge Street, at right angle. After dark, a vehicle came around the corner, entering Bridge from Lorne, crossed the railway track, and ran over a body the driver could not possibly see. Robbie Reid was dead on arrival at hospital. Was he dead before he was run over? Whatever the driver's culpability, the leader of those who beat Robbie went to jail for several years. Ruth was most upset by this tragic incident and wrote to the *Sackville Tribune Post* severely criticizing the Town for the lack of police presence at night. She got a vigorous reply, criticizing her for holding the police in any way responsible for the death of Robbie Reid.[16]

Aboushagan Road and Various Ventures in Sackville

In 1990 Ruth found another place even a bit further out of town, on Aboushagan Road. It had been foreclosed by the Royal Bank, whose people were only too willing to sell. Ruth thought this even more ideal than the Fawcett house because it had eighteen acres of brush/bush, rising up to a clearing; a man-made pond which attracted beavers and ducks.

From the time of Ruth's return from Ontario to Sackville in 1987, she wanted to get into the cinema business, preferably managing or having her own theater. She focused her attention on the Vogue Cinema in Sackville, once owned by Frank Cole, one of our neighbors. His daughter also had an interest in acquiring ownership and Ruth lost out in that bid, but found employment there as a projectionist. She learned to work the antiquated projector and found the strength to drag the heavy films up a narrow staircase. The owner offered Ruth the business in November 1991. The big stumbling block was an attempt to extract a large "goodwill" item, a large chunk of money up front.

When Ruth rejected that, and all else failed, it turned out that Wayne Harper, a local business man, purchased the company and Ruth worked for him for some time, indeed until she left in order to pursue a cinematic possibility in California. While she was working for Wayne she began to write movie reviews for the Sackville Tribune Post under the title "Room with a View." These were actually much appreciated as Ruth showed her writing talent and her broad knowledge of films and theater.

In the early 'nineties Ruth tried several other ventures without realizing success. She was thirty-four years of age in 1993 when we began seriously to consider moving to Calgary to be near Robert,

---

16 Ruth CJ Penner letter and Editorial (8 May 1991)

Angie, and Justin. Though she had not actively discouraged our move, it left Ruth on Aboushagan Road feeling somewhat abandoned.

Ruth in Ontario

Ruth with Merlin, her doll collection, antique furniture, Belleville, 1998

Ruth got what seemed like a secure position in Ontario with Belleville's Bellestar Cinema. With the manager's help she obtained her license as a projectionist. In May 1997 she was making her own way, living at first in an old brick house with adequate room for her furnishings, her books, dolls, and Merlin, the lovable stray from Main Street, Sackville.

Justina and I helped her to buy a house at Dunbar Street. What happened a year later was somewhat shattering. While there were some early signs that Bellestar 3 Theatre was failing to produce the anticipated income, what was worse, on June 6th, 1999, Norman Stern, the owner, notified Ruth that he would be closing the Theatre on the 24th. Actually, Ruth was prepared to buy, and did so, and we helped her on the further assumption that under different ownership and a different plan, Bellestar would make enough money to make the purchase payments for the equipment, as well as the mortgage on the house. A Belleville Rotarian and realtor helped as intermediary.

It was not too long, however, before Ruth discovered that her clientele seemed to be drying up. The first reality of this hit her early in October 1999. If Norman Stern could not make a go of it in Belleville at top prices for tickets, how would Ruth make it at discount prices? We did ask that question, but hope lives eternal! None of this was helped by the fact that Belleville built a huge modern Cinema near Wal-Mart.

Ruth in Nevada

While trying to find gainful employment in Belleville, Ruth sent out resumes in response to ads for 'cinematic experts.' In one case she was actually flown out to California while employed part-time in Kingston. She however did not want to take over a cinema in Barstow, below Las Vegas, which seemed like a barren place (so we had reason to think!). But on the basis of these possibilities we got a lawyer to assist in establishing her **academic credentials**, the equivalent of a Bachelor of Commerce degree, so that she could get a job in the United States with benefits on the basis of a non-immigration work permit. Eventually, in late April 2002 she was offered a job with a firm, Wallace Theater Corporation, Portland, OR. This took her to Carson City, the Capital of Nevada, just below Reno and Lake Tahoe where she would be manager of a ten-plex theatre. Signing a two-year contract seemed reasonable, but waiting for months for her lawyer to finalize the immigration status was irritating.

Once this was realized the Belleville realtor was able to sell her house surprisingly quickly. In June Justina was there with Ruth to enable her getaway and eventually drove with her to Carson City. Her car, now a 1988 Oldsmobile ranch wagon type, with over 300,000 kilometers performed beautifully all the way without trouble, heavily filled with everything immediately necessary. It was a very long trip by car (with Merlin) to Lethbridge (in very heavy rain, as it turned out) and then, without stopping in Calgary, they crossed into Montana at Sweet Grass, making the passage over the mountains in snow, and arrived in Carson City. Justina stayed to help with the search for a place to live and the start of a difficult job, as it turned out. We drove down to visit Ruth in September and stayed ten days. Carson City is a very pleasant place. Ruth found a nice house in Indian Hills, not far from all the Super stores, south of Carson. While there we visited Lake Tahoe, Virginia City, and Genoa, the place where the Mormons first settled long ago.

I close Ruth's story here by saying that she spent the next years in Nevada in cinema management on a work permit.

PART III

RETIREMENT YEARS

Chapter Eleven

Our Years in Calgary

This chapter tells briefly how we settled into Calgary and soon felt this was now home, and what a circle it has proved to become. A glance at the list of the eighty invited guests at our Diamond Anniversary in 2009, after fifteen years residence, would indicate the breadth of our friends and fellowship, far beyond what we could ever have dreamt when we first came to Calgary or we could have realized in another location. Among them were friends from our residential area, Church, Rotary, long-time friends, relatives, and White Hat Greeters from the Calgary Airport of which Justina is one. They came from Wiesbaden, Germany, London, UK, from Vancouver to Winnipeg, and Alberta. Because of this great diversity among our friends, recorded in pictures by Terry Allen and Linda Friesen, Justina and I as emcees introduced everyone before Brunch so that, as one guest said, by the end of it 'we felt we knew everyone.'

Terry Allen, photographer of our 60th Anniversary event, with Justina, his wife Sharon, Sherry Rainsforth (Austin), myself, 2009

Getting Settled and 'Warming' the House

What seemed different from our move to the East in 1965 when very few family members came to visit was that we were barely in the house in Rundle when company began to come. Relations and friends came from all directions to welcome us, even though it was a hot summer day. It was a busy time, given that I was still in the last research and writing (and map-making) stage of my India Mission book. Following that, we even managed an enormous amount of necessary shopping to get started in a new location.

Since we had these long-time friends and close family in Calgary, we thought we should have a "house-warming." We planned this for August 28, 1994 when, after some speeches and a prayer by a friend, Robert gave a beautiful rendition on the violin of "Bless This House!" accompanied by Leonora Pauls on his portable piano.

Grandma Justina

As in the Maritimes, life with family usually took on huge proportions during Advent and Christmas. Therefore, we were happy on December 11, 1995 to welcome Jonathan William as a second grandchild, but it meant that Justina, called on to do the grandmotherly thing, was tired before the crunch came with Christmas dinner for all the 'family' and some extras. On top of all that, we had a dinner for four couples between Christmas and New Year's, and my cousin, Frieda Wiebe, St. Catharines, Ontario, came for a few days. All of this suggested that

Robert, Angie, Justin with guitar, and Jonathan, 2006, in our house

entertaining would henceforth take more energy than Justina could be expected to deliver.

Robert and Angie lived a five-minute walk from our house, on Rundlelawn Way. At first, as our guest book shows, the family came for a meal about once a month. What became a familiar and much anticipated event was the boys' coming for sleepovers. Justin, born in 1992, came alone at first, but when Jonathan was only two he wanted to come too. This became something very significant for Justina as grandmother. I may not have recorded each such occasion, but these overnights were quite frequent until about June 2006 when I noted that there was "this long overdue overnight." But I also noted that Justin at age thirteen, nearly fourteen, was five feet, eight inches tall.

That seems to have been the last overnight.

Oh dear! A sad day! After that the boys became teenagers, their interests changed, much else changed. Justin, otherwise a strong reader, became totally engaged in *Facebook,* and was seriously dating by age seventeen, while Jonathan, a brilliant student, a drummer of greatly developed skills, transferred to Bob Edwards School, Marlborough, in order to enter French Immersion. As a result of his abilities and dedication to his studies, he was chosen as head of his class and then as head each year of the entire school until he graduated. Once he moved to Lester B. Pearson High School located in Village Square, 52nd Street, Jonathan became involved in expensive animation projects which seemed to absorb all his time. Meanwhile, Justin had gone to Forest Lawn High School where he excellent in drama. He did Grade Twelve at the Henry Wise Wood School in the South West.

In a word, it became more difficult to keep up the purely social engagements with the family.

When Robert and Angie waited thirteen years to have their first child, we hoped to live long enough to see them grow up, graduate from high school, if not university. Now in 2015 they are twenty-two and nearly twenty and we are 89 and 90. We are thankful to have been here to see Justin, as was his choice, to become eventually a fully qualified journeyman carpenter, trained at Southern Alberta Institute of Technology (SAIT). Jonathan finished his intensive one year course at Vancouver Film School and had a job to go to in Vancouver on the Monday after his Friday graduation. Justin moved in with Lauren who works for the City, while Jonathan, as noted in a previous chapter, found his companion for life among a small group of Mennonite young people from Abbeydale Christian Fellowship.

From 1992 to 1998 Justina shared the family's attention with the other grandmother to the boys, Lea Parkes. She was unfortunately divorced by her husband and thereupon moved from Dartmouth to Calgary to be near Angie and her family. Lea died from complications on July 29, 1998. Angie was able to arrange for a Memorial Service in the Chapel of the Peter Lougheed Centre conducted by Rabbi Moshe Saks.

The New Orbit, Social and Intellectual

About a year after moving to Calgary I was asked to give a paper at the annual convention of the American Historical Society of Germans from Russia (AHSGR) meeting. For this occasion in July 1995 I chose the 1929 emigration episode that involved my grandfather Peter J. Wiebe and his family. My paper entitled "Let my people go: a catastrophic episode in German/Russian emigration: 1929" was published in the *Journal* of this Society. That, as it turned out, led to our continuing involvement with the Calgary Chapter of that Society and expanded our social and intellectual life.

For a short time we took guests to the Royal Tyrrell Museum at Drumheller, AB. When tired of taking people through we let them go on their own. While we got the picnic lunch ready for their return we wondered if they, inside, were trying to reconcile Bishop Ussher's chronology for the creation of the world [4004 BC] with what the dinosaurs were telling them.

The Eventful Years of 1995 and 1996

We found our new travel orbit to BC and within Alberta exciting. Our new western orbit brought us closer to the Manitoba Steingarts, and made possible the organization of the first Steingart Reunion. Justina's mother was the eldest of the children of Heinrich Steingart. The reunion was held during the last weekend of August 1995 on the campus of Canadian Mennonite Bible College, Winnipeg. For this I wrote "A Brief History of the Steingart Family" which I sold at $2 to cover basic costs. Justina's family came from Ontario and most of the Steingarts from Manitoba, Minnesota, and Alberta, about 80 all told. It was considered a great success, but we never had a second. As Justina and her cousin Mary (Steingart) Epp learned, such a reunion takes a great effort, and no one else came forward in Alberta to plan a second.

After that the contacts with Steingarts were few and far between. But when Frank, the last of the ten Steingart siblings, died on March 14, 2008, just six days short of 93, his widow Agnes phoned Justina to ask her to give the eulogy at the funeral in Steinbach General Conference Church. Justina went and her eulogy was much appreciated by Agnes and everyone related to the Steingarts.

We went to the Maritimes in May 1996 in order to take in Convocation at Mount Allison, to visit, in turn, David and Yvette Silverberg in Wolfville, NS, the Northfield Settlement *Kleinegemeinde* near Kennetcook, the Siegfried Janzens, Petitcodiac, and some friends in Sackville. This turned out to be a wonderful trip, very gratifying in nearly every way. As an Emeritus Professor we returned for Convocation in 2002 and 2010.

At the end of August 1996 we decided to accept Frieda and Vern Heinrichs' invitation to attend the wedding of their daughter, Anne Marie, in Toronto and Guelph. We were not sorry to have gone to this expense as we were able to see many of our former friends from Ontario, England and elsewhere.

Relations with Mennonites in Calgary

Our close relations with Fresno and the Mennonite Brethren continued until the India MB mission story was completed and published in 1997. In Calgary we could have gone to any mainline church. Instead, we looked for a Mennonite Church home.

The story of our church shopping and decisions regarding membership and participation in First Mennonite Church, Richmond Road, in preference to any Calgary congregation within the MB conference could easily fill a chapter. Unfortunately, what began in euphoria in 1995 turned into disappointment. There were more problems in the congregation than we had been led to believe. Some members of our Monday evening Bible study group had suggested that I should get involved to help resolution. I found myself disliking intensely the steps that were being taken by some few to force out a talented Associate Pastor. Once the Associate had taken his family out of First Mennonite and had gone into doctoral studies and university teaching, we decided to withdraw from the congregation in favor of Grace Presbyterian Church in Calgary's Beltline. Our involvements however had in part issued in the calling of a crisis-in-the-church minister.

At Rundlelawn Close, NE

Since 1994 we have filled about 600 lines in our guest books. This included our immediate family, those invited for special events like birthdays, Rotary Dinner Club guests, six at a time, and visitors from afar staying overnight.

In 1997 quite unexpectedly we had Dr. David Ewert as an overnight guest. David Bergen, while completing his ministry at First Mennonite, invited Ewert to conduct Bible expositions, `deeper life services` they were called. As no one else offered to billet him, Justina and I did and thus got to know more about him as teacher, author, and family man. My connections and correspondence with David Ewert went back to the year 1956–57 when I wrote an undergraduate thesis for the Mennonite Brethren Bible College. He was there to guide me and edit the whole. After that I kept up with his thinking by reading his articles in the *Mennonite Brethren Herald*, especially on eschatology in which he disparaged dispensationalism. Otherwise, he remained a distant figure to us, as he moved about advancing his academic standing and teaching at MBBC, Eastern Mennonite College, Harrisonburg, VA, and Mennonite Brethren Biblical Seminary, Fresno. When he published his story at age 70 in *A Journey of Faith: An Autobiography* (1993), some of us thought this premature, since he was still going strong as a Bible expositor. He lived to be 88.

During that visit Ewert told us that he was working on a series of biographical sketches of his former colleagues, mainly at MBBC, Winnipeg. When I asked whether he would be doing a certain colleague also, he said "no" because he was excluding some who had been objectionable to him personally and theologically. In his book, *Honour Such People*, 1997, Ewert included Cornelius Wall, Henry Janzen, Bernard Sawatsky, John A. Toews, Jacob Franz, Jacob Quiring, and Frank Peters.

On a more pedestrian note with reference to hosting guests, there came a time when we began to reconsider how much we could do as hosts. The ones who stayed the longest, and overstayed their leave, were a family related to Justina from Detmold, Germany. This was in 1998. They brought their three children (15 to 7) and were here 25 days. During that time, we made two trips with them in a Grand Caravan rental, one to Tacoma, WA, to see their friends, and the other to Luceland–Superb–Saskatoon, SK, to visit his relations. To their credit, they were prepared to work and to share costs. He repaired our basement wall (from the outside); the family helped paint our fence, and they even painted the neighbor`s fence for $100. We supplied them with old clothes for the job.

That however did not make it easy for Justina who provided beds and bed linen, did laundry, put food on the table for people who could not adapt to our table manners! The children actually wanted their mother`s dishes served in one pot (*Eintoepfer* meals) where they needed just to reach to the center of the table and help themselves.

It was not too long after that I formulated the guiding rule that we do not have overnight guests for more than one day and two nights, three nights at the very most! Why? Because it seems that it only takes a few days for fatigue to take over, and it does not take much for emotions to take over when fatigue kicks in. In order to prevent excessive unbearable fatigue for either of us, we had to let it be known: short visits only. In fact, by the year 2002 it was obvious that we were not really interested in having overnight guests except on very rare occasions.

Actually, as we got older (having reached our future!) and given our limited facilities, I began to agitate for eliminating overnight situations altogether. While I finally had my way, we made exceptions with the Dyck family from Winnipeg. Ron and Irene and their children, especially Karen when she was working here in Calgary with Samaritan's Purse, continued to be welcome. They caused us no work and were glad to rough it, so to speak, as long as we could be together for a short time. It was always a good time, and we had the advantage of always being welcome in Winnipeg, even for pickup and drop-off at the airport.

Justina as a White Hat Volunteer

We were not long in Calgary when Justina applied to join the White Hat volunteers that made themselves very noticeable in the Calgary International Airport (YYC, the identifying symbol). They made their first appearance on the arrivals level on July 1, 1991. They were dressed proudly in white Stetsons and red vests, ready to greet arriving passengers with a hearty 'welcome!' They had been selected and assembled for this volunteer service by

Justina in dress of a White Hat Greeter, YYC, 1998

Elizabeth Wesley who was authorized by the Administration of YYC to do so. Justina was trained and assigned to the Tuesday afternoon shift – from two to six – with about six others.

While YYC boasted over 200 White Hat Volunteers in 2002, today there are more than 400, many of them being trained for the opening of the greatly expanded Calgary International Airport in 2016. Like the original forty-nine, they are eager to provide a memorable airport experience. As Debbie Stahl who took over the program in 2008 stated, "these White Hat Volunteers are a true testament to Calgary's warm western hospitality and spirit of volunteerism. Their enthusiasm, dedication, genuine care, and desire to go the extra mile, make YYC one of the friendliest airports in the world!"

YYC is probably the only airport in North America or the world that has a program remotely similar to the White Hat Greeters who dot this airport in four-hour shifts, manning certain stations, or walking about, or driving the club cars shuttling visitors who have arrived at YYC.

From Justina I have heard hundreds of stories of what her assistance as a German-speaking volunteer meant to arrivals: young families, grandmothers from afar, and others. Occasionally she will spot a "Mexican Mennonite" from Grassy Lake area and go up to them, dressed as she is, and surprise them with "Do you speak Low German!" To them she has become 'de Pannasche!'

This is her mission, her service to others, in advanced age. Her ready smile, her helpfulness, her willingness to redirect the bewildered passenger to the proper location has made her a lot of friends, whether among passengers or YYC staff, reaching into the concierge's office, ticket agents and flight attendants. Many refer to her by name and, by the way, do things for her when they can. This circle widened at YYC to include friends among the White Hatters. Two of them became 'daughters' – forging remarkable relationships – AnneLiese and Maureen. More below.

I know how meaningful this service has been to Justina because I volunteered from the first to drop her off at the Airport for her stretch of duty and pick her up again, often parking to join her for something to eat in the Food Court. Actually, the cost to me for two trips or more a week to YYC is more than $500 a year just for gas, but then that is one justification for keeping a vehicle!

Justina's Mission and her Friends

One of the most remarkable things about Justina has been her ability to make friends. Even then, she has often lamented that she has never had many with whom she would want to share her innermost thoughts. But she has always had some, though the relationship may be long distance. One of these is Frieda Dick Heinrichs, as mentioned, Toronto and London, another Rozella Friesen, Charlottetown, and even more longstanding, Katie Fast Harder, Chilliwack. This latter friendship began when Katie was seven and Justina six. They met in 1933 in the Inter-Lake District of Manitoba where their fathers were teachers in one-room schools about fifteen miles apart – Moosehorn and Camper. Both Frieda and Katie came to our 60th anniversary in 2009.

Just as remarkable, perhaps, is the phenomenal increase in the number of friends Justina garnered during our years in Calgary. We live in the North East, east of 36th Street with its Calgary Transit rail. The large Sunridge Mall, Lougheed Hospital, London Drugs, and the huge Safeway Store are just across those tracks. Then there is also the Salvation Army's Thrift Store. In each of these establishments, somehow, clerks at various levels of responsibility have become attached to Justina. She often went with a short shopping list but returned two hours later with little in her shopping bag. This is where she walks Thursday noon to look up these friends again and again, to listen to their stories. She often comes home to tell of meaningful encounters.

New opportunities through Rotary

I was inducted into the Rotary Club of Calgary South on February 16, 1995, having been sponsored by Ray Kelly and George Seaborn, as mentioned. At the time this Club had about 165 members from many walks of life, professionals and business men, and over the years they have developed a Club exceptional for a good combination of 'service above self' and fellowship with joviality. Thus, once a week I had lunch with men from the 'oil patch' and other businesses whose income far exceeds mine, but I was made to feel comfortable with them. Many of the Club members' friends are Rotarians and they care for each other until the last rites are necessary. Some of the Rotary funerals or memorial services have been among our most meaningful experiences. The special luncheons, dinner club, working projects, and meetings are enjoyable as well as educational to attend. The friendships formed seem more worthy of one's trust than some we have experienced in other social or religious settings.

Friends in Rotary: Len Hamm, Rick Jakubec, Murray Flegel, Mel Gray, and Bryan Targett, 2009, photo by Terry Allen

We Rotarians in Calgary counted ourselves privileged to have **Rotary International 1996** come to town. Given the ample facilities of the Stampede grounds, we could host more than 25,000 guests, the greatest number ever at a RI convention in North America. With the help of David and Diane Lamsdale, we hosted five couples at our place for Hospitality Night, Monday, June 24. They came from three different American states, others from Brisbane, Australia, and Cape Town, South Africa. We managed to visit with the Novosibirsk singing group who were hosted by Don Campbell of the Rotary Club of Calgary.

Justina and the Partners of Calgary South

Chapter Eight of my history of the Rotary Club of Calgary South tells the story of the women, the spouses, of the members of the Club. It is the only Club that has them, numbering about one hundred. First they were part of **Inner Wheel**, which had spread over the United States and the Commonwealth. After some years they decided to leave **Inner Wheel** in favor of becoming the **Rotary Anns** of Calgary South. When our Club belatedly took in women members in 1998, they changed their name to **Partners**, but maintained their full loyalty to the members and projects of Calgary South. Justina became involved with the Partners, was asked to organize a Book Club, and took her turn in the Executive, becoming President in 2003-2004. For this, on her 80th birthday, I wanted her to have a Paul Harris Fellowship (PHF) in recognition of her significant contributions as a volunteer, both in Calgary as well as in Sackville, NB. A PHF signifies a donation of $1,000 US to the Rotary Foundation. Money from the interest generated by this huge RI fund is used for scholarships at the masters and doctoral level in the first instance.

Family Reunions

In 1998 the Wiebe family in St. Catharines, Ontario, called for a family reunion of all the descendants of the Peter J. Wiebe who came to us in Manitoba in March 1930. The reunion day, August 23, 1998 arrived and cousins Frieda and John had received a good response from all the families: Wiebe, Penner, Unrau, and grandchildren. The reunion was well planned with a suitable worship format, Natalie Lerch singing, Paul Wiebe playing classical guitar, videos, short presentations, and food and fun, of course. I had brought along copies of my study of the Wiebe family which had grown out of the family memoir I had been working on since moving to Calgary. Most importantly, Frieda managed to prepare a 'Peter Wiebe Family Tree' and she organized a composite family photo.

Justina did not want to go to Florida in 2002 because of the humidity there. So I went alone in February and spent six days with my Penner siblings at Cathy's in Bradenton, Florida. All told we enjoyed our special time and had fun, especially with brothers-in-law Ed Reimer and John Clairmont present, always at ease and ready for some laughter. We had some fun with the concept 'emeritus' professor. Cathy and John, Americans, found this difficult to understand, even upon full explanation, or to accept. They insisted wrongly, as it turns out, that this was 'not done at Mennonite colleges!'

Oh well, we're Canadian, eh!

Golden Wedding Plans

In some ways the anniversaries got better and better. Early in February 1999 we received confirmation from Vern and Frieda Heinrichs that **the Fiftieth** would be held on Sunday, June 20, 1999 in Rosedale, Toronto, at noon. Their guests included siblings and closest friends from the Neufeld side and our side. At one point in his scheduled remarks Jack Neufeld said, off hand, "and isn't it nice that the Heinrichs are paying for all this." Living in Belleville, Ruth could be present, while Robert and Angie waited for our planned event in Calgary.

After that we took Peter and Katie Harder, who had come from Chilliwack, BC, to Ottawa to show them our Capital City. In turn they gave us two nights in the prestigious Chateau Laurier. On the way back we stopped in Kingston to visit Justina's brother Henry and his wife Vera who were too ill to come to Toronto. They both died in the year 2000.

On our flight home to Calgary, because Justina let it slip that this was our anniversary, this brought us some free champagne and a visit to the flight deck. After all that, we packed our Van and drove across the Prairies to Roland, Manitoba, where the Neufelds celebrated their Fiftieth with their family and friends. The Heinrichs were there too from Toronto. Then we hurried home and

The Triangle started in 1962: Vern and Frieda Heinrichs, right: Peter and Justina; Jack and Ruth Neufeld, left upper, at 88 Elm, Rosedale, 1998

made final plans to celebrate our Fiftieth on home turf. Here in Calgary in the Alberta Room of the Sheraton-Cavalier Hotel we had about fifty guests including Robert and Angie, Justin and Jonathan, and Justina's relations from Alberta. Maria Letkemann, MD, came from Wiesbaden, Germany, and Jack and Ruth Neufeld had driven over from Carman, Manitoba.

We had Robert's string quartet made up of Robert, regular violist Arthur Bachmann, and substitutes for second violinist Craig Hutchenreuther and cellist Tom Magee. They did a half hour concert, beginning with Mozart and ending with the Beatles song: 'Will you still love me when I'm sixty-four?' Robert served as master of ceremonies, told some good stories, several of our friends spoke, John Pauls sang a number

Ruth with us at Golden Anniversary, Rosedale, 1999

as good as ever he does, accompanied by Leonora, and everyone enjoyed themselves.

The Sixtieth

This Sixtieth Anniversary Program in the McKnight Ballroom, Sheraton-Cavalier Hotel on August 9th, 2009, did not come about in a day. It took more like six months of planning. We wanted to make this an enjoyable party and yet make a statement of who we were as we had done twenty years earlier at our Fortieth in Sackville, NB. We certainly wanted only those as guests with whom we really felt comfortable. Over time we had to draw the line, given our budget capability and our program plan. We felt it necessary to draw the line at nieces and nephews.

Because a few people wanted to know the date six months in advance we sent out a "keep this date [August 9, 2009] open" notice. This also went to all our siblings on both sides. If any of them were prepared to go to the expense of a long trip and hotel accommodation, they would be welcome, except that we would need to know by a dateline to be determined. Meanwhile, Justina`s sister Susie died on April 7 and Justina went to her funeral in Vineland. This left only Mary who kept saying that the Coombs would be at the cottage then. We understood and accepted that. None of my siblings were planning to come.

What we planned to do as things became clearer was to be our own master of ceremonies and to introduce all of our eighty guests before we enjoyed a sumptuous brunch. They were seated at ten tables of eight, carefully grouped. Champagne was served each guest in time for the toast to be given by Robert. Following the Brunch, our minister Victor Kim gave a seven-minute meditation using a new and then crumpled $20 bill as his illustration of what can happen in a marriage. He ended by flattening out the bill as an illustration of our example. John Pauls, now from Vancouver, accompanied by Leonora, sang two meaningful numbers. We also managed to have a fourteen-voice choir to sing one of our favorites in German, Robert conducting and Leonora at the pianoforte.

For additional music Robert and his sons Justin and Jonathan put on quite a show. They did themselves proud and concluded the program, literally, in a purple haze: Robert, violin, played Bach/Gounod's *Ave Maria*, accompanied by a recording. He next played jazz, Herman Hupfeld's *As Time Goes By*, and then on electric violin and guitar, and the drums, the trio did Jim Hendrix` *Purple Haze*.

Our guests loved it.

Robert Conducting pickup choir, Diamond Anniversary, 2009: Leonora Pauls behind at the keyboard, Irene Dyck, Katie Harder, Elsie Thiessen, Frieda Heinrichs, Angie Parkes, Sylvia Regehr, hidden, Justina; the men: Ernie Thiessen, John Pauls, Colin Redekop, Ted Regehr, Ron Dyck, hidden, Peter

The Freiwilliges (Open Mike)

Obviously we cannot include all of the statements offered. Among these were our grandson Justin, Frieda and Vern Heinrichs, Mel Gray from Rotary, and Debbie Stahl from White Hatters. Robert gave the Official Toast:

Mom and Dad, honored guests, family and friends, when I was talking with my immediate family about what to say on this occasion of my parents' 60th Wedding Anniversary, Justin said something that I thought was quite perceptive. He said that you can tell a lot about the grandparents from the way the grandchildren have turned out. And why is this? It's because the very best of what the grandparents cherish and value gets distilled and strengthened and comes down through the generations that follow.

Mom and Dad, you married in a time when rather than throwaway or replace an item, time was taken to repair what needed attention. So one of the reasons that your marriage has lasted for sixty years is that you have tended and nurtured your relationship, rather than following the modern trend to run off and find a new one. Through your example I have learned the value of commitment, not only to my wife Angie and to our children, but for all that life has to offer. I had the dogged determination to keep on playing the violin, in part I suspect because through you I learned that some things are worth sticking to over the long haul.

In you I see two people who, commendably, are not joined at the hip. There is space in your togetherness, enough to accommodate the writing of books or travelling to different parts of the world. I admire your community service through Rotary International and the wearing of a white hat (you can always tell that those are the good guys), the hospitality that you extend to others, and Mom especially for your openness to people and remarkable ability to go to depth with strangers in the shortest time possible. You walk a path of faith: faith in God, faith in each other, and faith in your community which you give to generously.

Between the two of you I see a deep and abiding love, free from the artifice of romance, strong enough to look beyond the faults in each other, strong enough to have seen you through sixty years together.

I wish you all the best in the years to come. May you continue to enjoy the gifts of good health, keen minds, and relatively unimpaired mobility (don't worry, the glass of champagne won't impair you too much). While sixty years may seem like a long journey, may there still be new horizons ahead for the love between you to grow.

And now the time to toast has arrived. The last word goes to my sister Ruth, whose thoughts and good wishes are with us today. Her words remind me that despite my serious bent, there is room for lightness, even on this occasion.

Please join me in a toast to my parents, Peter and Justina Penner.

"A little ditty in celebration of sixty years'
By Ruth Penner

There once was a boy from Siberia
Who married a girl from Ukraine
They settled in Sackville and raised a few kids
And now they can make quite a claim

Sixty years they can now celebrate
For solemn vows they did take
To love and honour, cherish and obey
(Well, maybe not that last part, eh?)

Friends from all over, too many delights
They've traveled the world and seen a few sights
London, Moscow and Calcutta too
[Budapest] and Vienna, what a beautiful view

You have now all here gathered to help them rejoice
To laugh and to party, to praise them with voice
May you raise up your glasses and join me in praise
Happy 60th dear parents, have the best of all days

From your loving daughter, Ruth

There were also meaningful toasts from Karen Dyck, who thought of us as 'the coolest relatives' and Katie Harder, friend to Justina of 77 years. In February 2010, Katie gave a brief address to her senior's group at the Greendale MB church in BC. She spoke of this lasting, special friendship in terms of a James Russell Lowell quotation: *Each year to ancient friendships add a ring, as to an oak.* "This past fall my friend Justina Penner, formerly Janzen, and I celebrated our long years of unbroken friendship or in the poet's words added another "ring" – it was the seventy-seventh! She then retold the story of that friendship, beginning in the fall of 1932 in Moosehorn and Camper, Manitoba, where their fathers were teachers for some years.

While the Harders came to visit us once in New Brunswick and came to our Fiftieth at the Heinrichs in 1999, we took advantage of their hospitality more frequently over the years, especially as I was invited to join the Yarrow Reseach Committee which met annually in Abbotsford for ten years beginning in 1998.

Three 'Daughters'

After about fifteen years in Calgary, we have derived much satisfaction and joy from the informal but meaningful 'adoption' of three daughters, AnnaLiese, Maureen, and Sherry. You see, it was almost inevitable, given Justina's proclivity for making friends that she would not discourage certain persons younger than herself to consider her as a mother figure. When Justina joined the White Hat Volunteers as a greeter at the Calgary International Airport (YYC) about 1998, and was assigned to the Tuesday afternoon shift, she met **AnnaLiese**, who is German. Once AnnaLiese had shared her story of addiction, recovery, and extensive volunteer work with Justina and found a sympathetic listener, she soon began to call her "Mutti" (one expression of mother in German) and relies on Justina in significant ways.

Two of our 'adopted' daughters, Maureen Proctor and Sherry Rainsforth (Austin), 2009

When Justina began going to YYC on Sunday afternoons to help with the reception of German speakers coming off the Frankfurt flights she met **Maureen,** the daughter of an Irish father and a Metis mother, and brought up Catholic. When her husband died of cancer in 1995, he left her without children, in good health, and siblings living quite far away. As her summer car she drives a red Mustang convertible dating from 1995. She has many friends, loves to entertain, but turned actively towards volunteering, joined the Red Hat Society and the White Hatters. About 2007 Maureen started calling Justina 'Mom' and they became very attached to each other. By the time of our Sixtieth, Maureen had become an integral member of our adoptive family, giving tremendously helpful assistance to Justina because she is so knowledgeable, hard-working, efficient, and supportive.

Sherry and I met in the Rotary Club of Calgary South sometime after she was inducted in 2001. She was married to Randy, a successful engineer who unfortunately got flesh-eating disease and died, shockingly, within a few hours. That was in 2004. Following this tragic loss, both Justina and I came close to her, not knowing that about three years later she would begin to hint that she would like to be 'adopted' by us even though she had a biological family only four hours away.

We discovered gradually that her career began as a chemistry teacher. She earned a PhD in Educational Administration (postsecondary governance) and subsequently held senior administrative positions in several universities in British Columbia and Alberta. In this connection she had the chance to travel to many parts of the world including Eastern Europe, Australia, United States and South East Asia.

She was a member of the downtown Rotary Club in Edmonton when she took the job as Director of Conservation, Education and Research for the Calgary Zoological Society. Next, she became president of an Alberta consulting company involved in a series of diverse projects related to governance and regulatory authorities, strategic planning, policy development, corporate communications, and executive coaching. Sherry is younger than Maureen, has no children, but her weekday life is taken up with business responsibilities and at other times with her own circle of friends and her biological family in Bow Island. She has made a strong commitment to Rotary and as a sign of her performance and contributions to Calgary South, and her engaging personality and ability, she was elected as the first woman president of the Rotary Club of Calgary South for the year 2012-2013. At the time of writing she was engaged to be married to her friend Steve Austin of the Rotary Club of Calgary.

It must be obvious to all that we are blessed indeed.

Chapter Twelve

Involvements and Travels

Voluntary Service, Lithuania, 1997

In 1997 I was invited by the Abbotsford office of Lithuania Christian College (LCC) to teach as a volunteer in this recently established Christian college in Klaipeda (the former Memel) on the Baltic coast of Lithuania. Within a period of six years or so it had made tremendous advances with the support of the DeFehr Foundation of Canada, Winnipeg, and the assistance of long term and short term volunteers.

The simple idea was that a few key officers, professionals from North America and Lithuania, evangelicals all, were needed to administer the school. It was assumed that qualified professionals from Canada and the United States, mostly those in retirement, would be found to pay their own way for travel, housing, food needs, visa costs, and medical insurance. Their simple reward would be a sense of contributing to mission and to the development of a Christian University (in a Catholic country). Friends and acquaintances of ours had been there on that basis and had found the experience gratifying. So they said. As a result of some experiences there and a discussion with the executive secretary in Abbotsford, I wrote a somewhat critical assessment of LCC which I thought was deserved at that time.

While for us the experience was not wholly good, when asked to report to our home church in Calgary and other locations, we tried to be entirely positive. We had slides, prints on a stand-up fold-out, and we had a table for show and tell: books, a large map, tablecloths, banners, hangings, and amber. We could also show the 1995 calendar of Baltic Sea paintings by Edvardas Malinauskas, the most famous Lithuanian painter of seascapes. We lived in the Karklu Dorm, a ten minute-walk from the LCC Dorm which housed half the staff and the administrative offices, also some classrooms. This dorm, originally built during the centralizing Soviet regime, was completely renovated with money and volunteers from North America at a cost of about $500,000.

Our favorite was a "Currents Events" class in which I was expected to use current affairs topics to upgrade their English skills: comprehension, vocabulary, writing and speaking skills. We told First Mennonite Church about the table in our flat in Karklu laden with Canadian and Lithuanian food for a Christmas party with that class. Underneath that table covering was dried straw (hay) that a member of the class had brought with her from her home in Kaunus. An indigenous custom dictates the drawing of straws to help predict what the next year will bring. (I drew a short straw with some tassels on it. Interpreted, this meant that I might not live too long, but I would probably get home safely!)

The Rotary Connection in Lithuania

We were well on our way to being persuaded to engage with LCC along the lines described, when a friend in Rotary, Terry Allen, told me I could apply to Rotary International for travel and per diem support. Terry argued that I would surely qualify for funds from the RI Voluntary Program if I was going to teach two history courses at LCC, while Justina, a member with me of the Partners of Calgary South Rotary would be working in the Library. It was also necessary to have the Rotary Club of Klaipeda sponsor me in order to get financial assistance. This was made possible when an English speaking member, Mindaugas Karalius, a shipper who lived in Palanga, stood as my sponsor and proved most helpful and hospitable. I attended this Club every Tuesday by walking to their meeting. The current

President and a medical doctor member spoke German; the Mayor and a few others spoke English, enough to get by. By the end of the term I was told they would like to have me as a full-time member.

Amber (*Bernstein*) Museum, Palanga

Not far away in Palanga, a former castle built 100 years ago by a Polish count (under the Tsarist system), was remodeled to house the Amber Museum. It contains 25,000 pieces of amber, Lithuanian gold. We brought home a sampler in a magnifying glass which shows a dozen stones which have captured Jurassic insects from ages and ages ago. It was Justina`s Christmas gift to me.

Palanga also has an airport with flights for business men to various centers surrounding the Baltic, like Minsk, Warsaw, St. Petersburg, and Copenhagen. In the 1970s members of the Politbureau of the Soviet Union found this park a good alternative to Yalta. Premier Brezhnev liked Palanga, it was said.

Palanga's streets, the park, and the beaches are elbow to elbow with people during the summer months. The beaches are superior, a hundred kilometres in length from Kaliningrad (the former Koenigsburg) to Riga, and all along Klaipeda and Palanga. From the beach opposite Klaipeda, after walking across the Slip (huge sand dunes which act like a dike against the sea), one can see ships entering the harbor; north of Palanga we saw a statue of three women looking out to sea for the return of their husbands (or lovers).

Klaipeda, Old and Recent

The statue of Anne of Tharau, restored in 1989, recalls the poet Simon Dach (17th C). It stands in cobble-stoned Theater Square in front of the building where Hitler spoke in 1939, after marching through Poland. He naturally reclaimed Klaipeda (Memel) as capital of *Klein Litau*, part of East Prussia for seven hundred years.

We were living not far from a house of classical lines which was used as the palace of King Frederick of Prussia following his defeat by Napoleon who was on his way to Moscow in 1812. Among the many sites we visited was a famous Clock Museum. Had I stayed longer I could have helped Martinus, the curator, prepare a new brochure or booklet in English.

We enjoyed watching three seasons out of our window at Karklu overlooking the basketball court. Gorgeous summer and fall it was; the trees, maple and chestnut were wonderful; and Klaipeda had a walk-through boulevard, from the marriage palace at the west end to the sculpture park on the east side, showing some of the older architecture. Here and there the red brick of the Prussian style stood out, especially on the campus of Klaipeda University and in the old Post Office with its Carillon Tower.

The market, seven days a week, with its meat and flower building and the flea market, so called, also had many who sold out of the trunks of their cars. Everything under the sun was available. There was also a huge car market for exchange and upgrading!

The Janzen Family Reunion, 1997

On the way home from Lithuania we stopped to visit Justina's *Aussiedler* cousins in Germany once again, this time in order to celebrate Christmas with them. After all, five years was a long time for Justina, having gotten used to seeing some of them every few years. This time we flew from Frankfurt to Duesseldorf which was only two hours by car from Bielefeld. On this occasion, staying with Peter and Susanna Janzen in Heepen (part of Bielefeld), we were surprised with the promise of a Janzen family reunion at Willingen, a Christian retreat centre and ski resort south of Paderborn. We felt quite overwhelmed. Not only would we be together from Friday evening to Sunday noon, but we could take photos of the whole group and individual families and start a family tree, something we did not have until then.

When we left Sunday after lunch, we were faced with a steep decline covered with snow which had fallen overnight. There was no snow blower and the people running this Centre had not graveled the hill saying they wanted to remain *"naturfreundlich"* (environment friendly). But that did not alter the fact that we had to get fourteen automobiles down that very steep decline safely. That took about two hours – men holding and pulling back with ropes, thus moving the cars down slowly and keeping them in the center of the road. What a hoot! There were no fender-benders and no injuries.

After this, back in Bielefeld with Peter Janzens, we also took in the ``*Kristkindel Markt*`` (Christmas market). This was most enjoyable as great Christmas music was being piped in for the shoppers.

Travelling with Peter Wiebe, Leopoldshoehe

On our visit to Germany in 2001 we were invited to Leopoldshoehe, near Bielefeld, where Peter Wiebe, son of Tina (Janzen) Wiebe, offered to take us to Warin, Mecklenberg, to visit his brother-in-law, Gunter Killer. On the way he wanted to look up the village of **Wiebendorf**. This proved very interesting, though no one in the village had any inkling how Wiebendorf got its name. I could only conjecture that a Wiebe family lived in the area in say, the seventeenth century, during the migration of Dutch Mennonites to the Danzig area.

Gunter and his wife showed us around Warin, though the castle of the *Herzog* of Mecklenberg was of greatest interest. We were taken to the coast of the Baltic Sea, and learned how good it is to take a boat from one of these ports to the main cities along the east coast, especially for our interest, Klaipeda, Lithuania. On the way home, driving on the *Autobahn* between Hannover and Bielefeld, Peter drove his five-year Audi over two hundred kilometres an hour. This was not entirely comfortable.

The Letkemann Family on the Rhine

The only family missing from the Willingen event was the Letkemann family whose male members, Heinrich, Peter, and Johann, lived near the Rhine River, from Wiesbaden to Neuwied. Once we had met the Peter Letkemann family, resident in nearby Taunusstein in 1992 it was hard to obliterate them from one's memory: Peter and Nadia (a lovely Russian mother who knew little German) with six children, four girls and two boys. We were introduced to them by Sarah and Peter Braun, Frankenthal, Phalz, Sarah being the cousin of both Peter and Justina.

Peter Letkemann Family at Larissa's wedding: two sons, four daughters: Eugene, Paul (with Tina), Leona, Peter, Larissa and Wadim, Nadia, Irene and Natalie, 2004

The Letkemann family attend a Baptist (MB) Church [17] in Wiesbaden. Though the church acts as a morality guide, the Letkemann family are cheerful, outgoing, and acculturated to the region's industry,

---

17 In the Soviet Union many Mennonite congregations joined with those Baptists that were registered with the Government.

business, and the latest styles. We always felt at ease with them. This photo shows the entire Peter Letkemann family on the occasion of Larissa's marriage to Wadim in 2004.

At home we broke our hospitality rule several times for the Letkemann family. We had a visit from Larissa and Natalie some years ago. This proved most enjoyable. We also had Paul and Tina here for several days in 2005. Natalie (Letkemann) and her husband Paul Tjart, with Paul's brother Peter and wife Lillian, who were living in Indiana, came in 2011, bringing their little darling Sarah.

To Cambridge with the Heinrichs

In 2001 we went to London to visit both Roy and Audrey Smith who had moved from Richmond to Teddington, and Vern and Frieda Heinrichs who until recently spent part of each year in their flat in Mayfair. On this occasion Justina and Frieda cooked a complete Indian meal and we had the pleasure of having the company of famous mystery novelist P.D. James, a member of the House of Lords, who is a close friend of the Heinrichs. After that Vern and Frieda took us to Cambridge to be guests of Sir David and Lady Rachel Willcocks. This plan seems to have arisen out of Justina`s earlier invitation from Frieda to be present when Sir David Willcocks was in Toronto from Kings College, Cambridege. Being able to share breakfast with him was a great privilege for her. Once in Cambridge, we saw Sir Richard conduct one of his choirs in Kings College Chapel. Then we were privileged to have dinner around the Willcocks dining room table. Dennis and Susan Wright from St. John's, Newfoundland, were there too as Susan was touring with her prize-winning choir in England and was privileged to show off their talent in the famous Chapel.

Like many other lovers of choral music, Justina was saddened to hear of the death, at age 95, of Sir David in September 2015

The Wiens Family, Cousins of the Steingarts

What follows is the story of how Justina learned about the Wiens equation we never knew about: Two families in the Ukraine were joined together by marriage in 1897 and were separated in 1926-1927 by emigration. They did not meet again until 2003 and then only as second cousins. Why did it take so long?

For us this story was unique. This is part of the Steingart story, the family we celebrated in Winnipeg in 1995. The patriarch is Heinrich Steingart (1873-1957) and his first marriage was to Gertruda Wiens (1878-1922), the daughter of Abram and Justina (Toews) Wiens, Neu=Halbstadt, Sagradowka. Heinrich, it is conjectured, came to Sagradowka from the Molotschna as a young man, and found employment with Abram Wiens who had the equivalent of two farms (zwei Vollwirtschaften) and two of the best houses in this village of Neu=Halbstadt.[18] In time Heinrich was attracted to the young Gertruda and they married in 1897. Heinrich's presence and physical strength and probable know-how was appreciated because Gertruda came from a family where poor eyesight ran in the family. She had only one sister, and two brothers who were not of great help on the farm: Abram developed epilepsy, and Aron had poor vision.

What made Gertruda's case even more helpless was the fact that her father died in 1899, and her mother Justina in 1908. Gertruda and her siblings were thus orphaned. For these reasons Heinrich became a guardian to his brothers-in-law, as well as a tower of strength in the business of farming and therefore stood a good chance to inherit some of that property held by the Wienses.

Meanwhile, this marriage between Heinrich and Gertruda proved really fertile, in that Gertruda bore him ten children between 1899 and 1921– four girls and six boys. The eldest was Justina (1899-1992) the mother of my wife Justina Janzen Penner (1926 -). My Justina finally made the connection with a nephew of Gertruda, one Heinrich Wiens, but not before the year 2001.

---

18 Mennonite villages were compacted into two rows of houses on ample lots, while their acreages were assigned in the area surrounding the village. Mennonite villages were about fifteen kilometers apart.

Another sad part of the story was the death of Gertruda in 1922. She succumbed to the terrible scourge of typhoid which ravaged the villages during the famine years of 1921-22, a story well-known. This left all those children motherless. Her sister had married and went to Brazil; her epileptic brother had died (1918); and her poor-visioned brother Aron had meanwhile married Helene Regehr (1917), just in time to face the uncertainties of the Leninist Revolution.

Heinrich, badly needing a mother for his children, soon married Aganetha, the widow of Abram Walde, the one who suffered death at the hands of the Brigand Machno in 1919 in the village of Orloff, Sagradovka.[19] That marriage in 1923 brought five more children into the family. They also added a daughter, Nettie, born in 1925. This considerably enlarged family, where some had already married, took the revolutionary alarms to heart, sold what they could and emigrated to Manitoba in 1926-1927 where they settled on a small farm near Steinbach, Manitoba.

The Cousins Who Were Left Behind

Back in Russia, Aron and Helene (Regehr) Wiens, living elsewhere during the emigration years, were eventually forced into Stalin's Collective of the First Five Year Plan (1928-1932), where Aron, of poor vision, carried the mail from house to house. By this time, they had six children: Helena, Aron, Heinrich, Anna, Justina (Christel), and Jacob. How different was their lot!

In short, while Aron's wife Helene died in 1940, the others welcomed the German occupation of the Ukraine in 1941-1943. When, however, the Wehrmacht was defeated at Stalingrad, General Paulson ordered a retreat of his diminished troops. About 300,000 German-speaking settlers, inclusive of 30,000 Mennonites, also took what they could manage and joined this retreat in what for them became known

---

19 The Brigands took 213 lives during the nights of November 29-December 1, 1919 in eight Mennonite villages of Sagradowka, as listed at the end of Gerhard Lohrenz, *Sagradowka*. Rosthern, SK, Echo Verlag, 1947

as the 'Great Trek' of 1943 via Poland in the direction of Germany. Young Aron (born 1920) and Heinrich (born 1925) were impressed into the German army. Aron was taken as a war prisoner by the Soviet army, but eventually got to Germany, while Heinrich, captured by the Americans in Austria, was badly treated at first, and held there until his repatriation in 1946 into Soviet military hands with the cooperation of high-ranking American generals. This, Heinrich said, was like 'a sentence of death' and many around him chose suicide.

The rest of the family, Aron, and his daughters were repatriated and sent to Arkangelsk on the Arctic, where Aron died in 1945, while Helena the eldest, who never married, took the young Jacob in her care. These siblings all suffered the long years of the Gulag experience, until they were freed of the *Spetskomandantura* (Stalin's deportation regime) when Khrushchev came to power in 1956. All were able to move to a warmer climate, mostly to Kirgizia, where they found work, marriage partners, and worship opportunities.

Repatriated, Heinrich was sent on a 39-day railcar ride to the Pamir Mountains, north-east of Hindu-Kush. He was eventually assigned to a uranium mine where he worked for twenty years. Here he met his wife, an Anna Boschmann, whom he married in a civil ceremony. Together, they had a family of four children, three daughters, and one son, Helena, Anna, Agnes, and Heinrich.

Pathos in the Story

The pathos lies in the fact that the Wiens family members knew very little of the experience of others in the Soviet Union, and certainly knew nothing whatsoever of their relations in Canada, such as those Steingart siblings that for years had called Heinrich and Aganetha (Walde) Steingart their grandfather and grandmother. That large Steingart and Walde family had scattered over Canada. Whoever gave the Wienses a thought?

Heinrich and Anna Boschmann Wiens with their children came to Germany in 1988 under the repatriation program of Germany. They were received at Nuernberg and were assigned to Tuttlingen on the Danube river, in Baden-Wuertemburg. All the children, by then in their thirties, got good jobs. Four of Heinrich's siblings had preceded him and were settled 600 kilometers away in Hamm-Heesen, west of Bielefeld, Westphalia.

Once settled, Heinrich began to seek Steingart relatives and found an address for Aron Janzen in Coaldale. "Surely they will respond if I write them," he thought. They unfortunately did not. The letter of 1992 was apparently mislaid and left unanswered.

It was not until 2001 that Justina heard about Heinrich in Tuttlingen, and resolved to contact him. When she did, Heinrich was simply overjoyed and began to write something of his story. His ability in German as a "Low German Mennonite" (as he called himself) was fortunately much greater than many other *Aussiedler* had demonstrated.

Finally, Justina and I resolved to visit Heinrich and his siblings in October 2003. For this we rented a car and took to the Autobahn. Great experience it was, first south to Tuttlingen and then north to visit Helena, the eldest, born in 1918, then eighty-five years of age. Our appearance in Hamm-Heessen was 'a miracle,' she called it. As I editorialized: "The yearning for a communication, the knowledge that someone cared about a family that had been unfortunate in its passage through life, chosen or fated for punishment, loss, suffering, and lack of concern, or so it appeared, was profound. They were all so grateful. They lacked for nothing, one can say, except this touch of family, humanity, a sense of belonging restored!"

Chapter Thirteen

Voluntary Service with Rotary in Siberia

Three years after our Lithuania venture, in October, 2000, I went to Barnaul, Siberia, for a period of two months to do English as a second language (ESL). I was not qualified to do ESL at the most basic level, only to help those who had had some English. My sponsorship was made possible under Rotary International's Voluntary Program and by the fact that Rotary had been able to move into Russia, including Siberia, at the very end of the Communist regime, about 1989-1990.

My way was paid for two months. I was given hospitality by a Russian Rotarian, Oleg, a physicist at Altai State University, and his wife Ludmila, a high school physics teacher. They accommodated me in their seventh-floor two bedroom flat (Khruchev-style apartment block). People preferred these to the traditional cottages along the streets nearby. At least the apartments had heat and running water, an elevator and garbage disposal. Ludmila gave me good meals and Oleg had made the arrangements for me to help two different classes of adults who already had some elementary English. He also chauffeured me wherever I needed to go.

When some of the *Ruszlanddeutsche* (Germans in Russia – formerly Lutheran, Catholic, and Mennonite) in Barnaul heard about my coming and that I was equally facile in German and was hoping to visit my birthplace about four hundred kilometers away to the west, this doubled the interest for all the people I met. As a result my life was enriched by many experiences, encouraged as I was by the Barnaul Rotary Club to take advantage of these opportunities.

I was now in south-western Siberia, in the district of Altai, extending from Slavgorod in the west as the leading city for the Mennonite villages set in the vast Siberian *Kulundasteppe*, where I was born, to Gorno Altai in the east, nestled in the foothills of the Altai Mountains. Barnaul, a city of 650,000 with its 45,000 to 60,000 students attending the various parts of the Altai State University (ASU), sits at the center of this Region. It was only at the end of my two months that I managed to visit Akademgorodok, just south of Novosibirsk. I will leave that experience for later.

More Unusual Than Imagined

I had unexpected media exposure. People from the press wanted to know about my intended visit to my birth village and area. As a result there were two stories about me in Slavgorod's *Zeitung fuer Dich* ("Newspaper for You"), as well as in the Barnaul city newspaper (Russian). The mother of one of my students, Denis (who did well in three languages), interviewed me for a Barnaul German Radio program. This was aired in two instalments, while at a Russian/German cultural event I had a chance to speak briefly.

Oleg and Ludmila took me to see their *dacha* amidst a village of summer *dachas* (with their saunas and gardens) alongside the Ob River. We stopped at open markets; experienced the unusual phenomenon of Russian women hitchhiking alone along the highways, to get to town or the market. My hosts stopped for one such hitchhiker who climbed into the back seat beside me.

I was invited to visit ten schools where English was taught. One of these was the Barnaul School for Visually Impaired Children, whose Russian staff is shown. Invariably I had an exchange with the students and tried to answer their many questions. One class of children in a school for the gifted kept me going with questions in English for ninety minutes.

Staff of School for Visually Impaired, Barnaul, Siberia; Olga Polyanski, host, seated between the musicians, 2000

Meeting Johannes Schellenberg, 80, of whom I knew nothing, turned out to be important. He took me to meet his Russian wife, showed me the city, the German House, and then surprised me totally by signing over to me a copy of his history of my birth village Orlovo (in Russian). As a young man he had taught school there before becoming an editor of the regional newspaper. Perhaps the most significant thing he did was to take my host Oleg and me to visit the Barnaul archive housing the records of the repressive measures forced on *Ruszlanddeutsche* and Russians in the Altai by the NKVD (Russian secret police) during the period 1929-38. Archived here are about 42,000 cases of people who were repressed in the 1930s. Oleg, a Russian of about fifty years, away from home at the time while studying in the south, grew up without being aware that such things had taken place right there in his Altai region, in Slavgorod, at the Friesen mill converted by the NKVD into a jail. He came away appalled at the perpetration of those horrendous Stalinist crimes against humanity, including many more Russians than Germans. "Good God," he exclaimed, "what did these innocent people do to deserve such treatment?" Those archival resources were mostly in Russian, but some, even the minutest records of those repressive measures involving Germans were written in German.

Visit to My Birthplace

During a school break from my classes in Barnaul, Oleg and Boris, also a Rotarian, took me 400 kilometres west and south to Protassowo, one of the forty or so Mennonite villages planted in the Kalundasteppe between 1908 and 1912. This visit was brief, only five full days until my friends came to take me back to Barnaul at 140 kilometres an hour, a pretty bouncy ride!

Protassowo was the home village of my mother's cousin, Heinrich Krecker (sort of Low German for the family name Kroeker), who left for Germany with his family in 1993. During our visit to Justina's cousin in Bielefeld a few years after that, Heinrich and his wife Justina came from the village of Rietberg to meet us there. Heinrich offered to phone friends in Protassowo in case I could make arrangements to go to Siberia. In short, that is how I came to be welcomed and hosted by the Kornelius Baerg family in 2000.

One year later we were able to visit the Krecker family in Rietberg. Heinrich told me about collective life in the village of Protassowo. His story took me back to 1929 when Stalin's Collectivization was in full swing. The Mennonites asked: shall we voluntarily comply, thus losing our independence, or shall we resist, or even attempt flight to Moscow in hopes of getting out of Russia? That was the question. Unlike my grandparents the Wiebes and about 15,000 others who tried in 1929 to get out of Russia by seeking exit visas in Moscow, the Krecker family did not attempt to escape collectivization. They were spared a worse fate. Only about 5,500 got away via Germany, among them my grandparents. All the others (perhaps 10,000), were forcibly returned and subjected to severe repressive measures; many men were sent to Gulag locations for ten years hard labor, or were simply taken to Slavgorod, interrogated by the **NKVD** in the old Friesen mill converted to a prison (*die Gelbe Muehle*, the Yellow mill!), and then shot.

Even with compliance the Krecker family did not escape the Stalinist scourge. During the purges of 1937-1938, Heinrich's father was taken away as a 'Kulak' and never heard from again (as was an uncle of mine, Peter P. Wiebe). The family that remained, widow and son, was tied to the Karl Marx/Friedrich Engels *Kolkhoz* and that is where Heinrich grew up, married Justina Arndt, and they made do with his wages for an eight-hour day.

The Heinrich and Justina Krecker (Kroeker) family, Rietberg, Westphalia: Ludmila, wife of the tallest, Kolya, Oxana, Victor, Justina, Maria and Frank Dyck, Alexander, Heinrich, Peter and Justina, Andreas and Maria, Helena, Anna and Elizabeth; Abram Dueck, Alexander Braun, Waldemar Fischer, 2003

How did Heinrich manage? He learned mechanics, was attached to the Machine Tractor Station where he became the Head Mechanic. He was charged with keeping the Collective's farm machinery running for working the land, seeding and harvesting. All of them learned Russian as the official language, and spoke Low German at home and to their Mennonite friends. The children attended the Collective's composite school, probably to grade eleven, and medical needs were supplied by the State. Heinrich told how they always had a vehicle (a Lada), and over a thirty-year period, they built their second house for the growing family with the tallest sons in the village. In this photo the father of the eight children is behind me and I am nearly six feet tall. His tallest son is fully seven feet, and works as a window-installer. The two daughters wearing head coverings indicate that they are church members.

Obviously the children had all been taught to share in the chores in the busy household, tending to the garden and to their animals. Perhaps they were also assigned tasks in the Collective as they grew up. Of utmost importance was the quarter hectare (half acre) that every household had immediately behind their lot. Here they raised their own vegetables, and the manure created by perhaps two cows, pigs, hens, and ducks made their garden tremendously productive. Once in Germany the parents retained their Low German and their married children took lessons in German as provided.

The Baerg Family, Religion and Language

I was extremely sorry to learn that Heinrich had moved to Germany with his entire family before I visited his village in 2000. He would have been able to take adequate time to visit more former Mennonite villages. He lamented this also.

As it was, Kornelius Baerg took time from his job of supervising the Collective's sausage-making plant in Protassowo to take me around. First we went to Orlovo where I had to have my picture taken on that first street of 1908, and to meet Ivan Fast who remembered my grand-father Peter J. Wiebe. We toured the leading City of Slavgorod where I was introduced to Peter Isaak, leader of the very large Mennonite church, now emptying as members moved to Germany, as well as to the Mayor, a former Party functionary, who seemed professional by comparison. He gave me a carved spoon as a take-away souvenir.

It was a revealing visit. The parents and eldest Baerg daughter could speak German and Low German, but the younger siblings spoke only Russian. Two daughters had just gone to Germany to stay with relatives, hoping to find husbands! Protassowo in 2000 was no longer a Mennonite village, but a Russian-speaking community. The provision for German was too late for them when President Boris Yeltsin declared the region a German national area in 1992 and German was permitted in the schools. But, as the Volga Deutsch Principal and his Dean of Students, a Mennonite, explained, the language level in the prescribed texts was far too difficult for the children. It was a fact that literary German, once the language of home, church, and the town square in earlier Mennonite villages was gone. The mother-tongue of Mennonites and Volga Germans now became their 'second' language.

Yet it was the Low German language that saved any Mennonite culture for many of the older generation. It was also a language which no one could take away from them, even in the Trudarmee (Labor Army [Arbeitsarmee]) or in the Gulag. It was also the language which gave us instant rapport when we visited those relatives of ours who came to Germany as Aussiedler [Justina's cousins].

The 'Siberian Initiative'

As the end of my two months was approaching, I asked Oleg whether I might spend the last three days in Novosibirsk. Without much ado he was able to find a Rotarian member who would host me for those days. Elena lived in Akademgorodok (Academic Town) which had the Soviet Union's largest Scientific Centre east of the Ural Mountains. It was founded in 1957 just south of Novosibirsk in a deeply forested area – an attractive place.

Like Schellenberg in Barnaul, Elena was a pleasant surprise in Akademgorodok. She, an Economist, in the short time I was there managed to arrange personal tours of several unusual museums: one holding pieces of every precious stone found in Siberia, huge, indicating the enormous wealth of that vast land, and the other holding

Siberian mummies. When I asked whether I might meet some of the historians on campus, Elena, knowing the timetables being used, hurried me over to the History office where I was introduced to Andrej Savin. Fortunately he was fully German-speaking, was between classes, but had no more than twenty minutes. He already had an impressive list of articles about Germans in Siberia, including joint authorship with Detlef Brandes, Duesseldorf, Germany, of *"Sibiriendeutsche im Sowjetsystem 1920 – 1941"* (*Siberian Germans in the Soviet System, 1920-1941*). Hardly could I know at that moment that he would be willing to research Soviet archives to find items of great significance to all Mennonites.

I soon discovered that Russian scholars seemed to have a head start in telling the story of the Stalin Terror. Savin was one of them. Many articles and books had been written during the previous fifteen years in Siberia. After meeting Savin and thinking of the research that could and should be done, it seemed obvious to me that those with complete Russian language skills and knowledge of the archives, and the ways of Russian archivists, would do better at digging out the sources of interest to Mennonites than persons from abroad with weak language skills and facing many frustrations.

Much must be omitted here, but I got an encouraging response from Mennonite historians from Western Canada and from Paul Toews in Fresno when I told my story of how I managed with the help of a Rotarian in Akademgorodok, outside of Novosibirsk, to make contact with several historians and to discover Andrej Savin to whom I spoke in his office.

Paul Toews wrote me in May 2006 that he continued to think of my encounter with Andrej Savin as "extremely fortunate. Your sense that he was someone with whom we could work has led to this very significant 'Siberian Mennonite Research Project' which I hope will continue...." Of the nearly 500 page book released in March of that year entitled *Ethno Confessions in a Soviet State: Siberian Mennonites, 1920-1980: Annotated Listing of Archival Documents and Materials, Selected Documents* Paul wrote: this is a "very impressive work. In fact I think it is the most significant work done in "Russian" Mennonite history by the new generation of post-Soviet scholars in the Commonwealth of Independent States (CIS)."

For this reason it is a pleasure to recall that in 2001-02 the persons I photographed here launched what came to be called a "Siberian Initiative." As a result of these advances and a growing interest in Siberia, Royden Loewen, Chair in Mennonite Studies, University of Winnipeg, chose a committee to spearhead the organization of a Mennonite History Conference projected for 2010 in succession to the history conferences that had been organized in the Ukraine a decade earlier. The outcome of this activity, supported by Russian scholars, was a successful conference held at a University in Omsk with good Mennonite scholarly participation from abroad. When Volume 30 of the *Journal of Mennonite Studies*, published early in 2012, came to my desk, Royden Loewen not only provided the names of the Winnipeg committee as well as that of the Omsk University that ultimately put this all together, but he was good enough to write that "special mention is extended to Professor Peter Penner who inspired the idea of the conference in the region of his birth, but in the end was unable to attend."

'Siberian Initiative' group: Lawrence Klippenstein, James Urry, Ted Regehr, Dave Giesbrecht, Walter Unger, Paul Toews, in Winnipeg, 2001

Germans from Russia, AHSGR, Leader, SK

As already told, not long after settling into Calgary life in 1995, I was asked to give a lecture at the Convention of the American Historical

Society of Germans from Russia (AHSGR). Twice more was I invited to speak at the annual convention of the AHSGR, first in Yakima, WA, in June 2003; and much later in 2009 when the Calgary Chapter hosted the convention in Medicine Hat, Alberta.

As a result of this involvement we were invited to share in the German Festival organized by Tim Geiger, a well-to-do grain farmer at Leader, Saskatchewan. This is a main center for many Germans from Russia who came to Canada before World War One, during Clifford Sifton's time as Immigration Minister in the Wilfrid Laurier government (1896-1911). Geiger's people did not want to join the AHSGR or the parallel group in Fargo, ND, but were willing to organize a festival in Leader in 2004. We were amazed to find up to six hundred persons gathered in this town of no more than six hundred residents. All told, it was a phenomenal success and worthy of a second try some years later. We supported the efforts of our Calgary Chapter – Leona and Gerry Mann and Mabel and Fritz Kiesling – to bring the Chapter's Library of books to the Festival. We were billeted by the young Mennonite family of Steve and Debbie Bueckert, both school teachers locally, with children Christi and Daniel. We went back two more times and each time Debbie insisted that we stay with them rather than stay in the local hotel.

Chapter Fourteen

Research and Writings in Retirement

During the nine years, beginning in 1988, that I worked on the story of the Mennonite Brethren missionary effort in India, a whole host of other topics interested me. Articles, reviews, and other books in the making kept me busy. As the Old Testament writer of Ecclesiastes observed at the end of chapter twelve: "Of the making of many books there is no end; and much study is weariness to the flesh."

The India Mission: Discovering the True Story

What follows is an account of what it meant to try to give readers an understanding of what Mennonite Brethren tried to accomplish in Andhra Pradesh, India, between 1885 and 1975. The Mennonite Brethren were only one of many church conferences that had been sponsoring such missions since the beginning of the modern missionary age associated with the name of William Carey in 1792. In fact, the large field in Andhra Pradesh assigned to the Mennonite Brethren was surrounded, as it were, by Lutheran, Baptist, and Catholic missions, to name a few.

Paul Toews, the director of the Centre for Mennonite Brethren Studies, Fresno, gave me a working carrel where I could leave my research work overnight. The records in Fresno were found to be complete and profuse: missionary correspondence, India missionary council records, Board correspondence and minutes, besides a complete run of the Hillsboro, Kansas-based *Zionsbote* (Messenger of Zion, 1880s to 1960s) in which many missionary letters were printed verbatim until about 1953.

What I was not prepared for was how distressful the unfolding of the story would be for me personally. The many stressful situations discovered in the files and the cover-ups were almost too much. I soon concluded that any tragic situation that proved embarrassing to missionary or board – like accidental deaths involving India personnel – was not told, while any tragic event which could be turned to the glory of God and would encourage giving was told. How was I ever going to deal truthfully with personal empire-building, ego-tripping, the pecking order, or the causes of missionary shipwreck after one term?

Well, after starting on this project, I had three years of teaching to reflect on that problem. I spent much of the intervening months writing letters and arranging for interviews as I had opportunity to travel. During the 1990 Mennonite World Conference in Winnipeg I interviewed Donald Unruh who was a 10-year old in 1952 when his father was faulted for the drowning of an Indian servant. The incident had to be reported to the Board in Hillsboro. An ex-missionary, an eyewitness of that tragedy, told me that the India Missionary Council decided the story would go no further. And the Board in Hillsboro thought the same. After those nearly forty years Donald was prepared to tell me in detail what I had almost been afraid to ask about.

Along the way other retired missionaries were most helpful in answering direct questions that grew out of my reading of the missionary correspondence.

The Trip to Shamshabad, Andhra Pradesh, India

While in Winnipeg at the Mennonite World Conference in 1990 we were able to meet the Mennonite Brethren delegation from India. Given that I had already initiated correspondence with Dr. P.B. Arnold, President of the India MB Conference, about visiting India on the occasion of the 100th anniversary (1889-1989), it was simple to get a reinforcement of the invitation to be there. Justina then persuaded me that she should go too. When the Sears Travel Agent in Moncton, New Brunswick, was able to get Justina on the same flight as mine, and at a 'sale price,' we decided to do this together.

A resting place at entrance to Abe Friesen's Nalgonda: M.C. Emmanuel, under the Banyan tree, the sacred cattle omnipresent

The Air Canada agents at the Halifax Airport, surprisingly, put us into Executive Class to Heathrow, and then into First Class to Bombay (Mumbai). Following an interesting overnight stay in the JAL Hotel, we flew by airbus to Hyderabad, where M.C. Emmanuel, whom we knew from Winnipeg, met us. His assistance in so many ways was immeasurable. He introduced us to Bethel Church, Hyderabad, and saw us ensconced in the well-preserved Ritz Hotel.

For Justina this was another of those trips of a lifetime. She coped with uncomfortable situations on Sunday, October 7, 1990, with common sense and Christian courtesy. M.C. Emmanuel (since deceased) rented a car (an Ambassador) and took us to his home to meet his family, also gave us a tour of Hyderabad. Also, with his son Menno driving, he took us to old missionary compounds in remote villages which had been built first around 1900 by A.J. Friesen and A.J. Huebert, some of the first missionaries from Russia.

This experience was beyond our wildest dreams. To see the church buildings and the contrasting bungalows these two built, and to meet such a large part of the one congregation, and eat with them, using fingers only, was beyond our expectations. The highlight for Justina was being asked to speak to the children of a Mother Teresa School that was nearby.

From this experience Emmanuel took us to Shamshabad, one of the earliest mission compounds. These usually consisted of a bungalow for the missionary 'in station,' a church, school, and hospital, or just a dispensary. On this compound there was also a Bible institute that was named after Daniel Bergthold, another of the first American missionaries to arrive on this field.

There we were welcomed by a special lady named Chandraleela, the hostess of the old Ladies' Bungalow built by the American missionary John Lohrenz. She took care of us until the weekend of the great celebration. The women on the compound in Shamshabad liked Justina because she took a warm interest in them and wanted to see where they lived and how they managed. At the Celebration on the weekend where I had a chance to speak and show my slides of the mission, Justina discovered that she was the only white woman in that congregation of about 4,000. The women seated around her were pleased to see her wearing a lovely sari.

Return to Fresno

In 1992, having retired, I decided to return to Fresno to complete the research, especially in the *Zionsbote,* the German-language review. I also made hard copy of documents that seemed most important and which I brought with me to Sackville. We took the long road home, eighteen days, around the Deep South, taking in New Orleans, the Georgia coastline with its historic buildings, and many other things worth seeing. We had the opportunity to visit with Herb and Margaret (Penner) Schwarz who live near Harrisonburg, VA. Margaret is the daughter of John and Anna Penner, about whom I had written in connection with their work at Mahbubnagar and Suryapet. She was one of the last persons to be interviewed. I had already contacted her sisters and her brother Waldo in Ontario. Herb Schwarz was my forerunner in Toronto in 1962.

Because we were contemplating a move to Calgary, I hastened to complete a first draft so that by April 1994 Paul Toews was reading some of my chapters and was glad to see that I had gotten away completely from the "providential and piety" framework of earlier books by other authors. By October 1994 I was ready to give him the manuscript which would be read by three 'experts' for a thorough testing as to content, tone and image, organization, and conclusions.

I discovered later that these were Elmer Martens, Paul Hiebert, and Paul Wiebe. Elmer had experience on the Board, Paul Hiebert had been in India as a missionary and had become a noted anthropologist, while both Hiebert and Wiebe were India MKs (missionary kids, as they were called). Paul Wiebe was the principal of the American Kodaikanal International School. All were authors of a variety of works in theology, missiology, and sociology, respectively. After making all the corrections and revisions that I thought it possible to make, I needed to finalize the choice of photos, limited as I was to about thirty-five, and to have a cartographer at Fresno State University make two maps to help the reader place the mission in its geographical setting in Andhra Pradesh.

All of this resulted in a fine-looking book published under a title chosen by Kindred Productions (or by Paul himself): *Russians, North Americans, and Telugus: The MB Mission in India, 1885-1975* (1997). In all, of 400 pages, I had 100 pages of endnotes, maps, two sets of photos nicely arranged, a complete list of missionaries with biographical details, and an Index.

Missionaries from Ukraine: Standing: John and Anna Penner, Katharina Huebert, Aganetha Neufeld,; seated: Franz and Marie Wiens, Abram Huebert, Abram Friesen; three Wiens boys: Henry, Frank (on lap) and Jacob, 1914

Altering the Image of the Mission

When I first started I had no guarantee that the Historical Commission of the Mennonite Brethren Conference would accept the manuscript that might result. What the Director wanted from the beginning, however, was that I should finally 'demythologize the India mission.' I had intended and I was encouraged to tell an honest, open, story. As the son of a chief administrator of the Mission, Paul Toews saw incongruity between image and reality. When I became distressed again by what I was discovering in the missionary correspondence, I was quite determined to do what Paul wanted: 'demythologize' the Mission. This I did by letting all the human interest aspects of life and death, word and work, and the rhythm of life between the plains and the hills, unfold, or unravel.

Paul and Kevin Enns-Rempel, Archivist, did not challenge the openness and honesty with which I dealt with the story, even though hardly a missionary or board member remained on the pedestal! The missionaries provided a great human interest story in line with

Shakespeare's maxim: "All the world's a stage and all the men and women merely players." No one of us would have done any better. My interviews with those that only lasted one term convinced me that to have 'failed' in India was not a disgrace.

Of course I could not leave this work without a "legacy" chapter to end the manuscript. While I could not end without pointing to the colonial remnants in the struggle for control of property and institutions, I could write of the positive legacy in the India MB church with its enormous potential where and when the Spirit of God is in control.[20]

The Response

What could I say? I waited in vain for some missionary to write to say 'thank you', or 'what in God's name did you think you were doing! You have destroyed the image of the India Mission.' My guess is that they did not like it well enough to say thank you, or they were too embarrassed by the documented truthfulness of the whole to criticize or, in fact, few read it. I also waited in vain for a word of appreciation from the Historical Commission as such.

There were several published reviews. There was a good word from Katie Funk Wiebe, Wichita, KS, writer of some fame, on my treatment of the women and her disbelief at all the stories that had been covered up. The most significant review came from the pen of Clarence Hiebert, Tabor College, Hillsboro, published in *Direction*, the Review of the MB Biblical Seminary, Fresno. This is an excellent review, though he ends on a critical note, as indeed, I suspect, nearly all missionaries would if indeed they read the book.[21] As anthropologist Jake A. Loewen, Abbotsford, said to me, I was a bit too clinical!

---

20 Paul Wiebe has most ably written about that Legacy in his *Heirs and Joint Heirs, Mission to Church Among the Mennonite Brethren of Andhra Pradesh*, Kindred Productions, 2010

21 *Russians, North Americans and Telugus in India: The Mennonite Brethren Mission in India, 1885-1975*. Direction, Vol. 28 No. 2 (Fall 1999), pp. 262–65

A daughter of one of the missionaries, Carol Hamm, wrote a brief review for the *Mennonite Brethren Herald*. Here is part of her review:

"Penner's concern is to present a truthful account; thus, there is a need to reveal previously undisclosed facts. He handles these with sensitivity and impartiality, revealing the many complex factors at work without negatively judging those involved. He appreciates the unusual circumstances faced by India missionaries: the harsh climate, the separation of families, the feeling of exile from home and the difficulties in communicating with the home board. Penner succeeds in portraying missionaries as "unforgettable characters" and "real human beings." He must be commended for highlighting the often glossed-over commitment and contribution of single women to the work of the mission."

A third review was found in Amazon advertising entitled "An unusually frank look at a mission effort," July 2, 2000, by a Customer:

> Penner has written a rare history of missions because he neither sanctifies nor demonizes the work and workers in south India. It seems like most of the mission books I've read either attack missionaries as zealous destroyers of culture OR as saints who could do no wrong. Those of us who work in missions know that the story is much more complex than that. To be frank, I am the only person I know who has good things to say about this book! (I've only spoken with about five people who've read it from cover to cover but I'm picking up on a trend.) I prefer that my heroes be real people and I don't find it intimidating to learn they have flaws or weaknesses.... Reading it with my personal framework, I found Penner's book surprisingly inspiring. I can also understand why others would find it hard to read and you should be forewarned if you are a child of one of the missionaries mentioned. This book has such a narrow potential audience—mostly Mennonites with an interest in India and some missiologists—that I have to commend Penner for taking the risk of writing frankly.

A lesser historian and writer would have succumbed to the temptation to write another "feel good" book on missions. Lastly, I want to commend Penner on his skill as a writer which is much better than most books published at this level.

Imagine how thankful I was when the late Hugo Jantz, my friend from MBBC days, wrote me in August 2002 saying he had come upon this book in a store, bought it, took it home and read it through (practically) in one sitting. After doing so, he wrote: "This book alone makes you a very important and lasting gift to the Mennonite Brethren Church and far beyond, in my opinion. I congratulate you!"

Robert Frykenberg, my scholarly friend from Madison Wisconsin, and one who grew up in India with Paul Hiebert and Paul Wiebe and thus learned to know the Mennonite Brethren mission, expressed himself this way with reference to this study: "The nexus of faith and learning that has epitomized" [Penner's] career "can best be seen in the study of the MB mission in Andhra Pradesh. This, indeed, was one of his finest works ... This research brought together the accumulated and finely honed scholarly skills, both historical and theological, that Peter Penner possessed."

The Rotary History

In the background of these research activities there was always the weekly Rotary meeting with its inestimable fellowship. Rotary's members are chosen from business, holding positions as managers and up, and the professions. The aim is to bring together persons, men and women, from as many occupational classifications as possible, each willing to subscribe to the motto: Service above Self!

Given that the Rotary Club of Calgary South had had persons in the Club who were conscious of the need to maintain the records, it was relatively easy for leading members to think that a fifty-year history (1955-2005) should be produced, especially so when they came to recognize that they had a professional historian in their membership, namely myself. Thus it was that Bryan Targett as President in 2001 asked me to consider undertaking this task.

What pleased me above all was that here I was given complete trust by the Executive and a supervising history committee to do with the records as I saw fit. The result was to tell the history of this vigorous club, setting it into the context of Rotary's founding in 1905 and being chartered in 1955 by Calgary`s First Club, organized in 1913.

To assist me, early in 2002 Robert (Bob) Brawn, extraordinary entrepreneur in the oil and gas industry in Alberta, gave me a large office at Fifth Avenue and Third Street. George Adam, our only remaining charter member, who had carefully organized all the records, saw to the transfer of all the accumulated records to this fourth floor office; and Mel Gray provided a complete computer system in order to undertake this project.

Having the working office downtown allowed me to take the train instead of the car. There was a ten-minute walk from the house, train travel of seventeen minutes from Rundle Station, and five minutes-walk to my 'office.' This was a good combination for exercise and working hours. What is more I had access to the Plus Fifteen (the street crossover walk) for coffee and some recreation. I reported to my committee quarterly as I purposed "to publish a readable, understandable, and enjoyable history of Calgary South which does justice to its background in Rotary, its membership and its partners, and is guided, essentially, by the Four-Way Test of honesty, fairness, goodwill, and integrity. I was able to complete the 380 page book within three years, including George Adam's list of members, a brief foreword from Bob Watson in which he coined the apt phrase to describe the character of this Club, *irreverent integrity.*

In his testimonial, Mel Gray wrote rather too modestly of his contribution:

> In 2005 our Club celebrated the 50th anniversary of its founding coincidently with the 100th anniversary of the founding of Rotary. In honor of these anniversaries Dr. Penner researched and produced a volume of history of our Club. Peter's work set a new standard of excellence

in Rotary historical presentations. I was pleased to provide Peter with a bit of assistance with the photos from our Rotary Club archives.

Manchester to Calgary South, 1955 to 2005: Rotary Fellowship in Action was published in the fall of 2004 (printed by Friesen's, Altona) and President Terry Allen organized a full-scale book launching for November 19th, held at Fort Calgary where the Elbow and the Bow rivers meet. The book launch drew about 200 people. My brief speech was followed by Justina, having been asked, unexpectedly, to say a few words. So she said offhand what she had just found in the *Readers Digest* that day: "behind every great man is a woman who rolls her eyes." That brought the house down. Trust Justina! This party, arranged by Terry Allen, brought us much pleasure and many friends.

Every member of the Club received a copy at a low price because Bob Brawn had given a substantial sum toward the expenses of printing this beautiful book with its four signatures of full colour photos. For some years every new member was given a copy in their packet of information. While 500 copies were ordered, there was an overrun of 82 copies.

GAMEO, 2002-2008

I was fortunate to be asked in 2002 to join the board of what was then the Canadian Mennonite Encyclopedia initiated by the Mennonite Historical Society of Canada. A full explanation of the development of the encyclopedia in 1996 is available on the internet. Beginning in 2005 various conferences began to join the effort to create the English-language Global Anabaptist Mennonite Encyclopedia Online (GAMEO). In January 2011 there were around 15,000 articles in GAMEO, providing "information on Anabaptist-related congregations, denominations, conferences, institutions and significant individuals, as well as historical and theological topics. Secular subject articles from an Anabaptist perspective and full-text source documents are also included."

The experience and fellowship with this group of representatives from Ontario to British Columbia was a good one. Nevertheless I felt in 2008 that I should resign as I was not pulling my weight. I conveyed to the editorial board of GAMEO that it was not easy to be the representative in Alberta. One had to cope with the great distances between the Mennonite communities. Those that actively support the Mennonite Historical Society of Alberta with its archive and library are relatively few in number. The Manitoba and British Columbia members on the board surely found their work more rewarding. So I lost interest in doing GAMEO-type research and writing. After all, I would be 84 in April 2008 and as the writer of Ecclesiastes would have said: there is a time to stay and a time to go!

I count it as a privilege to have contributed two full-scale researched books on the Mennonite Brethren Church (1987 and 1997), and countless articles and reviews on various aspects of the Canadian Mennonite experience; to have been a member of the GAMEO board for six years, and a member of the board of *Mennonite Reporter* for nine years (1982–1991).

The Yarrow Research Committee (YRC)

It was like a bolt out of the blue towards the end of 1998 to be asked by Harvey Neufeldt, son of Peter Neufeldt, to serve as an advisor on the "Yarrow Project" which he and Jake A. Loewen had been planning for some time. Because I had been part of the story from 1957 to 1960 and had written *Reaching the Otherwise Unreached: A History of the West Coast Children's Mission* (1939–59), I was able to join the first brainstorming session in March 1999 in Abbotsford, BC. Harvey Neufeldt, chair, lived in Tennessee, and Leonard Neufeldt, Harvey's cousin, retired from Purdue University, lived in Gig Harbour, Washington. The co-chairs Jake and Anne Loewen, hosts, lived in Abbotsford, and Len's sister, Lora (Mrs. Rolly) Sawatsky, in Chilliwack, but all had grown up in the Yarrow Mennonite Brethern Church when John A. Harder was pastor. These and others from Yarrow, a Mennonite town nestled below Vedder Mountain and near Majuba Hill, gathered around Jake Loewen to do this sociological/historical study of Yarrow for the years 1928 to 1960. Over a ten-year period during which the Yarrow Research Committee (YRC) published five volumes, I was able to contribute five chapters and wrote the minutes of the annual meetings for five years.

Yarrow Research Committee: Harold Dyck, Leonard Neufeldt, Jake and Anne Loewen, Esther Epp Harder, Agatha Klassen, and Harvey Neufeldt, 1999

Grace Presbyterian Church, 2008

In 2001 we withdrew our memberships from First Mennonite Church in favor of Grace Presbyterian Church. We were now worshipping in one of Calgary's oldest, most beautiful sandstone churches located in the Beltline. As Cindy Stephens of the *Calgary Herald* wrote on December 29th, "Standing strong and welcoming at the corner of 15th Avenue and 9th Street SW, Grace has faithfully served as a house of worship for many of our city's most prominent citizens, such as the Gunn, Bell, Snowden, Rozsa and Mannix families."

What was however most important for us at the time was the wonderful church music we could anticipate at Grace Church: a magnificent Casavant organ, a dedicated choir under professional leadership, hand-bell ringers, and strong congregational singing from a very good hymn book. We came to appreciate the preaching of Rev. Victor Kim, disciplining himself to use the Lectionary for his sermons. We have never been sorry we made the switch.

As part of the plans for the celebration of 100 years, there was a strong desire to have a written and published history. Several attempts were made to get a book started, but agreement was reached with the help of such persons as Elder Bob Ermter and the Minister that I should be asked to do it. As I told the *Herald,* this project gave me "an opportunity to fill my time usefully in these later years of retirement and thus make a contribution to a Church that I have learned to appreciate deeply."

During the years 2005 to 2008 I devoted full time to the writing and completion of a congregational history entitled *A Century of Grace, 1905-2005: Grace Presbyterian Church,* Calgary, Alberta. Without knowing anything about this congregation in advance, but working from records, I put in six hours a day, almost every day, for about thirty months. Designed locally by Karol and Barbara Fodor, this became a companion to the Hall of History, a comprehensive display of photographs and anecdotes compiled by Orma Potter and a committee of history buffs. I was allowed to use some of these photographs, largely donated by church members, which swelled the book to 540 pages, letter-head size.

Despite coinciding radiation treatments for prostate cancer in 2008, I was able to complete the project in time to have it ready for Communion Sunday in December, when we had book signing. Justina was presented with roses, and I was presented with Copy One, which I then held up in the service for all to see. The audience was startled to see such a large book, weighing nearly two kilograms. Here is part of what I said: "As some of you know, I have been a serious historian for many years, and I took this responsibility quite seriously. Actually, I found that soon after I started on this project, my historian's antennae went up rather sharply. I saw no reason to take a different approach with the story about fellow church members than I would with others. I have not omitted the warts and controversies, nor the cover-ups, or the self-criticisms from various directions.

"In conclusion, this has been a great privilege. There were times, I must confess, when I wondered what in God's name I had started and must now finish! But it has been a great experience. I have used my privilege as author to thank some in a special way. Tonight I thank you all for your support, and especially for the trust placed in me."

Each book was hard-bound and printed by Friesens at a cost of $63, but a substantial private donation reduced the pre-published price to $25. In all about 400 copies were sold, leaving about a hundred for subsequent distribution to new members and special guests.

What is Ahead for Us?

God alone knows, as we used to say. At the time of penning these final paragraphs, Justina and I have reached the age of 90 and 91 and have most recently moved into a retirement home. We both, thankfully, are able to enjoy reading, and we both have email correspondence. We both trust God for the future and thank Him for His guidance in the past. Justina has her mission as explained and wants to continue her volunteer service to YYC as a White Hat Greeter for as long as she can. This has brought her many admirers and she has become a friend to many. That aside, Justina's legacy will be her family and friends, as indicated elsewhere, and the good memory of her volunteerism, conversation, friendliness, willingness to share, to help. She is particularly glad, as am I, to receive a granddaughter in the person of Elizabeth who married our grandson Jonathan on October 24, 2015. They are young and they will carry forward our Mennonite name from within an Anabaptist-Mennonite church. While I probably will not start another book, I suppose my legacy for the long run will be my books, my other publications, and my significant archival collections left behind at the Centre for Mennonite Brethren Studies in Winnipeg and Fresno, and at Mount Allison University, Sackville, NB. As to my letters, daybooks, photos, slides, and other significant collections, I have deposited these at the Mennonite Heritage Centre at Canadian Mennonite University, Winnipeg.

Peter and Justina dressed for the 65th Anniversary, in our living room, Terry Allen's photo, 2014

We will maintain our membership in Grace Church and in the Rotary Club of Calgary South. The friends we have made in each body have been most supportive, not only because I was able to write satisfactory histories of each, but belonging to them has been a significant factor in gaining friendships that are real and lasting.

Testimonials

"It has been my privilege to occupy a "ring-side" seat on the career of Peter Penner with reference to the academic historiography and prominent research historians with whom Penner interacted as a scholar in the secular world. The nexus of faith and learning that has epitomized this remarkably complex and intricate life and career can best be seen in the study of the MB mission in Andhra Pradesh. This, indeed, was one of his finest works and, with his works on the British Raj in North India, constitutes the pinnacle of Peter's scholarly career. This research brought together the accumulated and finely honed scholarly skills, both historical and theological, that Peter Penner possessed." Robert Eric Frykenberg, Professor Emeritus of History & South Asian Studies, University of Wisconsin, Madison

"Penner has been a long-time member of the academy and a long-time committed churchman. Some see those as contradictory commitments, Penner's life shows their complementarity. This autobiography of Peter Penner is a vivid and powerful story of combining objective and dispassionate scholarly analysis with deep religious commitments." Paul Toews, Fresno, California, historian, former Director of CMBS, Fresno

(Regrettably Paul died of cancer, November 27, 2015. He is shown on page 241)

Henry Marsh whom I met when he was eighteen years old, is now Henry Marsh CBE, ME, FRCS, Neurosurgeon, and author of *Do No Harm: Stories of Life, Death, and Brain Surgery* (2014). I reached him in Nepal. Of the stories about Norman and Christel Marsh, 1968 and 1981, he writes: "I have read the sections of your book concerning my parents with great pleasure and if the rest of your book is of the same standard I have no doubt it will make fascinating and excellent reading." (page 91)

"Peter Penner's rich and varied life exemplifies bridge-building between the worlds of church and academy. Situated as he was on the physical 'edge' of Mennonite communities for much of his career, his perspective on their history and identity is full of insight. As pastor, teacher, scholar, and volunteer, he has brought a critical yet gentle and loving eye to a lifetime of service." Marlene Epp, Professor of History and Peace and Conflict Studies – University of Waterloo

"This compelling autobiography traces the life of Peter Penner from his birth in Soviet Russia and his journey through nine decades in Canada. It reveals a committed family man, whether Mennonite pastor or history professor, becoming a highly respected author and scholar. His account provides a fascinating insight into, not only the lives of Peter and Justina and their children, but also the institutions and organizations of which they were an active part. Both were dedicated volunteers in their communities and made a difference. This publication is a narrative of a challenging and positive pilgrimage; truly an evocative and humble memoir well worth reading."

Vern Heinrichs, Toronto friend, entrepreneur, philanthropist

Publications
Articles, Books and Reviews, 1951-2015

Abbreviations and Legend for the Mennonite Papers:

CM, *Canadian Mennonite*, Altona, MB, Frank H. Epp, editor, 1953-1970 [see note under *Mennonite Reporter]*

CL, *Christian Leader*, Hillsboro, KS; moved to Fresno, CA: W. Vogt, Orlando Harms, Wally Kroeker, Don Ratzlaff

CGR, *Conrad Grebel Review*, 1982-

Der Bote, Rosthern, SK, Winnipeg, MB, 1924-2007, D. H. Epp, German language organ of the General Conference Mennonite Church

Direction, Review of the Mennonite Brethren institutions in Winnipeg, Hillsboro, and Fresno

JMS, *Journal of Mennonite Studies*, Chair of Mennonite Studies, University of Winnipeg, Harry Loewen, Royden Loewen, 1983-

MBH, *Mennonite Brethren Herald*, Winnipeg, Editors: Rudy Wiebe, Peter Klassen, Harold Jantz, Herb Kopp, Ron Geddert, Jim Coggins, and Laura Kalmar, 1962-

MH, *Mennonite Historian*, Mennonite Heritage Centre and Centre for MB Studies, Winnipeg, 1974-

ML, *Mennonite Life*, North Newton, KS, in recent times, James Juhnke, John Tiessen,1946-2008

MO, *Mennonite Observer*, Winnipeg, MB, Leslie Stobbe and G.D. Huebert, editors, 1956-1961

MQR, *Mennonite Quarterly Review*, Goshen, IN: Harold S. Bender, today John Roth, 1927-

MRep, *Mennonite Reporter*, Waterloo, 1971-1997, editors Frank H. Epp, Dave Kroeker, Ron Rempel. .... name changed back to *Canadian Mennonite*, Dick Benner

MR, *Mennonitische Rundschau*, 1880s-2005; H.F. Klassen, Eric Ratzlaff, in more recent times: Schellenberg, Marsch, Hiebert, Penner, Dulder

MF, *Mission Focus*, joint journal of the Mennonite seminaries, Wilbert Shenk

Preservings, Journal of the Hanover Steinbach Historical Society, Delbert Plett, John Friesen, 1985-2006

1951

Brief testimony of my Bible school experience at Prairie Bible Institute,

1945-47, *Olive Leaf*, 5/6 (March 1951), 6, edited by Walter Wiebe, MBBC

1953

Editor of *The Rainbow*, MBBC Yearbook Committee, 1952-53

1955

"Preparation for Service via MBBC and Waterloo College [University of Western Ontario]," *Voice* of MBBC, 4/4, (July-August 1955), 23-24

1956

"A Timely Warning" [regarding faith healers Jack Cole, Oral Roberts, and Valdez], *MO*, 2 March 1956, 2, 3.

"Twenty-One Years of Witnessing at Lindal," *MO*, 9 March 1956, 5

"Harvest and Mission Festival at Lindal," *MO*, 5 October 1956, 3

"Carman Dedicates Basement Auditorium," *MO*, 7 December 1956, 1, 4

1957

"Many Visitors at Lindal [from Manitou, Winkler, and Winnipeg]" *MO*, 29 March 1957, 4

"These were more noble… [a devotional from Acts 17:11-2]," *MO*, 17 May 1957, 2

"Faith Healing or Fake Healing?" *CL*, 1 May 1957, 4-5; 15 May 1957, 4-5.

"Organize for Fellowship and Discussion [at Morden]," *MO*, 21 June 1957, 11

"First Baptism in Seven Years [Joyce and Johnny Rachul, Dorothy and Russell Brown, Doris and Ronnie Guderian, and Bertha Guderian, at Lindal]," *MO*, 26 July 1957, 1, 4

"Rethinking Revival," *CL*, 15 August 1957, 3, 7

1958

"Conductors gather to prepare for better service [in Winnipeg, with Horchs and Klassen, MBBC]," *MO*, 25 April 1958, 5, 8; also in CM, 18 April 1958, 5,6

"Chilliwack Bible School Presents Play on Race [at Oliver and Kelowna]," *CM*, 9 May 1958, 7

"The Heritage of Mennonite Brethren Young People," *MO*, 30 May 1958, 8; 6 June 1958, 11

"Dry Weather Reduces Berry Crop in B.C," *CM*, 25 July 1958, 3

"A Tour of our West Coast Children's Mission Stations," *MO*, 26 September 1958, 5

"The Future of the Bible Schools," *MO*, 26 September 1958, 11; also in CM, 26 September 1958, 3

"WCCM Establishes 11 Stations," *CM*, 3 October 1958, 4

"Organize Camp Society and Agree on Site [above Cultus Lake, Chilliwack, B.C.]," *MO*, 31 October 1958, 4

"School Principal [J. H. Friesen, E. Chilliwack Bible School] Ordained at East Chilliwack," *MO*, 21 November, 1958

"Discovering the Doctrinal Position of the Brotherhood," MO, 19 December 1958, 3

1959

"The Christian Case for Abstinence," CL, 27 January 1959, 19

"Inter-Mennonite Bible School Fellowship [Abbotsford]," MO, 20 February 1959, 14

"A Three Language Radio Voice of Mennonites [Frank H. Epp, Altona]," MO. 3 April 1959, 1, 12

"The West Coast Children's Mission of BC," CL, 21 April 1959, 17, 21

"Over 4 and ½ Thousand Mennonite Brethren in B.C," CM, 12 June 1959

"At Hepburn Conference: M.B. Mission Giving [for CIM] Increased by $80,000." CM, 17 July 1959, 4-5

"WCCM has Headquarters at Clearbrook," CM, 24 July 1959, 9

"A New Departure in Home Missions in BC," CM, 30 October 1959, 1

BOOK: *Reaching the Otherwise Unreached: A History of the West Coast Children's Mission, 1939-59*, **Winnipeg: Christian Press, 1959, illustrated, 125 pp.**

1960

"[George Konrad] Ordained at Matsqui, B.C," CM, 8 January 1960, 7

"Mennonite Educational Institute Holds Religious Emphasis Week," CM, 18 March 1960, 7

"Eleven Thousand Dozen Doughnuts [John M. Lerch and his Donut Stand, Wayne County Fair at Wooster, Ohio]," CM, 30 September 1960, 5

1961

"This is My Concern: Can We Produce Books?" CM, 6 January 1961, 2

"Reflections on Mass Revivalism," CM, 30 January 1961, 2, 4; also CL, 1 July 1961, 4-5, 19

"Yarrow's [Neufeldt, Sawatsky, and Martens] Triple Fatality [my editing of Bertha Loewen's article and Frank Epp's editorial)]," CM, 1 September 1961, 3, 12

"Science and Scripture at One Day Student's Retreat [Ontario]," CM, 13 October 1961, 5

Eulogy for my Grandfather in conjunction with *Lebensverzeichnis* [Obituary], Peter J. Wiebe, MR ([September] 1961)

1962

"Was This the Time for Self-Aggrandizement?" CL, 20 February 1962, 3, 21; also in MBH, 9 March 1962, 5

Letter re the new MBH, captioned "Dangers in the Herald," MBH, 23 February, 1962, 2, 12; 16 March 1962, 2

"Mennonites and Music [in Appreciation of Ben Horch]," CM, 27 April 1962, 2

Letter "Concerning anonymity in the 'Mailbag'," MBH, 27 April 1962, 2

"A Mennonite, a Baptist, Again a Mennonite [Dr. Walter Klaassen]," *CM*, 26 October 1962, 1-2

Review of C.H. Spurgeon, a Reprint by Eerdmans of *Soul Winner*, *CM*, 5 July 1963

Review of G. M. Bryan, *Whither Africa? CM*, 30 July 1963, 8; in *MBH*, 19 July 1963, back page

Review of Don Gilmore, *In the Midst [of Renewal]*, in *CM*, 14 December 1962, 9

1963

"Mennonite Graduate Fellowship Meets [in Waterloo]," CL, 22 January 1963, 17; also in *MBH*, 11January 1963, 17-18

"Brief Evaluation of the Fifth Annual Convention of Mennonite Graduate Fellowship," *CM*, 4 January, 1963, 5, 7

"Student Services Committees Talk Together in Chicago," *CM*, 8 March 1963, 1, 2; also in *MBH*, 9 March 1963, 2; *MBH*, 15 March 1963

Letter to *MBH* re H. Swartz' article "From Mission Station to Mission Church," *MBH*, 8 March 1963, 2

"Momentous Events in the Life of David Livingstone: The Overriding Passion of his Life was to Expose and Destroy the Slave Trade," *CM*, 5 April 1963, 5

"Enthusiastic Response to Inter-Mennonite Choir [Frieda Heinrichs' choir from Toronto sponsored by Conrad Grebel College]," *CM*, 12 July 1963, 1, 12

"Bountiful Heritage – Continuing Tensions – Personal Commitment:

Conformity vs Individualism [Address at Eden Christian College Graduation]," *CM*, 19 July 1963, 6, 10

"Unsophisticated Biblicism," [F.C. Peters' Address on the Baptism Decision in Winnipeg]" *CM*, 20 August 1963, 3, 4

Series for University Students:

I "Tension between Work and Worship," *CL*, 10 December 1963, 3, 20

II. "Towards an Appreciation of our University Students," *MBH*, 20 September 1963, 4; "Are We Aware of Our Students?" *CL*, 1 October 1963, 12; 29 October 1963, 13

III. "Conformity or Confrontation [re relevancy of our Anabaptist witness]?" *MBH*, 29 October 1963, p. 4-5; also in *CL*, 10 December 1963, p. 17, 19

1964

IV. "The Bible as Personal Authority [with permission to use F.C. Peters' article from *Voice]* *MBH*, 31 January 1964, 4-5

"Basic Issues Facing Young People in World of Culture [talk given at Christian Education Conference, Winkler, Manitoba, 15 February 1964]," *MBH*, 21 February 1964, 4

Review of C.E. Nelson, *Love and the Law*, *MBH*, 21 February 1964, back page

"The Minister's Course at MBBC, 1964," *MBH*, 28 February 1964, 6-7

"The Lord Save Us From 'Ecumania' says PBI Principal Leslie E. Maxwell," *CM*, 10 March, 1964), 5 [an exclusive interview with this famous leader at MBBC Missionary Conference]

Review of D. Martin Lloyd-Jones, *The Basis of Christian Unity*, *MBH*, 20 March 1964, back page

Letter to MBH [in reply to critics of D.P. Watt's letters re Rev. Bennett]," *MBH*, 26 March 1964, 2, 13.

"Basic Issues Facing Young People in the World of Culture," *MBH*, 21February 21, 1964), 4

V. "Reclaiming Marginal Men [first given in MBBC Chapel, Minister's Course, February 1964]," *MBH*, 13 March 1964, 4–5

Review of Helmut Thielecke, *Encounter with Spurgeon*, *CM*, 21 April 1964, 8

"The New Penetration: the Current Tongues Movement," *MBH*, 15 May 1964, 4–5; also in *CL*, 12 May 1964, p. 4-5

VI."What Does Student Services [of the MB Church] Do?" *MBH*, 22 May 1964, 4-5; also in *CL*, 9 June 1964, 12-3

"Shall We Concentrate on Glossalalia or Proclamation?" *MBH*, 29 May 1964, 4-5; also in *CL*, 26 May 1964, 3, 15; response from John H. Redekop, "What about Glossalalia?"10 July 1964, 2; 17 July 1964, 2

VII. "Academic Qualifications and Migration Evangelism," *MBH*, 26 June 1964, 4

VIII. "Comments on a Mennonite Campus Club," *MBH*, 11 December 1964, 4-5. (See full-length reply from Peter Enns, 29 January 1965, *MBH*)

Review of Martin Schmidt, *John Wesley: Theological Biography*, *CM*, 29 December 1964, 8

1965

Letter in response to John H. Redekop's "Exploitation in the Name of Christ [re subsistence salaries paid to home mission workers]," *MBH*, 28 May 1965

Letter in response Delbert Wiens' *New Wineskins*: "Is one editorial all we are to have?" *MBH*, 26 November 1965, 2, 14.

1966

Letter in response to Harold Jantz' "Frontiers [in Lindal] Not so New," *MBH*, 11 March 1966, 19

Review of Delbert Wiens' *New Wineskins for Old Wine*, "An Application of 'New Wineskins for Old Wine' to the Canadian M.B. Church Scene," *MBH*, 15 April 1966, 6-7

Letter on "Rediscovery of Anabaptism," *MBH*, 14 October 1966, 2

1967

"Spiritual and Moral Freedoms" *CM*, 13 June 1967, 16 (Contribution to special Canada Centennial Issue of the "Mennonites in a Multicultural State"), 9 April 1968, 4

1968

"Matching Issues [as discussed at Cleveland] and Resources [as seen at Urbana], in Mount Allison University Chapel]," *MBH*, 15 March 1968, 6-7

1971

"A Reunion [of Mennonite Brethren] in the Maritimes and Issues that Divide," MRep, 4 October 1971, 1-2

1972

"Ireland: More Violence Seems the Certain Outcome," MRep, 27 November 1972, 7

"Wheeling and Dealing in Allahabad [Uttar Pradesh, India]," MRep, 8 January 1973, 2

"The Church in North India," MRep, 19 March 1973, 2

"The Mennonite Brethren Church in India: 1) "The American M. B. Church," MRep, 28 May 1973, 2; and 2) "The India M. B. Church," 11 June 1973,. 2

"Lighting a Candle: Illiteracy, One of India's Major Problems," MRep, 1 Oct/73, 2

1974

The "Mennonites in the Atlantic Provinces" Series:

1) "Denominational Witness Cannot Flourish," MRep, 13 May 1974, 7

"Three Christian Approaches to India," MRep, 27 May 1974, 2

2) "Siegfried Janzen and Mennonite Migrations," MRep, 8 July 1974, 9

Guest editorial: "Do we need missionaries in the Maritimes?" MRep, 22 July 1974, 6

3) "Christian Service in Nova Scotia – A Decade Later," MRep, 22 July 1974, 7

4) Conclusion to "Christian Service...," MRep, 5 August 1974, 7

"Haileybury: School for Anglo-Indian Statesmanship," Bengal Past and Present. XCIII, Part 1, #175 (January/April, 1974), 39-57

1975

5) "Two Decades of Voluntary Service in Newfoundland," MRep, 3 March 1975, 7

6) "Nova Scotia Experiences the John Esaus," MRep, 17 March 1975, 7

7) Professionals [in the Maritimes] Probed About Religious Identity," MRep, 31 March 1975, 7; 28; April 1975, 11

Review of Frank H. Epp, Mennonites in Canada, 1786-1920: History of a Separate People, Macmillan, 1974, MRep, 20 January 1975, 12

Are you Armigerous? Only Proper Research Will Tell," MRep, 1 September 1975, 17

Review of J. B. Toews, The MB Church in Zaire, Fresno, 1978, MRep, 8 Jan/79, 8

Guest editorial: "Ethnicity and Evangelism: Mutually Exclusive?" MRep, 19 Mar/79, 6

"MAP is on the Move," MRep, 2 April 1979, 14

Guest editorial: "Conscience or Commitment before Country?" MRep, 28 April/79, 6

Letter in response to John H. Redekop's column re overdoing of history: "History Not Yet Overdone," *MBH*, 2 March 1979, 9-10; and JHR's response, 12 April 1979, 12

Review of Elizabeth S. Klassen, *Trailblazer of the Brethren: The Story of Johann Claassen, a Leader in the MB Church*, Scottsdale, 1978, *MRep*, 5 March 1979, 9

Review of James Juhnke's, *A People of Mission: A History of the General Conference Overseas Mission*, Newton, 1979, *MRep*, 23 July 1979, 8

Review of Paul Toews, ed., *P.M. Friesen and His History: Understanding MB Beginnings*, in *MBH*, 31 August 1979, 28

Review of David Lelyveld, *Aligarh's First Generation: Muslim Solidarity in India*, Princeton UP, 1978, in *Canadian Journal of History*, XIV, # 8 (December 1979), 488-49

Young Violinist [Robert G. Penner] has Challenging Summer [with National Youth Orchestra]," *MRep*, 15 September 1975, 8

"Professionals Meet in the Maritimes," *MRep*, 8 December 1975, 10

"Education in Uttar Pradesh, 1843-54: James Thomason's Role in Education." *Journal of Indian History*, 53 (December 1975), 523-556.

1976

Review of J. J. Toews, The MB Mission in Latin America, Fresno, 1976, MRep, 17 May 1976, 8

"Mennonites in the Atlantic Provinces," ML, 31/4 (December 1976), 16-20

Review of J.A. Toews, *History of the MB Church: Pilgrims and Pioneers*, Christian Press, 1975, MQR, 1976, 73-5

1977

8) "Ben Warkentin: Educator and Sage," *MRep*, 31 October 1977, 17

Review of Frank H. Epp, *Mennonite Peoplehood* (A Plea for New Initiatives) under my title "The 'Pinched Feet' of Mennonite Peoplehood," *MRep*, 14 November 1977, 8

1978

Review of Paul E. Toews, ed., *Pilgrims and Strangers: Essays on MB History*, Fresno, 1977, *MRep*, 15 May 1978, 10

Guest editorial, "Why I am a Mennonite!" *MRep*, 7 May 1978, 6

Review of Richard Arons, ed., *Genocide in Paraguay*, Philadelphia, 1976, *MRep*, 26 June 1978, 9

Review of Swanstrom's *History in the Making*, MBH, 22 June 1978, 28

Guest editorial, "Agribusiness and the World Food Situation," *MRep*, 4 September 1978, 6

"Maritimers to Meet at Thanksgiving," *MRep*, 18 September 1978, 12

"Seek Organization in the Atlantic Provinces," *MRep*, 11 December 1978, 4

"By Reason of Strength: Johann Warkentin [Winkler] 1859-1948", ML, 33/4 (December 1978), 4-9

1980

"Mennonites Meet at London, UK [at Judy Kehler Siebert's recital]," *MRep*, 28 April 1980, 8

"Colonization Evangelism Leads to New Brunswick Baptism [at Havelock/Petitcodiac]," *MRep*, 21 July 1980, 3

Review article comparing Juhnke's *A People of Mission* and Theron Schlabach's *Gospel vs Gospel,* in *MF*, September 1980,.65-6

"New Brunswick Home [OPAL] Opens its Doors," *MRep*, 29 September 1980, 3

"[John] Esau Returns to Zaire After 20 Years," *MRep*, 24 November 1980, 11

"The Jacob-Esau Epic Speaks to Alienation in Canadian Life," *MRep*, 8 December1980, 7 (given first as a sermon at Mount Allison University)

1981

Guest editorial: "Bodily Exercise [Terry Fox Run] Profiteth Much!" *MRep*, 5 January 1981, 6

"OPAL Home in NB Sees Staff Changes," *MRep*, 30 March 1981, 14

"Survey of Mennonites in the Atlantic Provinces," *MRep*, 22 June 1981, 4

Review of Lawrence Klippenstein, ed., *That There Be Peace: Mennonites in Canada and World War Two*, Winnipeg: The Manitoba Conscientious Objector's Reunion Committee, 1979, in *MQR*, July 1981, 271

"Who Are the Maritime Mennonites?" *MBH*, 7 August 1981, 6-7

Letter seeking help to write "story of home missions," *MBH*, 11 September 1981, 9

"Oldest Methodist Congregation [Pointe de Bute, NB] Celebrates," *MRep*, 26 October 1981, 14

"Our Debt to the Canadian Sunday School Mission," *MBH*, 23 October 1981, 21

Review of Harry Loewen, ed., *Mennonite Images: Historical, Cultural and Literary Essays Dealing with Mennonite Issues, MBH*, 6 November 1981, 25; also in *Studies in Religion*, 1981, 210-211

1982

"The World's Hungry Belong to Us," *MRep*, 17 May 1982, 5 [First given as a sermon in Sackville United Church, 18 April 1982]

Review of John B. Toews [Calgary], *Czars, Soviets, and Mennonites* (Faith and Life Press, 1982), in *CL*, 4 May 1982, 17-8

"Ukrainian Baptist [Dr. Sam Nesdoly from Acadia visiting Mount Allison] seeks 'Biblical Witness' in Canada," *MRep*, 31 May 1982, 10

"Guardian of the Way: the Farmer-Preacher Henry S. Voth, 1878-1953," *ML*, 37/3 (September 1982), 8-13

"With Glowing Hearts" series:

1) Peter John Esau, the Intrepid Missionary, *MBH*, 17 December 1982, 6-7; also in *MRep*, 1 November 1982, 9

2) The Dynamic of the Mennonite Brethren Church, *MBH*, 17

December 1982, 7; also in *MRep*, 29 November 1982, 10

3) Seeking a New Image, *MBH*, 31 December 1982, 20-21; also in *MRep*, 10 January 1983, 5

1983

4) Efforts Produce Diminishing Returns," *MRep*, 24 January 1983, 5

Editor of the *Bulletin* of Rotary Club of Sackville, NB, a weekly circulation for club members (1980s), housed in Archives of Ralph Pickard Bell Library Library, Mount Allison University

Review of Paul von Tucker, *Nationalism: Case and Crisis in Missions: German Missions in British India, 1939 – 1946*, Erlangen, 1980, *MF*, March 1983, 13-4

Review of Barbara Daly Metcalf, *Islamic Revival in British India, 1860-1900*, Princeton UP, 1982, in *Canadian Journal of History*, XVIII, # 2 (August 1983 303-04

"Getting Together [Ninth Annual Retreat of MAP] in the Maritimes," *MRep*, 9 September 1983, 17

"Some Chose Trees: A Remembrance Day Address [in Sackville, 1982]," *MRep*, 31 October 1983, 8

BOOK: with Richard Dale MacLean, *The Rebel Bureaucrat: Frederick John Shore (1799-1837) as Critic of William Bentinck's India*. Delhi, Chanakya Publications, 1983, 304 pages

1984

Review of Daniel G. Dancocks, *In Enemy Hands: Canadian Prisoners of War, 1939-45*, *CGR*, III, 3 (Fall 1984), 250-1

BOOK: Author of new Introduction to John Beames, *Memoirs of a Bengal Civilian*. Columbia, Missouri, South Asia Books, 1984, 2nd ed., i-xxi; Introduction to First Edition, Chatto and Windus, by Philip Mason, 7-10

1985

"Maritime MBs 'double in a decade'," *MBH*, 25 January 1985, 16

"Second M.B. Congregation [Campbellton] Holds Charter Service," *MRep*, 4 February, 1985, 12

"*Kleinegemeinde* Settlers Making a Mark in Nova Scotia," *MRep*, 18 February 1985, 5

Review of John H. Redekop, *Two Sides: The Best of Personal Opinion*, Kindred Press, 1984, *MRep*, 15 April 1985, 8

[Mennonite] Participants in Sixth Assembly of the Canadian Council of Churches [Halifax]" *MRep*, 27 May 1985, 4

"Warden [Hank Neufeld, Dorchester, NB] Speaks on Prisons," *MRep*, 24 June 1985, 16

Review of Stephen Neill's *A History of Christianity in India: the Beginnings to A.D.1707*, *MBH*, 14 June 1985, 29

"Maritime Journal: A Time to Gather Stones Together [for the Monument in Vineland for the

Bicentennial of Mennonites in Canada]" *MRep*, 19 August 1985, 12

"Holdeman Families Move to Nova Scotia," *MRep*, 19 August 1985, 14

"New Pastors in the Maritimes," *MRep*, 16 September 1985, 4

"Installation of Siegfried Janzens at Petitcodiac," *MRep*, 28 October 1985, 13

"New Leadership for the Eastern Vision," *MBH*, 4 October 1985, 16

Letter: "More on a planet for the taking?" *MBH*, 15 November 1985, 10

"10 Years of MAP," *MRep*, 25 November 1985, 16

"William Klassen speaks on Middle East [at Mount Allison]," *MRep*, 25 November 1985

Review of Farley Mowat, *Sea of Slaughter*, in *CGR*, III, 3 (Fall 1985), p. 309-311

1986

"MAP '86," *MBH*, 3 October 1986, 21

"What Flag Will the Mennonite Brethren Fly [in the Maritimes] and Who Will Unfurl It?" *MBH*, 17 October 1986, 2-3

"Mennonite Brethren have history of involvement in India," *MBH*, 3 May 1986, 15

Review of Walbert Buhlmann, *A Church of the Future: A Model for the Year 2000*, Maryknoll: Orbis, 1980, *MF*, 14 #3 (September 1986), 46

BOOK: *The Patronage Bureaucracy in North India: The Robert M. Bird*

and James Thomason School, 1820 – 1870. Delhi, Chanakya Publications, 1986, 380 pages

1987

BOOK: *Robert Needham Cust, 1821-1909: A Personal Biography.* Lewiston, N.Y., Edwin Mellen Press, 1987, 357 pages

BOOK: *No Longer At Arm's Length: Mennonite Brethren Church Planting in Canada, 1883-1983.* Winnipeg, Kindred Press, 1987, 178 pages, pictorial, letterhead size [see review by John D. Reimer, "Dealing with the Cramp in our Arm," *MBH*, January 8, 1988, 26-27]

1988

Chapter: "Operation Cataract, 1964," in *Why I am a Mennonite*. Editor, Harry Loewen, Chair of Mennonite Studies, University of Winnipeg, Kitchener: Herald Press, 1988, 194-203

1989

Letter, Dave McKay, editor, *Sackville Tribune-Post* (5 February 1989), 2, regarding the responses I got from my article, "Saints, Gamblers, and Mennonites," which described our experiences on the way from New Brunswick to California in the fall of 1988

"Visiting Mennonites in the Soviet Union," *MRep*, 18 September 1989, 12

"Karaganda, *die alte Eiche und viel mehr*," *MR*, 27 September 1989, 16

1990

Review of William Neufeld, *From Faith to Faith: The History of the Manitoba MB Church*, Kindred Press, 1989, in *MQR*, October 1990, 424-25

Biographical Sketch of Peter Penner, *Contemporary Authors*, Vol. 129 (1990), 340-1.

BOOK: *The Chignecto 'Connexion': A History of Sackville Methodist/ United Church (1772-1990)*. Sackville, N. B., Sackville United Church, 1990, 192 pages

Atlantic Provinces", *ME*, 5 (1990), 43

1991

"Baptist in All But Name: Molotschna Mennonite Brethren in India", *ML*, 46/1 (March 1991), 17-23

"The Holy Spirit and Church Renewal: Coimbatore [India], 1906" *Direction*, 20/2 (Fall 1991), 135-142

Review article of Victor Adrian, editor, *Committed to World Mission: A Focus on International Strategy* (Hillsboro, 1990), and Paul D. Wiebe, *Christians in Andhra Pradesh: The Mennonites of Mahbubnagar* (Madras, 1988), in *Direction*, 20/1 (Spring 1991), 115-8

1992

Twenty-one biographical articles, The Blackwell Dictionary of Evangelical Biography,1730-1860. Editor, Donald M. Lewis, Regent College, Vancouver, BC (1990-92)

1993

Chapter: "The Russian Mennonite Brethren and American Baptist Tandem in India, 1890-1940", in *Mennonites and Baptists: A Continuing Conversation*, Kindred Press, 1993, 133-146, 243-7, edited by Paul Toews

Letter to the Editor: "A Sign of Animosity?" *Sackville Tribune-Post* (8 September 1993), in the matter of the local protest against building a cairn to commemorate the Acadians who were driven out of the area in 1755!

1994

Four articles, *The Biographical Dictionary of Christian Missions*. Editor, Gerald Anderson, New Haven, Connecticut (1994)

1995

Letter to the Editor, "Redekop's disclaimer [of not being against members having more than two residences!] invalid," *MBH*, 21 July 1995, 9

"Let My People Go! A Catastrophic Episode in Russian/German Emigration, 1929," *Journal* of AHSGR, (Fall 1995) 38-45

1996

Review of Sam Steiner, Lead Us On: A History of Rockway Mennonite Collegiate, 1945-1995, RMC, 1995, MRep, 29 April 1996, 12

"Mennonite Brethren have history of involvement in India," MBH, 3 May 1996, 15 (with my photo of the India delegation to MWC, Winnipeg)

Translation (from German to English) of a little booklet by Jacob H. Janzen, Waterloo Mennonite Minister, on the life of David Toews, Rosthern, for Louise (Toews, Mrs. Blake) Friesen

"The Westernization of History," in CGR: A Journal of Christian Enquiry (Winter/Spring, 1997), 119-127 [This issue, edited by Arnold Snyder, published the papers given at the conference 'toward a global Mennonite/Brethren in Christ historiography' held at Elkhart in 1995.]

BOOK: *Russians, North Americans, and Telugus: The MB Mission in India, 1885-1975*, Kindred Productions, 1997, 413 pages, illustrated, documented, indexed

1998

Review of Calvin E. Shenk, *Who Do You Say That I Am: Christians Encounter Other Religions*. Scottdale, PA: Herald Press, 1997, 294 pages, in *Direction*, 27/2 (Fall 1998), 196-97

"The Heinrich Voth Family: From Minnesota to Winkler to Vanderhoof," in *Mennonite Historian*, 24/4 (December 1998), 1-2

1999

Review, Abraham Friesen, *Erasmus, the Anabaptists, and the Great Commission.* Grand Rapids: Eerdmans, 1998, 196 pages, in *MBH*, 8 January 1999, 31

Letter to Editor, "Furore over war [re Remembrance Day article by Norman Fehr]," *MBH*, 5 February 1999, 13

"Things new and old in Alberta," *CM*, 15 February 1999, 26

Edited (and wrote) two *Newsletters* of the Mennonite Historical Society of Alberta, Second Series, Volume I, # 1 (October 1998); Volume I, # 2 (March 1999)

Review, Jacob A. Loewen and Wesley J. Prieb, *Only the Sword of the Spirit*, Winnipeg: MB, Kindred Publications, 1997, 346 pages, in *Direction*, 28/1 (Spring 1999), 130-132

2000

Review of Abe Dueck, *Moving Beyond Secession: Defining Russian Mennonite Brethren Mission and Identity, 1872-1922*, Winnipeg: Kindred Productions, 1997, in *CGR* (Spring, 2000), 93-94

Foreword to *Knowing and Interpreting our Past: Alberta's Mennonite History* (Calgary: MHSA, 2000), 60 pages, edited by Judith Rempel

Interview on Tape by Madame Filistovich regarding my impressions and experiences during a visit to Barnaul and the German National Region, Western Siberia, on *Altaier Weiten* (German Language Radio, Barnaul), aired 25 November, and 1 December 2000

2001

Review of Gladys Blyth, *When God Opens the Door* [the story of the MB Mission to Port Edward and Prince Rupert] Belleville, ON: Essence Publishing, 1999, 437 pages, in *MBH*, 19 January 2001, 31

Obituary of Henry and Vera Janzen [Kingston, ON], in *MBH*, 2 March 2001, 29

Review of *Not Without Zeal: Lessons from Life: The Story of Henry R. Baerg*. Calgary: David and Elfrieda Dick (printed by Print Logistics), 2000. Pictorial, 192 pages, Letterhead size, in *MBH*, 11 May 2001, 30

"Beyond Expectations" (several versions of my report on Trip to Siberia) in Calgary Chapter, AHSGR, *Newsletter*, March 2001

Interview by Ulrike Fischer, "*Auf der Suche nach den Wurzeln, ein Kanadier erforscht seinen russlanddeutschen Hintergrund, Zeitung fuer Dich*, # 13 (30 March 2001), 8-9, Slavgorod, Altai, Western Siberia, Russia.

Letter to the editor in response, *Ibid*, # 18 (4 May 2001), 23

Three 500-word articles on **Bible schools in Saskatchewan** (1930s and 1940s), located at **Eagle Creek, Speedwell, and Hochfeld**: for the *Canadian Mennonite Encyclopedia Online* (CMEO), submitted to and posted on the Internet by Sam Steiner, managing editor, August 2001

"The Last of the Namakans", *MHSA Newsletter* (July 2001), 3-4, edited by Dick Neufeld

Letter, "B.C. historical society reflects reality" [regarding the MHS of BC's music event during May], *CM*, 8 October 2001, 14

"The One-Hand Clock in Orlovo, Siberia," in *Preservings*, # 19 (December, 2001), 121-122

2002

"What a Coup!" [the story of "Celebrating the Musical Heritage of Mennonites in the Fraser Valley," May 2001, staged by the MHS/BC], in *MHSA Newsletter*, (June 2002), 3, edited by Dick Neufeld

"The Stalin Terror and the Aussiedler", in *Journal* of the AHSGR (Spring 2002), 33-37

"Breaking the Silence," in *Journal* of the AHSGR (Winter 2002), 1-6

"*Was ich im Altai, Sibirien, gewonnen habe.*" Der Bote, 79/4 (13 February 2002), 30-31; 79/5 (27 February 2002), 29-32

"Dick Family Sponsors Siberian Mennonite Research Initiative" (announcements in the Mennonite media): *CM* (9 September 2002), 18; in *Der Bote* (11 September 2002), 10-11; *MH* 28/3; (September 2002), 9; in MHSA *Newsletter*, Second Series, vol. 5, # 2 0(October 2002), 8;

Yarrow Research Committee Series:

Three Chapters: "Chauncy Eckert, the CCA, and Early Settlement," in *Before We Were the Land's, Yarrow, British Columbia: Mennonite Promise*, Volume I, 129-142; and "The Foreign Missionary as Hero," and ""Glimpses of Elim Bible School, 1930-1955," in *Village of Unsettled Yearnings*, Volume II, 50-61, 80-86. (Victoria, B.C., Heritage Group, 2002), edited by Leonard Neufeldt, Lora Neufeldt Sawatsky, and Robert Martens

2002-2005

"Memoir of a No-Name Man": Unpublished Memoir for Archival Deposit, planned for CD only [Mostly written between 1995 and 2002], *this has 35 chapters and swelled (with pictures) to more than 800 pages, typescript, burned to CD*

2003

Letter to Editor, in *Newsletter of the Westmorland Historical Society*, 38/3 (April 2003), 21

Review of Tena Wiebe, *Neu=Samara: A Mennonite Settlement East of the Volga*, Jackpine Press, Edmonton, 2002, in Vol 21, *JMS*, 2003, 232-233

Chapter: "Ábram H. Unruh, (1878-1961)," in *Shepherds, Servants and Prophets: Leadership among the Russian Mennonites (ca. 1880-1960)*. Waterloo, Ontario: Pandora Press, 2003, 385-400, edited by Harry Loewen, Kelowna, BC

"What was life like in Siberia for descendants of the deportees of 1941?" in *Journal* of the AHSGR, 26/3 (Fall 2003), 4-13

"A Remembrance Day Speech," first printed in *Mennonite Reporter* in 1983, in MHSA *Newsletter*, 6/2 (November 2003), 1, 3, 5, 13-15

2004

BOOK: *Manchester to Calgary South, 1955-2005: Rotary Fellowship in Action*. Calgary: The Rotary Club of Calgary South, 2004 (designed by Fraser Seely, Calgary; printed by Friesens, Altona, Manitoba), illustrated, documented, indexed, 385 pages

Eight articles for *Dictionary of National Biography* (Oxford University Press), 2004:

Colvin, John Russell (1807-1857), administrator in India [*rev.*]

Elliot, Sir Henry Miers (1808-1853), administrator in India and historian

Gubbins, Martin Richard (1812-1863), administrator in India [*rev.*]

Hamilton, Sir Robert North Collie, sixth baronet (1802-1887), administrator in India [*rev.*]

Mansel, Charles Grenville (1806-1886), administrator in India [*rev.*]

Montgomery, Sir Robert (1809-1887), administrator in India [*rev.*]

Robertson, Thomas Campbell (1789-1863), administrator in India [*rev.*]

Thornton, Edward Parry (1811-1893), administrator in India [*rev.*]

Letter to the Editor, "Unmasking Translators" [of KJV and the RSV], *Presbyterian Record* (October 2004), 6

"The Changes in Mennonite Worship Music: A Betrayal?" MHSA *Newsletter*, 7/2 (October 2004), 6-9

2005

Letter to the Editor, "A tribute [to Dr. David E. Warkentin, Agincourt, ON, 1930-2005]," in *MBH*, 29 April 2005), 12

The Following Prepared for the CMEO (GAMEO):

Biographies:

Anne (Peters) Neufeld, Coaldale; John Esau, Educator, Missionary, Farmer, Debert [Truro], NS, including Agnes Sudermann Esau; Siegfried Janzen, Petitcodiac, who died at age 85 in August, 2005

Congregations:

"MAP", i.e. Mennonites in the Atlantic Provinces, 26 years, (disbanded)

Dartmouth MB (Crossroads Community) Church, 1967 to 2000 (disbanded).

Institutions:

West Coast Children's Mission of BC, 1939-59

"Germans in the Armies of the Tsar," *Newsletter* of Calgary Chapter, AHSGR (Fall 2005), 6-7 [re Volga Germans killed in the Russo-Turkish War of 1877-78]

2006

"Many are called, but few are chosen:" The Ministry of Grace Presbyterian Church, Calgary, Alberta, 1905-2005 (First Edition, April 2005), 72 pages

Review of Jeff Gundy, *Walker in the Fog: Mennonite Writing.* Telford, PA: Cascadia Publishing House; and Scottdale, PA: Herald Press, 2005, Pages, 296, in *MBH,* March 17, 2006, see Books section

Review of Hans Kasdorf, *Design of My Journey.* Fresno: Center for Mennonite Brethren Studies; and Nuernburg, Germany: VTR Publications, 2004, Pages, xix + 360 photo section, select bibliography, glossary, and index; in *JMS,* 24 (2006), 253-254

"Three Books, Three Rotary Stories," in RI District 5360, *Newsletter,* 1/8 (February 2006), edited by Marie and Steve Rickard, DG, 2005-2006

"Setting our Sights on Siberia," in *Preservings,* Issue 26 (2006), 72-77, edited by John J. Friesen

2007

Six Biogaphical Sketches for the *Bulletin of the Rotary Club of Calgary*: John Campbell, Chiropracter (1916-2007); Rev. John Flagler, Anglican Rector (1918 – 2010); John Kelly, Egg Hatchery Business (1913-2008); Clayton Carroll, Roadbuilder [e.g., Deerfoot Trail] (1920 – 2011); Bernie Tharp, Optometrist (1918-2010); Peter Penner, Historian (1925 –)

Review Article: James Urry, *Mennonites, Politics, and Peoplehood: Europe – Russia – Canada. 1525 to 1980.* Winnipeg: University of Manitoba Press, 2006, 400 pages, illustrated; and Abraham Friesen, *In Defense of Privilege: Russian Mennonites and the State before and during World War* Winnipeg: Kindred Publications, 2006, 520 pages, in *Newsletter* of MHSA, IX, # 2 (May 2007), 11-14

Two chapters: 1) "Herman Lenzmann: Navigating the Winds

of Change [Congo Missionary and Yarrow Pastor]," pages 121-148; and 2) "Is the Artist a Gift to the Church? The Singers from Yarrow [Holda Reimer Fast Redekopp, Bill Reimer, and Victor Martens]," pages 323-356; in Volume IV of the Yarrow Research Committee's series in the study of Yarrow, BC (1928-1960), entitled *Windows to a Village: Life Studies of Yarrow Pioneers* (Waterloo: Pandora Press, 2007), edited by Robert Martens, Maryann Tjart Jantzen, and Harvey Neufeldt

Letter to the Editor regarding the differences in preparation for baptism between Mennonite Brethren and General Conference in response to Ed Lenzmann (March issue), *Mennonite Historian* (September 2007), 8

"MHSC and GAMEO Meetings held in Calgary, January 18-20, 2007," in *Newsletter MHSA* (August 2007), 1, 3-4, edited by Dave Toews, Edmonton

"Grist to the Mill [was there a 'Canadian' mill in Russia?]," *Newsletter,* MHSA (December 2007), 5-7

Review of *The Ben Horch Story,* Winnipeg: Old Oak Publishing, 2007, 490 pages, by Peter Letkemann, in *Newsletter,* MHSA (December 2007), 9-12

Foreword to the English version of Hans Kasdorf's *Generations Come – Generations Go: Legacy and Destiny from History and Experience.* Masthof Press, Morgantown, PA, 2008, 227 pages letterhead size

2008

Book: *A Century of Grace, 1905-2005, Grace Presbyterian Church.* Calgary, Grace Presbyterian Church, 2008, 530 pages, design by Digital Art, Calgary, printed by Friesens, Altona, Manitoba

2009

Review of Heinrich Unruh, *Fuegungen u. Fuehrungen, Benjamin Heinrich Unruh (1881-1959): Ein Leben im Geiste christlicher Humanitaet u. Im Dienst der Naechstenliebe (mit einem Nachwort von Peter Letkemann [Winnipeg]).* Detmold, Verein zur Erforschung u. Pflege des Russlanddeutschen Mennonitums, 2009, in *Newsletter* of MHSA, 12/2 (September 2009), 7-9

"Remembering Erwen Fester, in *Newsletter* of Calgary Chapter, AHSGR, 17/3 (September 2009), 4

"Peter and Justina's Sixtieth Anniversary," in *Newsletter* of Calgary Chapter, AHSGR, 17/3 (September 2009), 5-6

BOOK: Editor: *From Kronstahl to Kelowna, The Story of David A. Schellenberg, 1894-1994,* published by David and Erwin Schellenberg, Kelowna, and Donna Schellenberg Jakubec, Calgary, printed by Prolific Graphics, Calgary, pictorial, maps, 95 pages

"How the German Language got silenced (stumped) in Russia," in *Journal* of AHSGR Volume 32, # 3 (Fall, 2009), 20-32

2010

"Review Article: Yarrow: Ten Years, Five Volumes," *Newsletter* of MHSA, 13/1 (Spring 2010), 16-19

Review of *The Voice of a Writer, Honoring the Life of Katie Funk Wiebe,* edited by Doug Heidebrecht and Valerie Rempel (Kindred Productions, 2010) in *Newsletter* of the MHSA, XIV, # 2 (Fall, 2010)

2011

A Review Article: *Leaders Who Shaped Us: Canadian Mennonite Brethren, 1910-2010* edited by Harold Jantz (Kindred Productions, 2010), 323 pages, in *Newsletter* of the MHSA, XIV, # 1 (March, 2011), 10-14

"Memories of My Time in London, England," in *Newsletter* of the MHSA, XIV, # 1 (March, 2011), 8-10; XVI, # 2 (June, 2011), 13-15

"Judith Rempel, an Appreciation," in *Newsletter* of the MHSA, XIV, # 3 (October, 2011), 1, 3-6

2012-2015

Personal Memoir in Preparation, about 88,000 words

2015

Review of Zacharias, Robert, *Re-writing the Break Event: Mennonites and Migration in Canadian Literature.* Winnipeg, Manitoba: University of Manitoba Press. 2013, 227 pages, in *MQR,* LXXXIX, January 2015, Number One

Select Bibliography

Epp, Frank H., *Mennonite Exodus: The Rescue and Resettlement of the Russian Mennonites since the Communist Revolution*. Altona: D.W. Friesen and Sons, 1962

Epp, Frank H., *Mennonites in Canada, 1786-1920: The History of a Separate People*. Toronto: Macmillan, 1974

Epp, Frank H., *Mennonites in Canada, 1920-1940: A People's Struggle for Survival*. Toronto: Macmillan, 1982

Fast, Gerhard, *In den Steppen Sibiriens* [In the Steppes of Siberia]. Private, 1957

Giesinger, Adam, *From Catherine to Khrushchev: The Story of Russia's Germans*. Winnipeg: Adam Giesinger, 1974

Journal of Mennonite Studies, Volumes 1-33, Chair of Mennonite Studies, University of Winnipeg, 1983-2015

Klassen, A.J., Editor, *Alternative Service for Peace in Canada during World War II, 1941-1946*. Abbotsford: MCC, Seniors for Peace, 1998

Regehr, Theodore, *Mennonites in Canada, 1939-1970: A People Transformed*. Toronto University Press, 1996

Reimer, Al, *My Harp is Turned to Mourning* (a Novel), Winnipeg: Hyperion, 1985

Reimer, Margaret Loewen, *One Quilt, Many Pieces: A Reference Guide to Mennonite Groups in Canada*, published by *Mennonite Reporter*, 2008 edition, 139 pages

Urry, James, *Mennonites, Politics, and Peoplehood: Europe, Russia, Canada, 1525-1980*. Winnipeg: University of Manitoba Press, 2006

CPSIA information can be obtained at www.ICGtesting.com
Printed in the USA
LVOW08s2312190816

501071LV00001B/5/P

9 781460 279342